CULTURAL STUDIES IN PRACTICE

General Editors: JOHN STOREY AND GRAEME TURNER

CULTURAL CONSUMPTION AND EVERYDAY LIFE

JOHN STOREY

Reader in Cultural Studies,
University of Sunderland

A member of the Hodder Headline Group
LONDON • SYDNEY • AUCKLAND
Co-published in the United States of America by
Oxford University Press Inc., New York

First published in Great Britain 1999 by
Arnold, a member of the Hodder Headline Group,
338 Euston Road, London NW1 3BH

http://www.arnoldpublishers.com

Co-published in the United States of America by
Oxford University Press Inc.,
198 Madison Avenue, New York, NY10016

The advice and information in this book are believed to be true and
accurate at the date of going to press, but neither the author nor the publisher
can accept any legal responsibility or liability for any errors or omissions.

British Library Cataloguing in Publication Data
A catalogue record for this book is available from the British Library

Library of Congress Cataloging-in-Publication Data
A catalog record for this book is available from the Library of Congress

ISBN 0 340 72037 9 (hb)
ISBN 0 340 72036 0 (pb)

1 2 3 4 5 6 7 8 9 10

Production Editor: Liz Gooster
Production Controller: Iain McWilliams
Composition by Scribe Design, Gillingham, Kent
Printed and bound in Great Britain by MPG Books, Bodmin, Cornwall

What do you think about this book? Or any other Arnold title?
Please send your comments to feedback.arnold@hodder.co.uk

For Jenny and Kate

Contents

General Editors' Preface

Cultural studies is a rapidly developing field of pedagogical practice and theoretical enquiry. Among its distinctive characteristics is the way its influence has spread across disciplines and research areas. While the effect of cultural studies on a wide range of disciplinary or sub-disciplinary fields has been substantial and in some cases profound, most publication in the area is less interested in that influence than in mapping the current hierarchies of positions and knowledges seen to define the field. The work of definition and clarification has preoccupied cultural-studies publishing for most of its history. This series hopes to move forward by mapping the ways in which the approaches and politics of cultural studies have affected both the detail and the overall shape of work within the humanities and social sciences today. The series will produce textbooks which critically describe and assess the contribution of cultural studies to specific areas of research and debate.

John Storey and Graeme Turner

Preface

Cultural consumption is a social activity and an everyday practice. It is through the practices we call cultural consumption that people make culture. In cultural consumption we articulate both our creative freedom to make culture and our dependence on the culture industries, which provide both the means and the conditions of our cultural creativity. Cultural consumption can be made to fulfil a wide range of social and personal purposes. What and how we consume may serve to say who we are or who we would like to be; it may be used to produce and maintain particular lifestyles; it may promise compensation in times of loss or provide a symbolic means to celebrate success and mark achievement; it can serve to meet both our needs and our desires; it can provide the material for our dreams; it can mark and maintain social difference and social distinction. Whatever else it is, this book argues, cultural consumption is the practice of culture.

The book's object of study is cultural consumption as it has been theorised and studied in work which has made a contribution (directly and indirectly) to cultural studies. It is not a study of consumer culture but a critical assessment of a range of 'theoretical approaches' to the study of cultural consumption. In this sense, then, the object of study is not how people make culture in the practice of cultural consumption, but how intellectuals and intellectual traditions have theorised and studied cultural consumption. Therefore, what counts as cultural consumption will vary from discipline to discipline, as each discipline constructs in discourse its own understanding of its object of study. In *The History of Sexuality* Michel Foucault tracks the discourse of sexuality through a series of nineteenth-century discursive domains: medicine, demography, psychiatry, pedagogy, social work, criminology, government. Rather than silence on matters sexual (which is what we might have expected given the stereotype of Victorian prudery), he encounters instead 'a political, economic and technical incitement to talk about sex' (1981: 22-3). He argues that these different discourses on sexuality are not simply about sexuality, they actually *constitute* sexuality as an object of knowledge. This is not to say that sexuality did not exist as a non-discursive formation in nineteenth-century Europe, rather it is to recognise that our 'knowledge' of sexuality, and the 'power–knowledge' relations of sexuality constituted by it, are discursive. Throughout the writing of this book I have tried to remain mindful of Foucault's insight. Therefore, what counts as cultural consumption in this study will vary considerably, as my focus moves from one critical perspective to another. In the final chapter, where I attempt to stake out a position, I am more circumspect and less catholic about what 'cultural consumption' is intended to signify. But until that point, the question of what counts as cultural consumption will remain open.

In the 'post-disciplinary' spirit of cultural studies, another aim of this volume is to bring together, in what is, hopefully, a fruitful relationship, work that up until now has largely remained separate, located in distinct disciplinary spaces: work on reception theory in literary studies and philosophy; work on consumer culture in anthropology, history and sociology; work on media audiences (both ethnographic and theoretical) in media studies and sociology.

In general terms culture is our relationship to nature (including the biology of 'human nature'). More specifically, it is how we live this relationship. It is the more specific definition which points to *cultures*, rather than culture, and to the possibilities of difference, negotiation and struggle. A fundamental part of this relationship involves the practice of cultural consumption. Culture is not a series of objects or texts, it is a dynamic practice of making and becoming, using for these purposes, among other things, the cultural commodities made available by the culture industries. Cultural consumption is fundamentally a social act; it is always affected by the social context and the social relations in which it occurs. What is of interest in cultural studies are the ways in which people use the texts and practices they consume to *make* culture. To paraphrase Marx on history (Marx 1977: 10), we make culture, but in conditions and from commodities which are not of our making. And to paraphrase him again (1973: 87), culture does nothing, it is people, real living people, who do things; culture is not a person apart, using other people as a means to its own particular ends; culture is nothing but the activity of people engaging in everyday life.

I have used the term 'cultural consumption', not, as in its usual usage, to refer to the consumption of culture (that is, the consumption of something already identified as culture), but to make the point that cultural consumption produces culture: that is, it is by the appropriation of the commodities of production (the commodities of the culture industries) that we make culture. Culture is, therefore, neither the products produced by the culture industries, nor simply their appropriation by consumers; it is always the result of an active combination of the two. I provide a more detailed account of this in my explanation of the work of anthropologist Daniel Miller (see Chapter 8, pp 159–63), especially his theory of 'objectification'.

According to the Canadian anthropologist Grant McCracken, 'The history of consumption has no history, no community of scholars, no tradition of scholarship. It is, in the words of T.S. Kuhn, "pre-paradigmatic". Or, perhaps more accurately, it is "neo-natal" ' (1990: 28). McCracken made this claim in an excellent book published almost a decade ago. Ten years is a long time in academic scholarship, and perhaps now the claim no longer has the same ring of truth about it. Nevertheless, I would like to think that the book you now hold in your hands will make a small contribution to making the statement even less true.

In broad terms, and in line with the general aims of the Cultural Studies in Practice series, this book will seek to provide a critical map of cultural consumption, one which both structures and describes the contribution cultural studies has made and can make to this area of research, pedagogy and debate. In this way, the book seeks not simply to reflect developments in the field, it also seeks to contribute to its further elaboration in ongoing debates on how best to understand the nature of cultural consumption. To avoid the twin dangers of misunderstanding and misrepresentation, I have allowed critical sources, when and where appropriate, to speak in their own words. This has the added advantage of allowing the student of cultural consumption a greater direct access to the material discussed. It also gives the book a certain 'dialogic', rather than 'monological', quality (Bakhtin 1984). However, the book is not intended as a substitute for reading first-hand the material discussed here. The value of this book, as I see it, is not that it provides the means to avoid further reading, but that it presents a critical map of cultural consumption and everyday life, and in doing this it also argues for a particular way to read the map. Armed with my map, and my suggestions on how to read it, my hope is that other students of cultural consumption will begin their own explorations.

Acknowledgements

I would like to thank the following people for help and support during the period of writing this book: Lesley Riddle, Jenny Storey, Kate Storey and Graeme Turner. I would also like to thank the School of Arts, Design and Media, University of Sunderland, for granting me sabbatical leave to complete this work. Similarly, I would like to thank colleagues in Media and Cultural Studies for bearing the burden of this particular absence, and for providing academic and intellectual support over the eight years I have been at Sunderland. I would also like to thank students past and present on the Media and Communication Studies degrees at the University of Sunderland, with whom I have rehearsed many of the ideas contained in this volume. Finally, many thanks to Juliette Crooks for her excellent work on the index.

1

Consumption in History

In this chapter I critically review some recent historical accounts of the development of cultural consumption. The chapter begins with some general points about the birth of a consumer society, and then moves on to an assessment of two very influential theoretical models, both of which seek to provide an explanatory account of its rapid and increasing success, the social-emulation model and the theory of the Romantic ethic.

The Birth of a Consumer Society

Although modern and postmodern consumption is now established as a field of critical enquiry, attention to early modern consumption is still in its preliminary stages. Ann Bermingham suggests that one of the reasons for this is to be found in a version of history made popular by some dominant versions of postmodern theory; that is, the claim that the consumer society is a product of late capitalism. Against this view, Bermingham argues the case for locating the birth of consumer society in the sixteenth, and certainly no later than the eighteenth century. As she points out, the coming to dominance of capitalism witnessed not only an expansion of production, but also a rapid growth in consumption. Moreover, the neglect of consumption in our understanding of these historical changes, she maintains, is a direct consequence of the influence of 'theorists of modernism [who] have assigned consumer society to the late twentieth century' (1995: 3). As she explains,

> One does not look for something where one has been led to believe it does not exist. In light of this, I would like to propose that the consumption of culture's seemingly 'neglected' early history has in fact been a culturally

suppressed one. Suppressed by a vision of modernity which has turned largely on an economic analysis of the social organization of production, and on an ideology of modernism which has taken upon itself the task of defending 'culture' against the very forms of mass consumption that we now seek to examine. In short, modernism's master narrative of culture has obscured the early history of consumption and its relationship to social and cultural forms, substituting in its place a history of culture focused on artistic production, individualism, originality, genius, aestheticism, and avant-gardism. This would help to explain why critics of postmodernism like Fredric Jameson, nostalgic for a more 'authentic' culture, see consumer society as part of the superficial, schizophrenic, 'logic' of late capitalism [Jameson 1984]. Indeed, it is only by operating outside the limits of modernism that we can see a 'consumer society' that is nearly four hundred years old. This vantage point reveals cultural and social formations which by the later eighteenth century had come to represent all that a nascent modernism both needed – and needed to suppress – in order to constitute itself. (ibid.)

Although Bermingham insists that we must reject the notion that consumer society is simply a phase of late capitalism, and instead see it as 'intrinsic to all phases of capitalism, even the earliest' (4), she does not argue that consumer society is a monolithic entity, unchanging since its inception in the sixteenth century. What is required, she argues, are histories of consumption which track it through the different phases in capitalist development. But she does not envisage these as yet unwritten histories of cultural consumption as providing only supplementary narratives, produced in order to complete the gaps and silences in the many histories of production. Her ambition far outreaches such a limited project: as she contends, '[t]he suppressed history of cultural consumption may help us to historicize dominant histories of modern production which mask with empirical data their deeper theoretical, moral, and aesthetic agendas' (ibid.). She argues for histories of cultural consumption that take as their object of study not just a past that can be empirically investigated, but also the past as present in a series of historical accounts of production. As she explains,

The modernist distrust of mass culture which has to a large extent both written the history of consumption and blinded us to its history, rests on a tendency to think in essentialist terms about culture, class, and identity. Accordingly, culture is high and pure, classes are homogeneous and stable, and identity is unified and transparent. All of these assumptions need to be questioned if we are to write a history of consumption since the seventeenth century. (14)

The histories of cultural consumption she proposes would raise many of the questions that the book you now hold is intended to address.

Histories of cultural consumption, which are able to break free of the confines of the modernist historical perspective, will undoubtedly recognise, as she claims,

> that one of the most extraordinary aspects of mass consumption since the seventeenth century, and perhaps the thing that distinguishes the modern period from any that preceded it, is the fact that consumption has been the primary means through which individuals have participated in culture and transformed it. (ibid.)

Moreover, as historian Joyce Appleby points out, such histories should show to be totally inadequate the claim

> that ordinary people – the masses – consume because they have been infected with artificial wants dreamed up by the international league of producers, [nor would it be adequate to] treat it [cultural consumption] as a residual category – what people do when they are blocked from nobler activities like philanthropy, meaningful politics and becoming mature. (1993: 172)

Although Bermingham and Appleby are among a growing body of historians working in the 1990s who have sought to establish the view that a consumer society first appears in the West in the sixteenth century, since the 1980s an influential body of work in historical scholarship has made the argument that it is to the eighteenth century that we should look for the origins of consumerism. J. H. Plumb, for example, asserts with great confidence that, 'During the eighteenth century extraordinary economic and social changes swept through Britain and brought into being the first society dedicated to ever-expanding consumption based on industrial production' (1982: 316). In similar fashion, Neil McKendrick, John Brewer and J. H. Plumb claim with conviction, 'There was a consumer revolution in eighteenth-century England' (1982: 1). As they explain,

> More men and women than ever before in human history enjoyed the experience of acquiring material possessions. Objects which for centuries had been the privileged possessions of the rich came, within the space of a few generations, to be within the reach of a larger part of society than ever before, and, for the first time, to be within the legitimate aspirations of almost all of it. (ibid.)

The consumer revolution of the eighteenth century was the result, they claim, of changes in ways of thinking, changes in retail skills, and changes in economic prosperity across all classes. McKendrick claims 'that consumer behaviour was so rampant and the acceptance of commercial attitudes so pervasive that no one . . . should doubt that the first of the world's consumer societies had unmistakenly emerged [in England] by 1800' (1982b: 13).

McKendrick is aware that the argument he seeks to make about the birth of a consumer society in the eighteenth century is one that must confront and challenge the influence of a deeply embedded prelapsarian myth – 'the idea that once there was a just and organic society in which men [and women] lived comfortable lives, athrob with job satisfaction and supported by a sufficiency uncorrupted by commerce or industry' (30). But as he and other historians are aware, it is very difficult to present pre-industrial Europe as an Eden before the fatal Fall into industrialism. McKendrick cites the Italian historian Carlo Capolla, 'After having bought their food, the mass of the people had little left for their wants, no matter how elementary they were' (quoted in McKendrick 1982b: 31). Similarly, we can add Raymond Williams's observation on what the Leavisites left out of their idealised view on a supposed pre-industrial 'organic' culture (see next chapter and Storey 1997), 'the penury, the petty tyranny, the disease and mortality, the ignorance and frustrated intelligence' (Williams 1963: 253).

Social Emulation

McKendrick identifies the practice of social emulation as a key factor in the dramatic birth of consumerism:

> In imitation of the rich the middle ranks of society spent more frenziedly than ever before, and in imitation of them the rest of society joined in as best they might – and that best was unprecedented in the importance of its impact on aggregate demand. Spurred on by social emulation and class competition, men and woman surrendered eagerly to the pursuit of novelty, the hypnotic effects of fashion, and the enticements of persuasive commercial propaganda. (1982b: 11)

The practice of social emulation, he argues, was facilitated by three factors. First, the close proximity of the different social classes played a key role, in that it provided possibilities for social mobility, social competition and, of course, social emulation. The second factor was what he calls 'the compulsive power of fashion begotten by social competition' (ibid.). He argues that the size and nature of London was the third important factor. As he points out, the population of London increased from 200 000 in 1600 to 900 000 in 1800, making it the largest city in Europe. In addition to this, by 1750 11 per cent of the population of England lived in the city, making London the European city with the highest proportion of total population living in its confines. When the number of visitors to London is added to the indigenous population (he estimates that up to 16 per cent of the adult population of the late eighteenth-century England would have spent some time in London), and then one thinks of how all these people may have been 'exposed to the influence of London's shops, London's lifestyle and the prevailing London fashions, its potential for influencing consumer behaviour was enormous' (21). In this way, he contends, London 'served as a shopwindow for the whole country, the centre of forms of conspicuous consumption which would be eagerly mimicked elsewhere' (ibid.). The poet Robert Southey, writing in 1807, had no doubts about the commercial appeal of the capital:

If I were to pass the remainder of my life in London I think the shops would always continue to amuse me. Something extraordinary or beautiful is for ever to be seen in them . . . There is a perpetual exhibition of whatever is curious in nature or art, exquisite in workmanship, or singular in costume; and the display is perpetually varying as the ingenuity of trade and the absurdity of fashion are ever producing something new. (quoted in McKendrick 1982b: 78)

McKendrick argues that social emulation and 'the manipulation of social emulation [through advertising[1] and sales campaigns] made men [and women] pursue "luxuries" where they had previously bought "decencies", and "decencies" where they had previously bought only "necessities" ' (98). Social emulation and the manipulation of social emulation were driven by the emergence in the eighteenth century of what he calls the 'Western European fashion pattern' (41), characterised by the rapid speed of change. He points to the key role played by manipulation:

potent as the force of fashion was, it needed to be released and mobilized and exploited before it could significantly add to aggregate demand. The conditions making this possible grew steadily more favourable . . . But it still required active and aggressive selling to reach that market and exploit its full potential. (63)[2]

Ann Bermingham is critical of the use of social emulation as a model for understanding the growth of cultural consumption. She thinks it an inadequate approach to the processes and patterns of cultural consumption in that it always assumes a top-down flow of cultural influence. As a model of explanation, she claims, it always 'reinforces the political view that culture is the province of the elite' (1995: 12). Moreover, such arguments, she observes, always draw their evidence from the self-understanding and self-presentation of dominant voices in past periods in history. Such unproblematic use of the views expressed by dominant voices may lead to a failure by historians to penetrate the surface discourse to reveal what might be the ideological stake that these voices have in specific arguments about social emulation. For example, as Bermingham makes clear, expressions of distaste at people supposedly consuming above their station might be driven by a fear that such an activity might lead to other, more socially threatening, ideas and practices (12). In other words, the reality might be that the dominant voices are really articulating their fear of where social emulation might lead, rather than identifying actual instances of it in practice. In addition to this, Bermingham also observes that '[t]he top-down model of emulation is also flawed in that it cannot accommodate situations where cultural forms seem to flow in the reverse direction' (ibid.). Ben Fine and Ellen Leopold, for instance, cite the eighteenth-century example of social emulation upwards: the frock-coat's movement from being the work wear of agricultural labourers to becoming the fashion wear of members of the royal family (1990: 172).

Fine and Leopold offer another type of objection to the social-emulation model as presented by McKendrick. They point out 'that the effect of directing attention to consumption through the market is to rewrite history favourably in terms of the rich and powerful, who act as the leading edge of change and as subjects to be emulated' (1990: 152). Further to this, they accuse him of wishing 'to revive the idea of the making of history by the wealthy as the leading and progressive edge' (155); he is accused of advocating a version of history in which 'economic progress is associated with the history of the rich or *nouveau riche*' (157).[3] Rejecting the view that social emulation is always a linear flow from top to bottom

> deprives luxury spending of its progressive attributes. The lower orders are no longer simply passive beneficiaries and transforming multipliers of consuming habits imposed from above, and spending by the upper classes is no longer required to serve as a catalyst in the transformation of goods from luxuries into basic necessities. (172–3)

> The concept of emulation (source of the trickle-down effect) . . . establishes a progressive role for the upper classes in the creation of consumer society. They are seen as the ultimate source of demand, introducing ideas for consumption goods

which are passed down through all other strata in society, transformed as they go from luxuries to decencies to basic necessities. There is an implication that the state of idleness made possible by unearned incomes may be warranted by the inventiveness of those so under-occupied in dreaming up demands for new luxury goods. . . . The belief that wealth produces 'breeding', which is itself the source of taste and refinement, is therefore used to justify the existence of the social pyramid. But the inequalities of that pyramid are entirely glossed over. (176)

However, although a 'bottom-up' model of cultural flow may correct the elitism of the 'top-down' model, it too would remain locked in a very limited notion of the meaning and social significance of cultural consumption. Therefore, although it is certainly true that specific practices of consumption may result from a desire to emulate other social classes, people can be observed to engage in cultural consumption for many other reasons. We should, as Bermingham suggests, move beyond social-emulation models and open up our gaze to see cultural consumption in terms of 'structures of appropriation, circulation, and bricolage, and the complex workings of aesthetics, fantasy, discipline, and sexuality' (1995: 13).

The feminist historian Amanda Vickery is also of the view that social emulation offers an inadequate explanation for the growth in consumption in the late eighteenth century. She argues that as a model of explanation it presents an 'unimaginative interpretation of human motivation' in its assumption that 'envy and wishful thinking are the norm' (1993: 275). Furthermore, she contends that it is a model, especially as used by McKendrick, that often operates with a very particular view of women, as on the one hand driven by a 'pathological desire to consume', and on the other 'simply innately covetous and congenitally wistful about the prospect of upward mobility' (277). For example, whereas Harold Perkin makes a general claim about the causes of the consumer revolution – 'the key to that demand was social emulation, keeping up with the Joneses, the compulsive urge for imitating the spending habits of one's betters' (1968: 110) – McKendrick is quite explicit about the gender of those doing the consuming:

Her increased earning released her desire to compete with social superiors, a desire pent up for centuries or at least restricted to a very occasional excess. . . . It was this new consumer demand, the mill girl who wanted to dress like a duchess . . . which helped to create the industrial revolution. (1974: 200, 209)

Vickery argues, in a view that supports Bermingham's point discussed earlier, that much of this way of situating women in the practices of cultural consumption derives from an uncritical reading of historical sources. As she explains, 'Generalizations about this homogeneously feminine consumer motivation are illustrated by uncritical quotation from eighteenth-century travellers' reports, satirical social commentary and moralists' diatribes. . . . Ancient prejudices have thus been passed off as actual behaviour' (277).[4] Mica Nava makes a similar point in a critical review of Janet Wolff's (1985, 1990) discussion of women's cultural experience in the nineteenth-century city. Nava seeks to draw attention to the potential difference between women's actual lived experience and the depiction of this in intellectual presentations of modernity. Much of Wolff's argument, according to Nava, is heavily reliant on 'the invisibility of women in the *literature* of modernity' (Nava 1997: 59). The problem identified by Nava is the way in which this invisibility is allowed to play a crucial but misleading role in explaining women's cultural experience of nineteenth-century urban life. As she explains,

> The absence from the literature is read as evidence of a 'real' absence rather than evidence of itself. A different reading of women's participation in modernity would have emphasized the constructedness of this literature. It would have highlighted the *intellectual* exclusion of women and the ambivalence of the authors about cultural change – the androcentrism of most of the texts about modernity. (59)

Vickery also points out how the social-emulation model has a tendency to foreshorten and impoverish analysis of consumption by 'assuming that beyond their material function goods only convey information about competitive status and sexuality and that consumables once possessed carry the same social and personal meanings for all consumers' (1993: 277). Against such a position she argues for a view of cultural consumption 'as a positive contribution to the creation of culture and meaning' (278). In her own research she seeks to 'move beyond the moment of purchase', to the way goods are 'used and the multitude of meanings invested in possessions over time' as they are placed in new contexts and in new relationships with other goods (281, 282). It is important, she maintains, if we are to fully understand cultural consumption, that we try to track items as they enter the personal economy of the consumer, where they may be given new meanings, as they are placed in shifting contexts and changing relationships; and they become part of the processes she calls '*inconspicuous* consumption' (284). As an example of these processes she cites research she carried out on Ellen Weeton Stock, a woman who worked as a governess in early nineteenth-century Lancashire. In a letter to her daughter Mary, written to accompany a number of family heirlooms, Stock wrote:

> The green ribbon is part of a boxfull my mother once had; they were taken in a prize which my father captured during the American war. . . . The piece of patchwork is an old quilt, I made it about 20 years ago; the hexagon in the middle was of our best bed hangings . . . they were chintzes my father brought home with him from one of his voyages. . . . I am thus minded, my Mary, that you might know something of the history of your mother's family. (quoted in Vickery 1993: 293–4)

Although Colin Campbell (1983) accepts McKendrick's argument about the birth of a consumer society in the late eighteenth century, and the central role played by women consumers, he is dismissive of the idea that this can be adequately explained by the social-emulation model. As he contends, 'the fact that modern societies are characterized by multiple and diverse elite groups presents a problem concerning who exactly one is to emulate' (284). Further-more, 'for those at the pinnacle, emulation is hardly an available motive and yet their pattern of consumption seems to lack none of the dynamic apparent among their emulators' (ibid.). Moreover, as Campbell has observed, 'behaviour which is imitative is not neces-sarily also emulative' (1993: 40). That is to say, a domestic servant may wear a dress similar to one worn by her aristocratic employer without this necessarily implying that she is seeking to be like her mistress. Although it is the case that domestic servants accepted new and second-hand clothes from their employers, the significance and meaning of such acceptance may not be entirely self-evident. As Vickery suggests,

> it is not clear that wearing a Lady's dress made a parlour maid look, feel or get treated like a lady. To presume she wished she was a lady might seem legitimate, but certainly does not follow from evidence that she accepted a second-hand dress. After all, second-hand dresses could be attractive simply because they had a high resale value. Besides, the strenuous efforts ex-servants made to retrieve their wages and wardrobe, including the threat of legal action, suggest that clothing was seen as an important part of their earnings, rather than merely the coveted equipment of social emulation. (1993: 284)

If social emulation is to have an impact on production it requires to be matched by emulative spending. McKendrick argues that domestic servants played a crucial role in the transmission of consumer taste and behaviour from the dominant classes in the metropolis to other classes in the provinces. In this way, he maintains, social emulation flowed downward from the rich to their domestic servants, then to industrial workers, and finally to agricultural workers. Working in this way, he argues, social emulation 'became an engine for growth, a motive power for mass production' (1982b: 66). But as Fine and Leopold point out, 'Emulative spending developing from below stairs appears highly improbable' (1990: 169). They cite the example of Barbara Johnson, who in the 1760s paid £7 15s 9d for material to make a day dress, at a time when her housemaid's basic annual salary would have been about £7 7s. It therefore seems highly unlikely that domestic servants engaged in emulative spending. The clothes they wore that echoed their employers' tastes were handed down from mistress to maid. Fine and Leopold offer two reasons for this. The first is the increasing pace of fashion among the dominant classes in late eighteenth-century England. The other reason presents a direct challenge to the very idea of social emulation: 'Employers often selected and purchased clothes for their servants to wear . . . [because servants'] clothes were a highly visible sign of their employers' wealth and status . . . [they] reflected his or her taste, not that of the servant' (170).

The Romantic Ethic

Colin Campbell (1983, 1987, 1993, 1995) argues that in order to fully understand the development of modern forms of cultural consumption we need to take into account what he calls the Romantic ethic. In what he describes as 'a very ambitious argument' (1987: 2), he maintains that Romanticism, the intellectual and artistic movement which developed alongside industrialisation, played a crucial role in the development and rapid growth of consumer society in the late eighteenth century.

Campbell begins his argument with a process the German sociologist Max Weber referred to as 'disenchantment' (1965). Weber used the term to describe a historical process in which emotions are gradually removed from the natural world ('the night was frightening') to be relocated in the inner-world of the individual ('she experienced the night as frightening'). This is an important part of the historical development of a growing separation of the subjective inner-world of the self and the objective outer-world of nature. It gradually produces a way of being in the world in which there is the objective world outside the self and the subjective response to it. As Campbell comments,

Objective reality and subjective response were now mediated through consciousness in such a way that the individual had a wide degree of choice concerning exactly how to connect them. Beliefs, actions, aesthetic preferences and emotional responses were no longer automatically dictated by circumstances but 'willed' by individuals. (1987: 73–4)

According to Campbell, this process reached a crucial stage with the development of Romanticism and what the Romantic poet Samuel Taylor Coleridge called for the first time 'self-consciousness' (73).

The importance of Romanticism for Campbell is that it was the first cultural movement committed to 'a radically different doctrine of the person' (1983: 286).

Romanticism . . . led to the creation of a distinctive ideal of character, one which, although most obviously applied to the artist, was also meant to serve for the consumer or 're-creator' of his [or her] products. Since the key characteristic of the divine was taken to be creativity, both in the sense of productivity and of originality, imagination became the most significant and prized of personal qualities, with the capacity to manifest this both in works of art and through an ability to enter fully into those created by others acting as unambiguous signs of its presence. (52)

The Romantic concept of the self involved the view that one should trust one's feelings; that one should seek within for guidance. This led to what we might call a commitment to experience; that is, a doctrine which maintains that one should seek out experiences and then learn from these experiences; and if one is an artist, one should express one's experiences so that others may in turn learn from the expression of experience. The Romantics believed firmly in the view 'that happiness comes from "self-expression" ' (285). Campbell argues that 'the romantic doctrine of learning through experiencing tended to emphasise the value not just of all feelings (whether positive or negative) but especially that of pleasure. . . . [what William Wordsworth called] "the grand *elementary* principle of pleasure" ' (286). This commitment to experiencing pleasure, Campbell argues, 'is a doctrine which provides an intellectual justification to the consumptive mode as via powerful experience we can come to know the world and ourselves' (287). It is this new way of thinking and being in the world, the Romantic self, with its redefinition of the individual and how to improve the individual through exposure to many new and different experiences, that Campbell sees as crucial to the development of a consumption ethic.

To establish an informing connection between Romanticism and this new consumption ethic, Campbell argues that the best place to look is in its 'development of new doctrines of art and the artist, doctrines which of necessity also applied to the consumer of these products' (288). Romanticism advocated an expressive theory of art; the work of art was seen as an expression of the artist's 'genius'; an embodiment of his or her experience, imagination and feeling (see Abrams 1953). But crucially for the development of a consumption ethic, Romanticism did not just advocate a new view of the production of art, it also insisted that consumption of art should be understood differently. The value of consuming Romantic art was in that it gave the consumer access to the artist's genius. Consuming Romantic art, in other words, involved the re-creation of the artist's experience, imagination and feeling. As Percy Bysshe Shelley argued in *A Defence of Poetry* (first published in 1821),

> A man [or woman], to be greatly good, must imagine intensely and comprehensively; he must put himself in the place of another and of many others; the pains and pleasures of his species must become his own. The great instrument of moral good is the imagination; and poetry administers to the effect by acting upon the cause. Poetry enlarges the circumference of the imagination by replenishing it with thoughts of ever new delight. . . . Poetry strengthens that faculty which is the organ of the moral nature of man, in the same manner as exercise strengthens a limb. (1973: 750)

The Romantic theory of poetry demands of readers an active and imaginative engagement with poetry, one, that is, which is capable of re-creating (in the act of reading) the experience, the feelings and the imagination of the poet. As Campbell explains,

> It is noticeable how such a theory [the Romantic theory of art] places almost as much emphasis upon the 're-creative' abilities of the reader as upon the original creative faculties of the poet, for whilst the latter must be moved by what he sees, and also capable of translating this experience into an affective, and hence effective, work of art, the former must possess sufficient imaginative skill to be able to use the words on the page to produce a convincing illusion. The reader is also, in that sense, assumed to be a creative artist, capable of conjuring up images which have the power to 'move' him [or her]. (1987: 189)

Campbell argues that the Romantic theory of art, with its belief in moral renewal through pleasure, 'led to the creation of a distinctive ideal of character, one which, although most obviously applied to the artist, was also meant to serve for the consumer or "re-creator" of his [or her] products' (193).

> Romanticism provided that philosophy of 'recreation' neces-sary for a dynamic consumerism: a philosophy which legit-imates the search for pleasure as a good in itself . . . [In this way it] served to provide ethical support for that restless and continuous pattern of consumption which so distinguishes the behaviour of modern man [sic]. (201)

In this way, Campbell argues, 'romantic doctrines provided a new set of motivations and justifications for consuming cultural products, ones which emphasized the value of the subjectively-apprehended experience of consumption itself' (1983: 289).[5] Having established the origins of the dominant mode of modern consumption in both the theoretical concerns and practical con-sequences of Romanticism, Campbell then elaborates a more detailed theory of contemporary cultural consumption. He begins by distin-guishing between two forms of hedonism, traditional and modern. What marks the difference between these two modes is an expansion of the field of pleasure from a location in quite specific experiences to a belief that it can be located in all experiences. The movement from one to the other is the result of a shift from seeking pleasure in 'sensations' to seeking pleasure in 'emotions'. As he explains,

> The key to the development of modern hedonism lies in the shift of primary concern from sensations to emotions, for it is only through the medium of the latter that powerful and prolonged stimulation can be combined with any significant degree of autonomous control, something which arises directly from the fact that an emotion links mental images with phys-ical stimuli. (1987: 69)

In other words, traditional hedonism sought pleasure in particular objects and practices, modern hedonism seeks pleasure in the meaning of objects and practices (76). Figure 1.1 presents Peter Corrigan's useful diagrammatic summary of Campbell's argument.

Traditional hedonism	Modern hedonism
Search for pleasure tied to specific practices	Search for pleasure in any or all experiences
Pleasure tied to sensations	Pleasure tied to emotions
Emotions not under control of subject	Emotions controlled by subject
Pleasure derived from control of objects and events	Pleasure derived from control of the meanings of objects and events

Fig. 1.1 Traditional versus modern hedonism. Source: Corrigan 1997: 16

According to Campbell, the shift from seeking pleasure in what is known to provide pleasure to seeking it in what has yet to be experienced as pleasurable had a dramatic effect on consumption. As he explains,

> The capacity to gain pleasure from self-constructed, imaginative experience crucially alters the essential nature of all hedonistic activity. . . . In the . . . traditional pattern of hedonistic conduct imagination does not have a significant role to play because the nature of anticipated pleasure is known from past experience. The expectation of pleasure triggers desire but what one 'expects' to enjoy is mainly what one 'remembers' enjoying. Novel objects or activities thus tend to be regarded with suspicion as their potential for pleasure is as yet unknown. In modern hedonism, on the other hand, if a product is capable of being represented as possessing unknown characteristics then it is open to the pleasure-seeker to imagine the nature of its gratifications and it thus becomes an occasion for day-dreaming. Although employing material from memory, the hedonist can now imaginatively speculate upon what gratifications and enjoyments are in store, and thus attach his [or her] favoured day-dream to this real object of desire. In this way, imagined pleasures are added to those already encountered and greater desire is experienced for the unknown than the known. (85–6)

Campbell sees this as the key to modern patterns of consumption:

> The introduction of day-dreaming into hedonism thus not only strengthens desire, but helps to make desiring itself a pleasurable activity. Whilst for traditional man [sic] deferred gratification had simply meant the experience of frustration, for modern man it becomes a happy hiatus between desire and consummation which can be filled with the joys of day-dreaming. This reveals a unique feature of modern self-illusory hedonism – the fact that the desiring mode constitutes a state of enjoyable discomfort, and that wanting rather than having is the main focus of pleasure-seeking. (86)

For Campbell the process is driven forward by the inevitable gap which always opens up between the attainment of an object of desire in actuality and the anticipation of its attainment in imagination. It is generally the case that the actual experience of consumption will fail to match the experience imagined in anticipation. In this way, 'The consummation of desire is thus a necessarily disillusioning experience', in that the gap between anticipation and reality will always produce, regardless of the pleasures actual experience of consumption may bring, a 'resultant recognition that something is missing' (ibid.). Although Campbell's argument is that consumers are driven from object to object, from anticipatory day-dreaming to disillusioning reality, longing for an object of desire which can be experienced in actuality as it is experienced in imaginative anticipation, his 'central insight [however] . . . is the realization that individuals do not so much seek satisfaction from products, as pleasures from self-illusory experiences which they construct from their associated meanings' (89). In this way, he argues,

> The essential activity of consumption is thus not the actual selection, purchase or use of products, but the imaginative pleasure-seeking to which the product image lends itself, 'real' consumption being largely a resultant of this 'mentalistic' hedonism. Viewed in this way, the emphasis upon novelty as well as that upon insatiability both become comprehensible. (ibid.)

In this way, it is the cycle of anticipation and disillusionment which drives the desire to consume. All that is required to keep the process moving is the appearance of *new* commodities for cultural consumption. Campbell's argument is a refutation of claims that modern consumerism is evidence of materialistic desire to consume more and more objects.

> The idea that contemporary consumers have an insatiable desire to acquire objects represents a serious misunderstanding of the mechanism which impels people to want goods. Their basic motivation is the desire to experience in reality the pleasurable dramas which they have already enjoyed in imagination, and each 'new' product is seen as offering a possibility of realizing this ambition. However, since reality can never provide the perfected pleasures encountered in day-dreams (or, if at all, only in part, and very occasionally), each purchase leads to literal disillusionment, something which explains how wanting is extinguished so quickly, and why people disacquire goods as rapidly as they acquire them. What is not extinguished, however, is the fundamental longing which day-dreaming itself generates, and hence there is as much determination as ever to find new products to serve as replacement objects of desire. (89–90)

It is the continual dynamic interaction between anticipated experience and actual experience, and the profound longing to close the gap between the two, which is the key to understanding the limitless nature of modern cultural consumption (*see* Fig. 1.2).

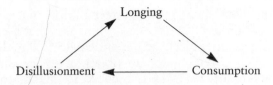

Fig. 1.2 Cycle of consumption. Source: Campbell 1987

Although Campbell acknowledges the ways in which advertisers may attempt to fuel this process, he rejects the view that they can in any way control the cycle of production and reproduction of longing. He recognises that 'advertisers [may] make use of the fact that people day-dream, and indeed feed those dreams' (91). But, as he insists, because 'the practice of day-dreaming is itself endemic to modern societies [it] does not require the commercial institution of advertising to ensure its continued existence' (ibid.).

To work as material for day-dreams, cultural commodities must be actively consumed. Moreover, in an important distinction, running counter to much 'common sense' about cultural consumption, Campbell is insistent that it is important 'to conceive of these cultural products as providing the material for day-dreams rather than as being day-dreams' (93). The activity of the consumer is crucial.

> [It] is important not only because the individual has to actively use the words, pictures, and sounds to construct an 'as-if' world for himself [sic] to inhabit, but also because the process of day-dreaming (which has in any case preceded contact with the cultural item in question) may well continue long after direct contact has ceased; images relating to a particular film or novel being brought to mind subsequently and embroidered in pleasurable fashion. (ibid.)

However, although cultural consumption is an active process, the essential activity of the consumer is in the imaginative process of seeking pleasure. This leads to a concern 'with the 'meaningfulness' of products', rather than 'a concern with *the* meaning of a product' (1995: 120).

Notes

1 Writing in 1759 Dr Johnson claimed that 'The trade of advertising is now so near perfection that it is not easy to propose any improvement' (quoted in McKendrick 1982b: 146). Johnson may have been wrong about the future, but McKendrick's summary of eighteenth-century advertising (compared to twentieth) suggests he was not so wrong:

The language was inevitably slightly different – teeth were artificial rather than false, waves were not yet permanent, hair was frankly dyed rather than genteelly colour-rinsed. The dominant approach was still verbal rather than visual. The claims were unhindered by even the loosest code of advertising ethics . . . so superlatives abound and the most remarkable combinations of virtues co-exist in a single product. The knocking copy of rivals was more direct – usually straightforward warnings of deceit and commercial theft. But the similarities were greater than the differences. There was the same insistent propaganda, the same constant repetition of brand names, the same exploitation of snobbery and social emulation, the same use of the famous and the authoritative to promote their products – royalty used their hair dyes, doctors recommended their medicines, dentists sanctioned their tooth pastes, fashion leaders enthused over their clothes styles. (183)

2 Colin Campbell (1987: 21–4) suggests that McKendrick has certain 'unresolved problems' in his account in that he wants to insist on the primary role played by the new fashion pattern in generating the consumer society of the eighteenth century while at the same time claiming that the fashion pattern itself was produced by market manipulation. This appears to be an argument in which cause produces effect and effect produces cause.

3 They also claim that 'The result is to construct a rationale in favour of contemporary consumerist society, however understood, and the role of those privileged within it' (152). Paul Glennie identifies another problem perhaps symptomatic of much historical work on cultural consumption, 'McKendrick's account was largely researched from sources relating to producers and traders, from which it is difficult to identify the new consumers, and how and why their demand changed' (1995: 167).

4 Colin Campbell makes an interesting point about the nature of some of these sources:

> most of these observers of the social scene were themselves either members or representatives of the superior classes, their jealous regard for their own privileges, combined with an intense anxiety about the stability of the social order (especially after 1789), meant that they were prone to see imitative consumption as inherently threatening. In other words their strident condemnation stemmed less from any knowledge that such conduct arose out of emulative desires than fear that it might, with the consequence that they condemned imitation for what it could represent rather than what it was known to be. (1993: 41)

5 Campbell is aware that Romanticism's influence on the development of a consumer society is to say the least ironic; especially so, given that its proponents' own perception of what they were doing involved a sense of being in conflict with the emerging industrial society in which they lived (see Campbell 1983: 293, and Campbell 1987: 209).

|2|

Cultural Consumption as Manipulation

The focus of this chapter is on three approaches to cultural consumption which have had in different ways, both positive and negative, an enormous influence on the development of cultural studies, especially in the UK. The first is the work of a group of German intellectuals (especially Theodor Adorno, Max Horkheimer and Herbert Marcuse) collectively known as the Frankfurt School. This section will also include a critical assessment of the political-economy-of-culture approach as a way of demonstrating the continuing influence of the Frankfurt School's work on contemporary cultural analysis. This is followed, in the second section, by a discussion of Leavisism (the work of F. R. Leavis, Q. D. Leavis and Denys Thompson). The third section contains a discussion of the early work of the French cultural theorist Roland Barthes. Although these three bodies of work represent quite different traditions and different approaches to cultural consumption, what connects them is, as I have already said, their influence on cultural studies, and what makes them of significance for the particular concerns of this book is the fact that, despite their many differences, all three operate with a model of cultural consumption as manipulation. The chapter concludes with a brief discussion of some of the problems with critical approaches which begin with the assumption that cultural consumption is best understood as a form of manipulation.

The Frankfurt School

The Frankfurt School is the name given to a group of German intellectuals associated with the Institute for Social Research at the University of Frankfurt. The Institute was established in 1923. Following the coming to power of Nazism in Germany in 1933, the Institute moved to New York, becoming a temporary part (until 1949) of the University of Columbia. The experience of life in the United States had a profound impact on the School's thinking on the production and consumption of culture.

In 1947 Theodor Adorno and Max Horkheimer coined the term 'culture industry' to designate the products and processes of mass culture. The products of the culture industry, they claim, are marked by two features: cultural homogeneity, 'film, radio and magazines make up a system which is uniform as a whole and in every part . . . all mass culture is identical' (1979: 120–1); and predictability:

> As soon as the film begins, it is quite clear how it will end, and who will be rewarded, punished, or forgotten. In light music [popular music], once the trained ear has heard the first notes of the hit song, it can guess what is coming and feel flattered when it does come. (125)

Furthermore, 'Under the regime of the Culture Industry . . . the film leaves no room for imagination or reflection on the part of its audience . . . the film forces its *victims* to equate it directly with reality' (1977: 353–4; my italics). In a later essay, Adorno elaborates the same theme that the outcomes of cultural consumption are determined by production: 'In all its branches, products which are tailored for consumption by the masses, and which to a great extent determine the nature of that consumption, are manufactured according to plan. . . . The culture industry intentionally integrates its consumers from above' (1991: 85).

Whereas in the perspective developed by the Frankfurt School's contemporaries in England, the Leavisites (discussed in the next section), the concern is that mass culture will lead to 'anarchy' (Matthew Arnold; see Storey 1985), thus bringing an end to cultural and social authority, the Frankfurt School can see only the development of a depoliticised social conformity and the iron grip of social authority. The Frankfurt School maintains that the culture industry, by producing a culture marked by 'standardisation, stereotype, conservatism, mendacity, manipulated consumer goods' (Lowenthal 1961: 11) had worked to depoliticise the working class; that is, it had limited its horizon to political and economic goals that could be realised within the oppressive and exploitative framework of capitalist society. Leo Lowenthal contends that, 'Whenever revolutionary tendencies show a timid head, they are mitigated and cut short by a false fulfilment of wish-dreams, like wealth, adventure, passionate love, power and sensationalism in general' (ibid.). In short, the culture industry discouraged the 'masses' from thinking beyond the confines of the present. Herbert Marcuse develops this line of argument, to suggest that capitalism, working through the culture industry, promotes an 'ideology of consumerism', which generates false needs,[1] and that these needs work as a mechanism of social control:

> the irresistible output of the entertainment and information industry carry with them prescribed attitudes and habits, certain intellectual and emotional reactions which bind the consumers more or less pleasantly to the producers and, through the latter, to the whole. The products indoctrinate and manipulate; they promote a false consciousness which is immune against its falsehood . . . it becomes a way of life. It is a good way of life - much better than before – and as a good way of life, it militates against qualitative change. Thus emerges a pattern of *one-dimensional thought and behaviour* in which ideas, aspirations, and objectives that, by their content, transcend the established universe of discourse and action are either repelled or reduced to the terms of this universe. (1968: 26–7)

In other words, by supplying the means to certain needs, capitalism, working through the productions of the culture industry, is able to prevent the formation of more fundamental desires. The inevitable result, or so it is claimed, is that the political imagination of working people is stunted. In this way, the Frankfurt School argue, work and leisure under capitalism form a compelling relationship: the effects of the culture industry are guaranteed by the nature of work; the work process secures the effects of the culture industry. The function of the culture industry is therefore, ultimately, to organise leisure time in the same way as capitalist industrialisation has organised work time. Work under capitalism stunts the senses; the function of the culture industry is to continue the process: 'the escape from everyday drudgery which the whole Culture Industry promises. . . [is a] paradise . . . [of] the same old drudgery . . . escape . . . [is] predesigned to lead back to the starting point. Pleasure promotes the resignation which it ought to help to forget' (Adorno and Horkheimer 1979: 142). In short, work leads to mass culture; mass culture leads back to work.

In 'On Popular Music' (first published in 1941), Adorno makes three specific claims about the music the culture industry produces. First, he claims that it is 'standardised'. Once a musical and/or lyrical pattern has proved successful it is exploited to commercial exhaustion. Moreover, details from one popular song can be interchanged with details from another. Unlike the organic structure of 'serious music', where each detail expresses the whole, popular music is mechanical in the sense that a given detail can be shifted from one song to another without any real effect on the structure as a whole. In order to conceal standardisation, the music industry engages in what Adorno calls 'pseudo-individualization':

> Standardisation of song hits keeps the customers in line by doing their listening for them, as it were. Pseudo-individualization, for its part, keeps them in line by making them forget that what they listen to is already listened to for them, or 'pre-digested'. (1998: 203)

It is Adorno's second claim – that popular music promotes passive listening – which brings us back to the question of cultural consumption. The Frankfurt School maintain, as we noted earlier, that work under capitalism is dull and therefore promotes the search for escape, but, because it is also dulling, it leaves little energy for real escape – the demands of 'authentic' culture. Instead refuge is sought in forms such as popular music – the consumption of which is always passive, and endlessly repetitive, confirming the world as it is. Adorno sees popular music as the 'non-productive correlate' to life in the office or on the factory floor. The 'strain and boredom' of work leads men and women to the 'avoidance of effort' in their leisure time. Denied 'novelty' in their work time, and too exhausted for it in their leisure time, 'they crave a stimulant' – popular music satisfies the craving.

> Its [popular music's] stimulations are met with the inability to vest effort in the ever-identical. This means boredom again. It is a circle which makes escape impossible. The impossibility of escape causes the widespread attitude of inattention toward popular music. The moment of recognition is that of effortless sensation. The sudden attention attached to this moment burns itself out *instanter* and relegates the listener to a realm of inattention and distraction. (206)

Popular music generates a kind of blurred dialectic: a mutually reinforcing relationship in which to consume it demands inattention and distraction, while in return, its consumption produces in the consumer inattention and distraction.

Adorno's final point is the claim that popular music operates as 'social cement' (ibid.). Its 'socio-psychological function' is to achieve in the consumers of popular music 'psychical adjustment' (ibid.) to the needs of the prevailing structure of power. This 'adjustment' manifests itself in 'two major socio-psychological types of mass behaviour . . . the "rhythmically" obedient type and the "emotional" type' (207). The first type dances in distraction to the rhythm of his or her own exploitation and oppression. The second type wallows in sentimental misery oblivious to the real conditions of existence.

In spite of its Marxist sophistication, the approach of the Frankfurt School to the cultural consumption of popular culture is, ultimately, a conservative discourse from above (a discourse of 'us' and 'them') on the culture of other people. Moreover, it is a form of analysis which leaves very little room for a critical engagement with cultural consumption, other than one, that is, in which we know all the answers before we ask the questions.

A perspective which has unproblematically inherited many of the limiting assumptions of the Frankfurt School is the political-economy approach to culture. Peter Golding and Graham Murdock offer this outline of its procedures and protocols:

> What distinguishes the critical political economy perspective
> . . . is precisely its focus on the interplay between the symbolic
> and economic dimensions of public communications [including popular culture]. It sets out to show how different ways
> of financing and organising cultural production have traceable
> consequences for the range of discourses and representations
> in the public domain and for audiences' *access* to them. (1991:
> 15; my italics)

The significant word here is 'access' – privileged over 'use' and 'meaning'. This reveals the limitations of the approach: good on the economic dimensions but weak on the symbolic. Golding and Murdock suggest that the growing tendency in cultural studies to engage in a 'romantic celebration of subversive consumption is clearly at odds with cultural studies' long standing concern with the way the mass media operate ideologically, to sustain and support prevailing relations of domination' (17). What I find particularly revealing about this claim is not the critique of studies of cultural consumption in cultural studies, but the claim about the assumed proper purposes of cultural studies. They seem to be suggesting, that is, that unless the focus is firmly and exclusively on domination and manipulation, cultural studies is failing in its stated task. Moreover, what is also quite explicit is the claim that there are only two positions of cultural analysis: either, on the one hand, romantic celebration, or on the other, a full recognition of, and total focus on, the ideological power of the culture industries – and only the second position amounts to a serious scholarly engagement. The logical conclusion to be drawn is twofold: first, all attempts to show people resisting ideological manipulation are forms of romantic celebration; second, left pessimism is the only guarantee of political and scholarly seriousness.

Political economy's idea of cultural analysis seems to involve very little more than detailing access to, and availability of, cultural texts and practices. Nowhere does it actually advocate a consideration

of what these texts and practices might mean (textually) or be made
to mean in use (cultural consumption). Moreover, as Golding and
Murdock point out,

> in contrast to recent work on audience activity within cultural
> studies, which concentrates on the negotiation of textual inter-
> pretations and media use in immediate social settings, critical
> political economy seeks to relate variations in people's
> responses to their overall location in the economic system. (27)

This seems to suggest that audience negotiations are fictions, merely
illusory moves in a game of economic power. Cultural theorists,
especially within cultural studies, who reject this view are dismissed
as being guilty of giving currency to 'an influential version of . . .
free market philosophy' (28). By reducing cultural consumption to
simple questions of 'access', the political-economy-of-culture
approach threatens, despite its admirable intentions, to collapse
everything back into the economic (for further discussion, see
chapter 8 below).

The Leavisites

The work of the Leavisites (I am concerned here only with the work
of F.R. Leavis, Q.D. Leavis and Denys Thompson) spans a period
of 40 years. However, their attitude to cultural consumption,
especially the consumption of popular culture, was formed in the
early 1930s with the publication of three works: *Mass Civilisation
and Minority Culture* (F.R. Leavis), *Fiction and the Reading Public*
(Q.D. Leavis) and *Culture and Environment* (F.R. Leavis and Denys
Thompson).

Leavisism is based on the assumption that 'culture has always
been in minority keeping' (Leavis and Thompson 1977: 3). Really
meaningful cultural consumption is always limited to a truly
cultured minority. As Leavis and Thompson explain,

> Upon the minority depends our power of profiting by the
> finest human experience of the past; they keep alive the
> subtlest and most perishable parts of tradition. Upon them
> depend the implicit standards that order the finer living of an
> age, the sense that this is worth more than that, this rather
> than that is the direction in which to go, that the centre is here
> rather than there. (5)

Unfortunately, the twentieth century has witnessed a change in the
status of this minority. No longer can it command cultural deference; no longer is its cultural authority allowed to go unchallenged.

Q.D. Leavis describes this as a situation in which 'the minority, who had hitherto set the standard of taste without any serious challenge' have experienced a 'collapse of authority' (1978: 185, 187). She longs for a return to a previous golden age when 'the masses' exhibited an 'unquestioning assent to authority' (191).[2] She quotes Edmund Gosse to confirm the seriousness of the situation.

> One danger which I have long foreseen from the spread of the democratic sentiment, is that of the traditions of literary taste, the canons of literature, being reversed with success by a popular vote. Up to the present time, in all parts of the world, the masses of uneducated or semi-educated persons, who form the vast majority of readers, though they cannot and do not appreciate the classics of their race, have been content to acknowledge their traditional supremacy. Of late there have seemed to me to be certain signs, especially in America, of a revolt of the mob against our literary masters. . . . If literature is to be judged by a plebiscite and if the plebs recognise its power, it will certainly by degrees cease to support reputations which give it no pleasure and which it cannot comprehend. The revolution against taste, once begun, will land us in irreparable chaos. (quoted in Q.D. Leavis 1978: 190)

According to F.R. Leavis, what Gosse had only feared had now come to pass. It is against the threat of continuing cultural decline that Leavisism proposes to develop particular strategies of cultural consumption: 'to introduce into schools a training in resistance [to mass culture]' (F.R. Leavis 1933: 188–9); and outside schools, to promote a 'conscious and directed effort . . . [to] take the form of resistance by an armed and active minority' (Q.D. Leavis 1978: 270).

In this way, the Leavisites were concerned to address what F.R. Leavis, writing in 1930, called the 'desperate plight of culture today' (1998: 13). They viewed the twentieth century as being marked by an increasing cultural decline. The century was characterised, they claimed, by the development of a culture of 'standardisation and levelling down' (Leavis and Thompson 1977: 3) which had its origins in the nineteenth century, with the devastating impact of industrialisation and urbanisation, but which had continued to develop in the twentieth.[3] To have any hope of reversing or even slowing down this process, they argued, would require special attention to matters of cultural consumption; in short, 'the citizen . . . must be trained to discriminate and to resist' (5). There are, however, certain forms of mass culture which are better avoided altogether. Popular fiction, for example, is condemned for offering addictive forms of 'compensation' and 'distraction':

This form of compensation . . . is the very reverse of recreation, in that it tends, not to strengthen and refresh the addict for living, but to increase his [or her] unfitness by habituating him to weak evasions, to the refusal to face reality at all. (100)

Similarly, Q.D. Leavis refers to such reading as 'a drug addiction to fiction' (1978: 152), and, for those readers unfortunate enough to become involved with romantic fiction, it can lead to 'a habit of fantasying [which] will lead to maladjustment in actual life' (54). For those not addicted to the cultural consumption of popular fiction there was always the danger of the cinema. The cinema's increasing popularity makes it a very dangerous source of pleasure indeed: 'they [films] involve surrender, under conditions of hypnotic receptivity, to the cheapest emotional appeals, appeals the more insidious because they are associated with a compellingly vivid illusion of actual life' (F.R. Leavis 1998: 15). For Q.D. Leavis, Hollywood films are 'largely masturbatory' (1978: 165). Although the popular press is described as 'the most powerful and pervasive de-educator of the public mind' (Leavis and Thompson 1977: 138), and radio is claimed to be putting an end to critical thought (F.R. Leavis 1998: 15), it is for advertising, with its 'unremitting, pervasive, masturbatory manipulations', that F.R. Leavis saves his most condemnatory tone.

The texts and practices of advertising are for Leavisism the very epitome of cultural decline. To understand why we must understand Leavisism's attitude to language. In their manifesto for good educational practice, *Culture and Environment*, Leavis and Thompson state: 'it should be brought home to learners that this debasement of language is not merely a matter of words; it is a debasement of emotional life, and the quality of living' (1977: 4). In this way, advertising is not just blamed for debasing the language, but is condemned for debasing the emotional life of the whole language community; reducing 'the standard of living'. They provide examples (mostly written by F.R. Leavis himself) for analysis. The questions they pose are very revealing of their general attitude. Here is a typical example, an advert for 'Two Quakers ' tobacco:

THE TOBACCO OF TYPICAL TWIST

'Yes, it's the best I've ever smoked. But it's deuced expensive.' 'What's the tuppence extra? And anyway, you get it back an' more. Burns clean and slow – that's the typical twist, – gives it the odd look. Cute scientific dodge. You see, they experimented . . . ' 'Oh! cut the cackle, and give us another fill. You talk like an advertisement.' Thereafter peace and a pipe of Two Quakers.

They suggest the following questions for school students in the fifth and sixth forms: '1. Describe the type of person represented; 2. How are you expected to feel towards him? 3. What do you think his attitude would be towards us? How would he behave in situations where mob passions run high?' (16–17). Two things are remarkable about these questions. First of all, the connection that is made between the advertisement and so-called mob passions. Second, notice the exclusive 'we'; and note also how the pronoun attempts to construct membership of a small educated elite. Other questions operate in the same way. Here are a few examples:

> What kind of person can you imagine responding to such an appeal as this last? What acquaintance would you expect them to have of Shakespeare's work and what capacity for appreciating it? Pupils can be asked to recall their own observations of the kind of people they may have seen visiting 'shrines'. (51)

After describing the cinema as 'cheapening, debasing, distorting', they ask: 'Develop the discussion of the educational value of cinema as suggested here' (144). Rather than encouraging 'discrimination and resistance', it is difficult to see how such questions would invite, with regard to the patterns of cultural consumption of 'other' people, anything other than a debilitating and self-confirming snobbery.

It is easy to be critical of the Leavisite approach to cultural consumption. However, it should be remembered that from a historical point of view, the tradition's work is absolutely foundational to the project of the study of cultural consumption in (British) cultural studies. Furthermore, the impact of the tradition is difficult to overestimate: for more than a century it was undoubtedly the dominant paradigm in cultural analysis. Indeed, it could be argued that it still forms a kind of repressed 'common sense' in certain areas of British and American academic and non-academic life. However, having said this, although it is true that the Leavisites helped establish an educational space for the study of cultural consumption, we should remain in no doubt about the nature of the kind of pedagogic practice they had in mind. The principal problem is its working assumption that cultural consumption of popular culture (the consumption practices of the many) are always presented, and are explicitly understood as, examples of cultural decline. Given this assumption, theoretical research and empirical investigation continued to confirm what they always expected to find. As Tony Bennett points out,

> It was an assumption of the theory that there was something wrong with popular culture and, of course, once that assump-

tion had been made, all the rest followed: one found what one was looking for – signs of decay and deterioration – precisely because the theory required that these be found. In short, the only role offered to the products of popular culture was that of fall guy. (1982: 6)

The Leavisites looked down from the splendid heights of high culture to the commercial wastelands of the cultural-consumption practices of other people down below, seeking only confirmation of cultural decline, cultural difference and the need for cultural deference, regulation and control. This was a discourse of how 'other people' found satisfaction in forms of cultural consumption which the Leavisites found distasteful – i.e. both the people and the commodities they consumed, because, ultimately, Leavisism is less about practices of cultural consumption and much more about 'the masses' and their lived cultures.[4]

Roland Barthes

Roland Barthes' early work on popular culture – with its concern with the processes of signification – introduces a very different way of seeing cultural consumption as manipulation. Barthes' aim is to make explicit what he feels too often remains implicit in the texts and practices of mass culture. His directing principle is to always interrogate what he sees as 'the falsely obvious' (1973: 11). As he explains in *Mythologies*, one of the founding texts of British cultural studies, 'I resented seeing Nature and History confused at every turn, and I wanted to track down, in the decorative display of *what-goes-without-saying*, the ideological abuse which, in my view, is hidden there' (ibid.).

Barthes uses Ferdinand de Saussure's (1974) structuralist model of language to produce a semiological analysis of French mass culture. He uses Saussure's schema of signifier/signified = sign and adds to it a second level of signification. In Barthes' deployment, as illustrated in Fig. 2.1, the sign of primary signification becomes the signifier of secondary signification. In *Elements of Semiology* he substitutes the more familiar terms denotation (primary signification) and connotation (secondary signification): 'the first system [denotation] becomes the plane of expression or signifier of the second system [connotation] . . . The signifiers of connotation . . . are made up of signs (signifiers and signifieds united) of the denoted system' (1967: 89–91).

Barthes claims that it is at the level of secondary signification or connotation that what he calls 'myth' is produced for consumption.

Primary signification/ Denotation	1. Signifier	2. Signified
	3. Sign	
Secondary signification/ Connotation	I. SIGNIFIER	II. SIGNIFIED
	III. SIGN	

Fig. 2.1 Primary and secondary signification. Source: Hall 1980: 130

Myths are the stories societies live by. They provide ways of conceptualising and understanding the world, and therefore they are crucial to a society's efforts (always in the interests of dominant groups) to construct and maintain a sense of self-identity (in terms of acceptable sameness and unacceptable difference). For Barthes myth attempts to become a society's 'common sense' – to produce and put into circulation modes of thinking in which what is cultural (i.e. made by humans) is understood as natural (i.e. a result of the 'laws' of nature). Barthes' concept of myth is very close to classical Marxism's understanding of ideology (see Marx 1998) in that, like ideology, myth is a body of ideas and practices which seek to defend the prevailing structures of power by actively promoting the values and interests of the dominant groups in society. Myth is successful to the extent it is able to naturalise and universalise the interests of dominant groups as if they were the interests of all members of society. To understand this aspect of Barthes' argument we need to understand the polysemic nature of signs; that is, that they have the potential to signify multiple meanings. He argues that all forms of signification can be shown to operate in this way. His most famous example of the workings of secondary signification is taken from the cover of the French magazine *Paris Match* (1955). He begins his analysis by establishing that the primary level of signification consists of a signifier: patches of colour and figuration. This in turn produces the signified: 'a black soldier saluting the French flag'. Together they form the primary sign. The primary sign then becomes the signifier 'black soldier saluting the French flag', producing the signified 'French imperiality'. Here is Barthes' account of his encounter with the cover of the magazine:

> I am at the barber's, and a copy of *Paris Match* is offered to me. On the cover, a young Negro in a French uniform is saluting, with his eyes uplifted, probably fixed on the fold of the tricolour. All this is the meaning of the picture. But, whether

naively or not, I see very well what it signifies to me: that France is a great Empire, that all her sons, without colour discrimination, faithfully serve under her flag, and that there is no better answer to the detractors of an alleged colonialism than the zeal shown by this Negro in serving his so-called oppressors. I am therefore faced with a greater semiological system: there is a signifier, itself already formed with a previous system (*a black soldier is giving the French salute*); there is a signified (it is a purposeful mixture of Frenchness and militariness); finally there is a presence of the signified through the signifier. (1973: 125–6)

At the level of primary signification (denotation) the cover of *Paris Match* presents a black soldier saluting the French flag. This produces, according to Barthes, at the level of secondary signification (connotation), a positive image of French imperialism. In other words, the cover illustration represents *Paris Match*'s attempt to produce a positive image of French imperialism. Following the defeat in Vietnam (1946–54), and the then current war in Algeria (1954–62), such an image would have been seen by many to be of some political urgency. Of course this is not the only way French imperialism might be given positive connotations. Barthes suggests other mythical signifiers the press might employ:

I can very well give to French imperiality many other signifiers beside a Negro's salute: a French general pins a decoration on a one-armed Senegalese, a nun hands a cup of tea to a bed-ridden Arab, a white schoolmaster teaches attentive piccaninnies. (138)

Barthes contends that 'myth has . . . a double function: it points out and it notifies, it makes us understand something and it imposes it on us' (126).

Myth has an imperative, buttonholing character . . . [it arrests] in both the physical and the legal sense of the term: French imperialism condemns the saluting Negro to be nothing more than an instrumental signifier, the Negro suddenly hails me in the name of French imperiality; but at the same moment the Negro's salute thickens, becomes vitrified, freezes into an eternal reference meant to establish French imperiality. (134–5)[5]

The ideological power of myth derives from its capacity to transform history into nature: 'Semiology has taught us that myth has the task of giving an historical intention a natural justification, and making contingency appear eternal. Now this process is exactly that of bourgeois ideology' (142). As Barthes eloquently explains, 'myth is constituted by the loss of the historical quality of things: in it, things lose the memory that they once were made' (155).

> In the case of the soldier Negro . . . what is got rid of is certainly not French imperiality (on the contrary, since what must be actualised is its presence); it is the contingent, historical, in one word: *fabricated,* quality of colonialism. Myth does not deny things, on the contrary, its function is to talk about them; simply, it purifies them, it makes them innocent, it gives them a natural and eternal justification, it gives them a clarity which is not that of an explanation but that of a statement of fact. If I *state the fact* of French imperiality without explaining it, I am very near to finding that it is natural and goes *without saying* . . . In passing from history to nature, myth acts economically: it abolishes the complexity of human acts . . . it organises a world which is without contradictions because it is without depth, a world wide open and wallowing in the evident, it establishes a blissful clarity: things appear to mean something by themselves. (156)

This is what is happening on the cover of *Paris Match*: the black soldier saluting the flag is 'naturalised' into a benign image of French imperialism. We are invited to share in the obviousness of it all: there is nothing to discuss, it is unmistakable that one implies the presence of the other. As Barthes explains,

> what allows the reader to consume myth innocently is that he [or she] does not see it as a semiological system but as an inductive one. Where there is only equivalence, he sees a kind of causal process: the signifier and the signified have, in his eyes, a natural relationship. This confusion can be expressed otherwise: any semiological system is a system of values; now the myth-consumer takes the signification for a system of facts: myth is read as a factual system, whereas it is but a semiological system. (142)

What makes the move from primary signification (denotation) to secondary signification (connotation) a possibility are the shared cultural codes on which both Barthes and the readership of *Paris Match* are able to draw. Without access to this shared code (conscious or unconscious) the operations of secondary signification (connotation) would not be possible. And of course such knowledge is always both historical and cultural. That is to say, it might differ from one culture to another, and from one historical moment to another. Cultural difference might also be marked by differences of class, race, gender, generation or sexual preference. As Barthes explains, reading closely depends on my culture, on my knowledge of the world, and it is probable that a good press photograph (and they are all good, being selected) makes ready play with the supposed knowledge of its readers, those prints being chosen which comprise the greatest possible quantity of information of this kind in such a way as to render the reading fully satisfying. (1977: 29)

Secondary significations (connotations) are therefore not simply produced by the makers of the image, but activated from an already existing cultural repertoire. In other words, the image both draws from the cultural repertoire and at the same time adds to it. This is a process of cultural consumption as manipulation in which we as readers are active and complicit participants.

Problems with the Cultural-Consumption-as-Manipulation Model

As the rest of this book will address, both implicitly and explicitly, a range of problems with the 'consumption-as-manipulation' model, I will conclude this chapter with just a few schematic points that can act as an introduction to the remainder of the book.

The Australian cultural critic John Docker finds the claims about the disabling influence of mass culture, as outlined by Adorno and Horkheimer, to be nothing short of 'preposterous, ludicrous' (1994: 41). He describes their attitude to establishing 'evidence' for the claims they make as 'disturbingly casual and even laughable . . . complacent, and . . . repellent' (ibid.). According to Docker, the work of the Frankfurt School (especially Adorno), and the 'modernist conformity' (55) of the early work of Barthes (especially *Mythologies*), displays an 'overriding modernist assumption, that we . . . can read off knowledge of audience responses and reception – the human condition of the mass of the population – from our (presumed) knowledge of mass culture texts' (46). He is even more dismissive of the work of the Leavisites. For example, he calls Q.D. Leavis's approach 'comical', and describes her approach to cultural consumption as that of 'an old-style colonialist ethnographer, staring with distaste at the barbaric ways of strange and unknown people' (25).

Michael Denning, who is generally quite positive about the work of the Frankfurt School, identifies a certain tendency in Adorno and Horkheimer to simplify the workings of the culture industries.[6] In a discussion of the production of dime novels as a part of the emerging culture industry in the nineteenth-century United States,

Denning rejects Adorno and Horkheimer's rather too easy correlation of the culture industry and mass deception, making the point:

> As in other capitalist industries, there are struggles both at the point of production, the writing of these dime novels; and at the point of consumption, the reading of cheap stories. So a history of dime novels is not simply a history of a culture industry; it also encompasses a history of their place in working class culture, and of their role in the struggles to reform that culture. (1987: 26)

In other words, Denning is insisting on taking seriously questions of both structure and agency (for further discussion on this issue, see Chapter 8). The trouble with much of the work of the Frankfurt School on mass culture (and evident in similar work undertaken from the perspective of political economy generally) is that it encourages a detailed understanding of the workings of production, while suggesting that a cursory glance will be more than enough to understand the practices of cultural consumption. There can be no doubt that the culture industries seek to manipulate and exploit consumers. But it is certainly not the case that the practices of cultural consumption can be seen as the total and always successful manipulation of passive subjects. What is needed is a more complex account. One that takes on board even some of the more obvious aspects of cultural consumption would be a start; for example, full recognition that a cultural commodity produced by the culture industries may not have sole access to an individual consumer; first, consumption always occurs in a cultural context (i.e. a social space often containing other people and other commodities, perhaps making counter-claims, or just seeking to undermine the appeal of a rival's products); second, consumers are not blank sheets of paper, but people who come to acts of consumption with a history of other moments of consumption.

Docker's criticisms of the Frankfurt School and of the early work of Barthes seem to suggest that how to determine the political effectivity of a cultural text or practice is ultimately an ethnographic question.[7] The nature and extent of impact a text will have on its consumer cannot be judged by formal analysis alone; the only way to decide this question is by examining how it is made meaningful by its consumers. According to the anthropologists George Marcus and Michael Fischer, ethnography is 'modern anthropology's major intellectual contribution to scholarship' (Marcus and Fischer 1986: 20).[8] They describe the ethnographic method as follows:

Ethnography is a research process in which the anthropologist closely observes, records, and engages in the daily life of another culture – an experience labelled as the fieldwork method – and then writes accounts of this culture, emphasizing descriptive detail. These accounts are the primary form in which fieldwork procedures, the other culture, and the ethnographer's personal and theoretical reflections are accessible to professionals and other readerships. (18)

Ethnography (including what passes for ethnography in cultural studies)[9] does not of course give direct access to why and how people consume and turn particular commodities into culture. What it does provide access to is people's accounts of what they are doing and why they do it. This means, regardless of descriptive accuracy, that ethnographic accounts are always reports on other people's reports of what they do and why they do it. Even with these qualifications, political economy might learn some modesty by reading Marcus and Fischer's account of the rescaling of anthropology as it moved from nineteenth- to twentieth-century practice. They describe how 'the nineteenth-century grand vision of an anthropological science of Man' was 'redrawn' under the impact of the twentieth-century practice of ethnography:

the nineteenth-century tendency to make sweeping global statements was rescaled. As an ethnographer, the anthropologist focuses his efforts on a different sort of holism: not to make universally valid statements, but to represent a particular way of life as fully as possible. (22)

Cultural studies has learned a great deal from anthropology. At the very core of cultural studies is a definition of culture borrowed directly from anthropology; that is, Raymond Williams's now famous phrase, culture as 'a particular way of life' (1965: 57).[10] Moreover, cultural studies shares anthropology's view that culture is both a constructed and a contested terrain.[11] Since the 1980s, the influence may have begun to run in a reverse direction. Marcus and Fischer, for example, point out that

The study of the mass-culture industry, popular culture, and the formation of public consciousness has emerged [within anthropology] as one of the most vigorous of new research directions . . . raising questions about cultural hegemony and how meaning structures are formed and negotiated by competing segments within a society. (153, 154)

They add that they would like to congratulate the Birmingham Centre for Contemporary Cultural Studies for having 'pioneered

some of the ethnographic techniques for exploring this topic'
(153).

Notes

1   For an anthropological critique of the notion of 'true' and 'false' needs, see
    Marshall Sahlins 1976.
2   The Leavisites looked back longingly to a cultural golden age, a mythic rural
    past, when there was a shared culture uncorrupted by commercial interests.
    This was a time before the cultural fall of the nineteenth century. The golden
    age in Leavisism tends to be historically rather mobile, but the Elizabethan
    period of Shakespeare's theatre is often cited as such a time of cultural coher-
    ence before the cultural disintegration of the nineteenth and twentieth
    centuries. F.R. Leavis writes of Shakespeare belonging 'to a genuinely national
    culture, to a community in which it was possible for the theatre to appeal to
    the cultivated and the populace at the same time' (1933: 216). Q.D. Leavis's
    comments on the organic relations between populace and cultivated are very
    revealing: 'the masses were receiving their amusement from above . . . . They
    had to take the same amusements as their betters. . . . Happily, they had no
    choice' (1978: 85). According to Q.D. Leavis,

    > the spectator of Elizabethan drama, though he might not be able to follow
    > the 'thought' minutely in the great tragedies, was getting his amusement
    > from the mind and sensibility that produced those passages, from an artist
    > and not from one of his own class. There was then no such complete
    > separation as we have . . . between the life of the cultivated and the life of
    > the generality. (264)

    Clearly, then, the golden age was not just marked by cultural coherence, but,
    happily for the Leavisites, a cultural coherence based on authoritarian and
    hierarchical principles. It was a common culture which gave intellectual stimu-
    lation at one end, and affective pleasure at the other. This was a mythic world
    in which everyone knew their place, knew their station in life.
3   The latest version of this moral panic (rehearsed by the media and fuelled by
    some American intellectuals) is perhaps so-called 'dumbing down'.
4   As Raymond Williams points out in *Culture and Society*, 'There are in fact
    no masses; there are only ways of seeing other people as masses' (1963: 289).
5   Barthes' formulation (1973) is remarkably similar to Louis Althusser's concept
    (1998) of 'interpellation' (see Chapter 7 below).
6   Michael Denning argues for the continued use of the concept of the culture
    industry:

    > The strength of the concept is twofold: it avoids a static and ahistorical
    > dichotomy between elite culture and popular culture, since it marks a
    > decisive break from earlier elite and folk cultures and emphasises the effects
    > of that break on both cultures; and it draws attention to the commodifi-
    > cation of culture – the restructuring of cultural production by wage labor,
    > a capitalist market, and a capitalist labor process which divides, rational-
    > izes, and deskills work. (1987: 25)

    Denning makes a valid point, one that is difficult to resist. My only disagree-
    ment is the use of industry in the singular rather than industries in the plural.
    In my view, seeing production in its complex and contradictory plurality

presents a much more usable model of what is involved in the processes of production.
7. Although his criticisms of modernist textual analysis point in this direction, this is not a move he himself makes.
8. The British anthropologist Bronislaw Malinowski is generally regarded as the founder of the ethnographic method, first outlined in the opening chapter of his first major work, *Argonauts of the Western Pacific* (1922).
9 This is the subject of Chapters 5 and 6 below.
10 The formulation was quickly modified in cultural studies to 'particular ways of life'; seeing culture as *cultures* situated in relations of domination and subordination, struggle and negotiation.
11 Another similarity might be added to the list: like anthropology, cultural studies has sought to build a readership for its work outside the confines of academia.

|3|

Cultural Consumption as Communication

The focus of this chapter is work which understands cultural consumption as a mode of communication. The chapter begins with a critical assessment of the foundational work of two early sociologists, Thorstein Veblen (working in the USA) and Georg Simmel (working in Germany). This is followed by a discussion of an influential study on the symbolic use of goods by social anthropologist Mary Douglas and economist Baron Isherwood. The monumental work of Pierre Bourdieu on cultural consumption and its use to mark and maintain social distinctions is discussed in the next section. Michel de Certeau is the subject of the penultimate section. The chapter concludes with a critical review of work in cultural studies on youth subcultures and fan cultures.

Veblen and Simmel

Around the turn of the nineteenth century, two sociologists, Thorstein Veblen writing in 1899 in the United States and Georg Simmel writing in 1903 and 1904 in Germany, published work which discussed what they believed to be new patterns of urban middle-class cultural consumption. Thorstein Veblen's key concept is 'conspicuous consumption', but to understand how this first becomes an important social practice, we need to begin with a brief discussion of the other term he made famous, 'conspicuous leisure'. Veblen argues that what he calls the leisure class developed initially through its predatory acquisition and ownership of private property. The more property it seized, the more power it accrued. Power, as the assertion of superior force, was in this way established as honorific. To own property, therefore, became a mark of honour. Veblen describes how this developed into a struggle for pecuniary emulation. The process was complicated, however, by the need to display to others one's pecuniary strength. In other words, to possess wealth was not in itself a sufficient means to gain and to hold the respect and the esteem of others. To win this, one had to display one's pecuniary strength. 'Conspicuous leisure', according to Veblen, became the principal means to openly display one's wealth and status. In other words, one communicated one's honour by conspicuously absenting oneself from useful work. This gradually, and inevitably, led to the view that productive work is a mark of weakness, in that it signified the absence of pecuniary strength. In this way, the leisure class's increasing exemption from productive work resulted in exemption itself becoming honorific. Therefore, to engage in productive work became generally a sign of inferior status.

Using conspicuous leisure as a means to mark and display one's social distinction worked very well in the compact communities of, say, rural Europe. Urbanisation changed this: in the company of urban strangers, conspicuous leisure was no longer a sufficient means to display one's pecuniary strength. The anonymity of urban life demanded a more obvious display of power and status. In the new urban culture, conspicuous leisure was replaced, Veblen maintains, by the practice of 'conspicuous consumption'.

Veblen identifies the way in which the new leisure class, as part of its strategy to secure and display its new social position, attempts to turn culture into nature; that is, it seeks to present what it has acquired through success in business as if it were something natural to itself. Central to this strategy is the need for members of the leisure class to put distance between themselves and the source of their wealth. They seek to present being rich as a form of being ordained by nature. Conspicuous consumption is the chosen means to communicate this fact to other social classes. Veblen argues against the view that conspicuous consumption is little more than harmless and irrelevant display. Such social display is the very pageant of power; from its prestige grows authority. Moreover, he insists that 'the leisure-class scheme of life . . . extends its coercive influence' throughout society as a whole (1994: 83–4). 'The leisure class stands at the head of the social structure in point of reputability; and its manner of life and its standards of worth therefore afford the norm of reputability for the community' (84). The example of the leisure class acts to direct social energies away from productive work and into wasteful displays of cultural consumption. Veblen cites the case of those he refers to as 'the scholarly classes'. Although they are the social equals of the non-scholarly classes, their presumed intellectual abilities and academic attainments, together with their public commitment to leisure-class canons of decency, give them a higher status than their pecuniary strength would normally warrant. As a result, Veblen observes, the scholarly classes

> are unavoidably thrown into contact with classes that are pecuniarily their superiors. The high standard of pecuniary decency in force among these superior classes is transfused among the scholarly classes with but little mitigation of its rigour; and as a consequence there is no class of the community that spends a larger proportion of its substance in conspicuous waste than these. (113–14)

Veblen also draws our attention to the ways in which the canons of conspicuous consumption exercise a distorting influence over ideals of feminine beauty. The delicate and the diminutive, for example, are promoted in order to display to the world that the women of the leisure class are incapable of productive work. In this way, women are reduced to symbols of 'vicarious consumption'. Woman is little more than a servant, whose task it is to exhibit in a public display her master's economic power. As Veblen explains, 'She is useless and expensive, and she is consequently valuable as evidence of pecuniary strength' (149). Women learn to conform to this standard, and men learn to read women's conformity as the very epitome of beauty.

Modes of male dress are not exempt from the dictates of the leisure-class canons of decency and good taste. Male apparel must demonstrate the ability to consume without economic restraint. It must also indicate that the wearer is not engaged in productive work. As Veblen explains,

> Elegant dress serves its purpose of elegance not only in that it is expensive, but also because it is the insignia of leisure. It not only shows that the wearer is able to consume a relatively large value, but it argues at the same time that he consumes without producing. (171)

The very fact that the leisure class denounces useful work as unworthy of human dignity makes this class a bulwark against what Veblen regards as the natural evolutionary flow of history. He maintains that in an industrial society a leisure class is at best a historical anachronism and at worse a parasitical burden. Such a society depends on productive labour, the very activity the leisure class has learned (and teaches others by example) to despise. Veblen's analysis is driven by a Darwinian model of cultural evolution. He refers to historical development as

> a process of natural selection of institutions . . . a natural selection of the fittest habits of thought and . . . a process of

enforced adaptation of individuals to an environment which has progressively changed with the growth of the community and with the changing institutions under which men [and women] have lived. (188)

The privileged position of the leisure class tends to protect it from the full force of economic exigencies. Moreover, given its leading role in terms of taste formation, it is able 'to exert a retarding influence upon social development far in excess of that which the simple numerical strength of the class would assign it' (200). In short, the existence of the leisure class is incompatible with the future development of an industrial community.

Veblen's model of cultural consumption is clearly predicated on social emulation; there is little sense here that what counts as 'reputability' might itself be a terrain of conflict. He presents a model of cultural consumption which assumes that those at the bottom or those in the middle will always seek to emulate those at the top of the social pyramid. Colin Campbell offers two further objections to Veblen's insistence that imitation and competition are the principal features of consumption:

> firstly, that individuals may gain success over their competitors through innovation rather than imitation (as many entrepreneurs have shown) and, secondly, that social groups (especially social classes) may actually be in conflict over the very question of criteria to be employed in defining status. (1987: 53)

His second point draws attention to Veblen's assumption that modern societies are consensually organised around a single status system: 'A more successful way of improving one's own social position may . . . be [in fact] to deny the moral validity of the claims of those above you, asserting in their place grounds for prestige which favour those like yourself' (53–4).

In an essay called 'The Metropolis and Mental Life' (first published in 1903), the German sociologist Georg Simmel identified a similar mode of behaviour in the new distinctive urban culture of Berlin at the turn of the century. Confronted by the perceived anonymity of city life, the new urban bourgeoisie used particular patterns of consumption to maintain and to display a sense of individuality. As he observed, 'The deepest problems of modern life derive from the claim of the individual to preserve the autonomy and individuality of his existence in the face of overwhelming social forces' (1964: 409). Faced with 'the difficulty of asserting his [sic] own personality within the dimensions of metropolitan life' (420), individuals are 'tempted to adopt the most tendentious peculiarities . . . extravagances of mannerism, caprice, and precariousness' (421). Simmel argues that the 'meaning' of such behaviour lies not in its particular content but 'in its form of "being different", of standing out in a striking manner and thereby attracting attention' (ibid.).

Simmel further pursued and elaborated these ideas in an essay on fashion (originally published in 1904). In this essay he argues that modern urban societies are marked by an increased tension between 'two antagonistic principles', which, he claims, have governed the historical development of the human race – the principles of 'generalization' and 'specialization' (1957: 542). Simmel sees these principles as manifest in two types of individual, the 'imitative' and the 'teleological'. As he explains, 'The imitator is the passive individual, who believes in social similarity and adapts himself [sic] to existing elements; the teleological individual, on the other hand, is ever experimenting, always restlessly striving, and he relies on his own personal conviction' (543). Fashion, driven as it is by a continuous social cycle of imitation and differentiation, is for Simmel an excellent example of these principles in social operation. Moreover, it is a process which depends for its success on the active involvement of both types of individuals, imitative (who follow fashions and thus satisfy their need to adapt) and teleological (who instigate them and thus satisfy their need to innovate).

In more general terms, the way fashion as a social practice is said to work is that subordinate groups seek to improve their social status by imitating the dress codes and forms of behaviour of their immediate superordinate group; the superordinate group is then forced to seek new fashions in order to maintain its social difference. As Simmel explains it, 'the fashions of the upper stratum of society are never identical with those of the lower; in fact, they are abandoned by the former as soon as the latter prepares to appropriate them' (543). In this way, he argues, 'Fashion . . . is a product of class distinction' (544). It is of course always more than the product; it also has a role to play as producer, in that by a strategy of inclusion and exclusion, fashion helps reproduce social power and privilege by marking and maintaining the social differences and distinctions upon which it in part depends. As Simmel points out, 'fashion . . . signifies union with those in the same class, the uniformity of a circle characterized by it, and . . . the exclusion of all other groups' (ibid.). It is not the content of fashion which matters, but the social differences it makes visible and helps maintain.

> Just as soon as the lower classes begin to copy their style, thereby crossing the line of demarcation the upper classes have drawn and destroying the uniformity of their coherence, the

upper classes turn away from this style and adopt a new one, which in turn differentiates them from the masses. (545)

Stephen Mennell provides a number of historical examples of this process in terms of social-class diet. As he explains, 'There are countless cases of foods being dropped by higher social ranks when adopted by lower' (1985: 303). For example, from medieval times white bread carried

> high prestige . . . the further down the social scale, the darker the bread. The upper classes regarded black and brown breads with aversion – it was even claimed their stomachs could not digest them – while the lower orders aspired to white or whiter bread. (303)

However, when in the nineteenth century white bread became the bread of the working class, the brown bread rejected by them soon became the chosen bread of the dominant classes.

The Canadian anthropologist Grant McCracken identifies three significant problems with Simmel's approach. First, he notes that the term 'trickle-down' (as Simmel's approach is generally called) is not an accurate description of the process Simmel observes. Rather than fashion dropping down the social structure, as the metaphor of 'trickle-down' suggests, its dynamic is in fact upward. As McCracken points out, the dynamic of fashion is better described as 'an upward "chase and flight" pattern created by a subordinate social group that "hunts" upper-class status markers and a superordinate social group that moves on in hasty flight to new ones' (1990: 94). The second problem he identifies is what he sees as Simmel's failure to recognise that the social groups at the top and bottom of the social structure would not engage at all in the dialectic of imitation and differentiation. The social group at the top would only differentiate, while the social group at the bottom would only imitate; it is only the social groups between these two (that exist in relations of both subordination and superordination) that would therefore engage in both imitation and differentiation. In addition, relations of subordination and superordination are not only defined by social class; these relations may exist in terms of, for example, gender, age or ethnicity. In each instance, the potential for a range of diverse mixes of other social differences combined with social class may complicate the nature and extent of both imitation and differentiation.

McCracken's third criticism is that Simmel's theory lacks a sense of the importance of cultural context. In order to understand the 'motive' behind particular examples of imitation and differentiation, we need to locate them in their specific cultural contexts.

McCracken gives the example of imitation in the practice of professional women in the USA in the 1970s, who adopted in the workplace the dress codes of their male colleagues (the business suit, or so-called 'power dressing'). As he explains,

> They imitate in pursuit of a social object: acceptance as a competent and equal partner in the world of work. Imitation is devoted to acquiring the symbolic complements in which competence and equality are expressed. Imitation then is not the simple pursuit of prestige nor the work of some generalised force; it is a culturally purposeful activity motivated by an appreciation of the symbolic liabilities of one style of dress, and the symbolic advantages implicit in another. (100)

Another problem with Simmel's argument (and also a problem with Veblen's model) is the view that modern urban societies have consensual hierarchies of taste, mirroring consensual hierarchies of social classes. In other words, those at the bottom or in the middle, it is assumed strive to be like those at the top. This is a linear model of cultural consumption, which excludes the possibility that classes, other than those at the top, might well choose to compete to be different, or that fashions could originate from both below and middle. This leads to another problem, as Colin Campbell observes, 'the fact that modern societies are characterized by multiple and diverse elite groups presents a problem concerning who exactly one is to emulate' (1983: 284). Moreover, making a point similar to McCracken's second criticism, he observes, 'for those at the pinnacle, emulation is hardly an available motive and yet their pattern of consumption seems to lack none of the dynamic apparent among their emulators' (ibid.).

Symbolic Goods

In stark contrast to the positions outlined by Veblen and Simmel, Mary Douglas and Baron Isherwood reject the view that 'emulation, envy, and striving to be better than the Joneses are the intentions which fuel consumption' (1996: xxi).[1] Instead of imitation and exclusion, they see cultural consumption as a form of expression more concerned with 'making visible and stable the categories of culture' (38). According to Douglas and Isherwood, because goods are expressive they can be used as a symbolic means to communicate with others. As they contend, 'goods are part of a live information system' (xiv).

Although 'Goods are neutral, their uses are social; they can be used as fences or bridges' (xv). As they explain, 'As far as keeping

a person alive is concerned, food and drink are needed for physical services; but as far as social life is concerned, they are needed
for mustering solidarity, attracting support, requiting kindnesses,
and this goes for the poor as well as for the rich' (xxi). The
symbolic value of objects in the 'information system' is not inherent in the objects themselves. Value is something 'conferred by
human judgments' (xxii). To understand the value of one object, it
is necessary to locate it in the information system as a whole.
Similarly, goods do not communicate by themselves, they communicate 'like flags' (xxiv), and thus require the active agency of
human subjects. But as they insist, 'consumption goods are most
definitely not mere messages; they constitute the very system itself.
Take them out of human intercourse and you have dismantled the
whole thing' (49). In this way, 'Consumption is the very arena in
which culture is fought over and licked into shape' (37). As they
observe,

> The housewife with her shopping basket arrives home: some
> things in it she reserves for her household, some for the father,
> some for the children; others are destined for the special de-
> lectation of guests. Whom she invites into her house, what parts
> of the house she makes available to outsiders, how often, what
> she offers them for music, food, drink, and conversation, these
> choices express and generate culture in its general sense. (37)

Rather than seeing the consumption of goods as 'primarily needed
for subsistence [economic theory] plus competitive display [Veblen
and Simmel]', they argue that the consumption of goods has a
'double role in providing subsistence and in drawing lines of social
relationships' (39). As a mode of communication, 'the essential
function of consumption is its capacity to make sense' (40); and
thus to 'make and maintain social relationships' (39). Moreover, we
must leave behind the 'false distinction' between goods that minis-
ter to physical needs (eating and drinking, for example), and those
which tender to our more aesthetic inclinations (reading poetry,
watching television, for example), because, as they insist, 'all goods
carry meaning' (49). Furthermore, 'any choice between goods is the
result of, and contributes to, culture' (52).

To fully appreciate consumption as a mode of communication,
they argue, we must think of it as a language: 'Forget that
commodities are good for eating, clothing, and shelter; forget their
usefulness and try instead the idea that commodities are good for
thinking; treat them as a nonverbal medium for the human creative
faculty' (40–1). The practice of consumption is a 'joint production,
with fellow consumers, of a universe of values. Consumption uses
goods to make firm and visible a particular set of judgments in the

fluid processes of classifying persons and events' (41). In this way, cultural consumption is a 'ritual activity' (45) in which people consume to communicate with other consumers, and the shifting accumulations of these acts of cultural consumption constitute the making of culture. What underpins this system and ultimately gives it meaning, what cultural consumption is in the end really communicating, is an underlying cognitive order. As they explain, 'the clue to finding real partitioning among goods must be to trace some underlying partitioning in society' (68).

The Making of Class Difference

In an argument that recalls the work of Veblen and Simmel, but is a great deal more sophisticated than both, Pierre Bourdieu demonstrates how particular patterns of cultural consumption are used for purposes of marking and maintaining social distinction. Whereas Douglas and Isherwood see cultural consumption as a neutral language of expression, Bourdieu maintains that it is a significant area of struggle between and within social classes. Bourdieu's model of cultural consumption, although sharing Douglas and Isherwood's view of cultural consumption as communication, insists that cultural consumption is not a polite conversation about an underlying cognitive order, but a heated debate about difference and distinction. He argues that what people consume does not simply reflect distinctions and differences embedded elsewhere, that cultural consumption makes visible, as Douglas and Isherwood suggest, but that cultural consumption is the means by which they are produced, maintained and reproduced. Like Veblen, he seeks to demonstrate how what social groups consume is part of a strategy for hierarchicising social space. Whereas Veblen was only concerned with the leisure class, Bourdieu focuses on French society as a whole. He argues that differences in cultural consumption (whether 'culture' is understood as text, practice or way of living) are always an important aspect in the struggle between dominant and subordinate classes in society.[2] He shows how arbitrary tastes and arbitrary ways of living are continually transmuted into legitimate taste and the *only* legitimate way of life. The 'illusion of "natural distinction"' is ultimately based on the power of the dominant to impose, by their very existence, a definition of excellence which [is] nothing other than their own way of existing' (1984: 255).

Bourdieu's interest is in the processes by which patterns of cultural consumption help to secure and legitimate forms of power and domination which are ultimately rooted in economic inequality. In other words, he argues that although class rule is ultimately economic, the form it takes is cultural; and that cultural consumption to mark social distinction, the making, marking and maintaining of social difference, is the key to understanding this. The source of social difference and social power is thus symbolically shifted from the economic field to the field of cultural consumption, making social power appear to be the result of a specific cultural disposition. In this way, the production and reproduction of cultural space help produce and reproduce social space, social power and class difference. Bourdieu's purpose, therefore, is not to prove the self-evident, that different classes have different patterns of cultural consumption, but to show how cultural consumption (from high art to food on the table) forms a distinct pattern of social distinction, and to identify and interrogate the processes by which the making and maintaining of these distinctions secures and legitimates forms of power and control rooted ultimately in economic inequalities. He is interested not so much in the actual differences, but in how these differences are used by dominant classes as a means of social reproduction. His project is to situate cultural consumption in the world of everyday experience. Only by producing a 'barbarous reintegration of aesthetic consumption into the world of ordinary consumption (against which it endlessly defines itself)' (100), will we fully understand the social and political role of cultural consumption. As he maintains, 'one cannot fully understand cultural practices unless "culture", in the restricted, normative sense of ordinary usage, is brought back into "culture" in the anthropological sense, and the elaborated taste for the most refined objects is reconnected with the elementary taste for the flavours of food' (1). Bourdieu insists that taste is always more than an aesthetic category. As he points out, 'taste classifies, and it classifies the classifier' (6). We are classified by our classifications and classify others by theirs. In this way, he would argue that similar things are happening when I 'value' a holiday destination or a particular mode of dress, as are happening when I 'value' a poem by T.S. Eliot or a piece of music by Philip Glass. Such evaluations are never a simple matter of individual taste, cultural consumption operates both to identify and to mark social distinction and to sustain social difference. While such strategies of classification do not in themselves produce social inequalities, the making, marking and maintaining of them function to legitimate such inequalities. In this way, taste is a profoundly ideological discourse; it functions as a marker of 'class' (using the term in the double sense to mean both socio-economic category and a particular level of quality). He argues that cultural consumption is, ultimately, 'predisposed . . . to fulfil a social function of legitimating social difference' (7).

The consumption of art is for Bourdieu the model for all forms of cultural consumption. At the pinnacle of the hierarchy of taste is the 'pure' aesthetic gaze – an historical invention – with its emphasis on aesthetic distance, and on form over function. Aesthetic distance is in effect the denial of function: it insists on the 'how' and not the 'what'. It is analogous to the difference between judging a meal good because it was economically priced and filling, and judging a meal good on the basis of how it was served, where it was served. . . . The 'pure' aesthetic gaze emerges with the emergence of the cultural field (in which texts and practices are divided into Culture and mass culture). One in effect guarantees the other. Bourdieu sees the art museum as the institutionalisation of the aesthetic gaze and the cultural field. Once inside the museum art loses all prior functions (except that of being art) and becomes pure form: 'Though originally subordinated to quite different or even incompatible functions (crucifix and fetish, Pieta and still life), these juxtaposed works tacitly demand attention to form rather than function, technique rather than theme' (30). For example, an advertisement for soup displayed in an art gallery becomes an example of the aesthetic, whereas the same advertisement in a magazine is an example of the commercial. The effect of the distinction is to produce 'a sort of ontological promotion akin to a transubstantiation' (6). It is the institutionalisation of such distinctions that produces what Bourdieu calls the 'ideology of natural taste', the view that genuine 'appreciation' can only be attained by an instinctively gifted minority armed against the mediocrity of the masses. Ortega y Gasset makes the point with precision: 'art helps the "best" to know and recognise one another in the greyness of the multitude and to learn their mission, which is to be few in number and to have to fight against the multitude' (quoted in Bourdieu 1984: 31).

As Bourdieu points out, 'it is not easy to describe the "pure" gaze without also describing the naive gaze which it defines itself against' (32). The naive gaze is of course the gaze of the popular aesthetic:

> The affirmation of continuity between art and life, which implies the subordination of form to function . . . a refusal of the refusal which is the starting point of the high aesthetic, i.e., the clear cut separation of ordinary dispositions from the specially aesthetic disposition. (32)

The relation between the pure and the popular aesthetics is needless to say not one of equality, but a relation of dominant and dominated. The popular aesthetic, in its stress on function over form, is necessarily contingent and pluralistic, contrary, and in deference to the absolute insistence of the transcendent universality of the pure aesthetic. Bourdieu sees the two aesthetics as articulating the two separate but related realms of necessity and freedom. Without the required cultural capital[3] to decipher the 'code' of art, people are made socially *vulnerable* to the condescension of those who have the required cultural capital. What is social is presented as innate, and, in turn, used to justify what is social. Like other ideological strategies, 'The ideology of natural taste owes its plausibility and its efficacy to the fact that . . . it naturalises real differences, converting differences in the mode of acquisition of culture into differences of nature' (68). Aesthetic relations thus mimic and help reproduce social relations of power. As Bourdieu observes,

> Aesthetic intolerance can be terribly violent. . . . The most intolerable thing for those who regard themselves as the possessors of legitimate culture is the sacrilegious reuniting of tastes which taste dictates shall be separated. This means that the games of artists and aesthetes and their struggles for the monopoly of artistic legitimacy are less innocent than they seem. At stake in every struggle over art there is also the imposition of an art of living, that is, the transmutation of an arbitrary way of living into the legitimate way of life which casts every other way of living into arbitrariness. (57)

Bourdieu's work on cultural consumption is underpinned by his view of education. Rather than being a means to lessen inequality, it functions to legitimate it. He argues that the education system fulfils a quite specific social and political function: that is, to legitimate social inequalities which exist prior to its operations. It achieves this by transforming social differences into academic differences, and presenting these differences as if they were 'grounded in nature' (387). The cultural tastes of dominant classes are given institutional form, and then, with deft ideological sleight of hand, their taste for this institutionalised culture (i.e. their own) is held up as evidence of their cultural, and, ultimately, their social, superiority. In this way, social distinction is generated by learned patterns of cultural consumption which are internalised as 'natural' cultural preferences and interpreted and mobilised as evidence of 'natural' cultural competences, which are, ultimately, used to justify forms of class domination. To fully understand this we need to understand how Bourdieu distinguishes between three types of capital – economic, social and cultural. In capitalist societies economic capital in the form of money, property, etc. is able to buy access to cultural and social capital. Hierarchies openly based on the accumulation of economic capital are vulnerable to challenge. Cultural and social capital is able to conceal and legitimate economic domination by reproducing it in the form of cultural and social hierarchies.[4]

Paul Willis uses Bourdieu's argument as a means to understand what he sees as a growing exclusionary cultural tendency in the 1990s, in which the aesthetic appreciation of 'art' has sought to distance itself, and those who 'really appreciate' it, from the 'uncultured mass'. A significant part of this process is a denial of the necessary relationship between aesthetic understanding and education; that is, that an aesthetic understanding of art has its foundations in education: the production and reproduction of the necessary knowledge on which aesthetic understanding is necessarily founded. Instead, Willis notes a growing tendency to present aesthetic understanding and the consumption of culture as something innate, rather than what it is, something learned. This produces in many people a sense of being 'uncultured'. But rather than seeing this as a question of non-access to knowledge – they have not been given access to the necessary code to 'appreciate' the formal qualities of high culture – they are encouraged to view 'themselves as ignorant, insensitive and without the finer sensibilities of those who really "appreciate". Absolutely certainly they're not the "talented" or "gifted", the elite minority held to be capable of performing or creating "art" ' (1990: 3). This produces a situation, Willis argues, in which people who make culture in their everyday lives see themselves as uncultured.

Against the growing influence of this cultural tendency, Willis argues the case for recognition of what he calls 'grounded aesthetics'. Grounded aesthetics is the process through which ordinary people make cultural sense of the world: 'the ways in which the received natural and social world is made human to *them* and made, to however small a degree (even if finally symbolic), controllable by them' (22). Grounded aesthetic value is never intrinsic to a cultural text or practice, a universal quality of its form; it is always inscribed in the 'sensuous/emotive/cognitive' (24) act of cultural consumption (how the text or practice is appropriated and 'used'). This is an argument against those who locate creativity only in the act of production: cultural consumption being merely the recognition or misrecognition of the aesthetic intention. Against this, Willis insists on cultural consumption as a symbolic act of creativity. His 'fundamental point . . . is that "messages" are not now so much "sent" and "received" as *made* in reception. . . . "Sent message" communication is being replaced by "made message" communication' (135). In the grounded aesthetics of popular culture, meaning is undecidable, always the result of a 'production in use' in terms of relevance (whereas in high or dominant culture, it is always already decided, a question of the correct interpretation arrived at on the basis of aesthetic contemplation). This of course means that a text or practice that may be judged to be intrinsically banal and uninteresting may, on the basis of its 'production in use' within specific relations of consumption, be judged to be of great cultural interest and originality. His position is a rebuke to both textualism, which judges on the basis of formal qualities, and the political-economy-of-culture approach, which judges on the basis of the relations of production. The 'symbolic work' of cultural consumption is never a simple repetition of the relations of production, nor is it a simple confirmation of the semiotic certainties of the lecture theatre.

> People bring living identities to commerce and the consumption of cultural commodities as well as being formed there. They bring experiences, feelings, social position and social memberships to their encounter with commerce. Hence they bring a necessary creative symbolic pressure, not only to make sense of cultural commodities, but partly through them also to make sense of contradiction and structure as they experience them in school, college, production, neighbourhood, and as members of certain genders, races, classes and ages. The results of this necessary symbolic work may be quite different from anything initially coded into cultural commodities. (21)

Textual Poaching

In *The Practice of Everyday Life*, the French cultural theorist Michel de Certeau is concerned with what he calls the 'ways of operating' of ordinary consumers as they move across the dominated landscape of cultural production. As he explains,

> The purpose of this work is to make explicit the systems of operational combination (*les combinatoires d'opérations*) which also compose a 'culture', and to bring to light the models of action characteristic of users whose status as dominated element in society (a status that does not mean that they are either passive or docile) is concealed by the euphemistic term 'consumers'. Everyday life invents itself by *poaching* in countless ways on the property of others. (1984: xi–xii)

He seeks to deconstruct the term 'consumer', to reveal the activity which lies within the act of cultural consumption or what he prefers to call 'secondary production'. Cultural consumption, he argues, 'is devious, it is dispersed, but it insinuates itself everywhere, silently and almost invisibly, because it does not manifest itself through its own products, but rather through its ways of using the products imposed by a dominant economic order' (xii–xiii). De Certeau offers the example of the ways in which indigenous Indians of what is now South America, 'subverted from within' (xiii) the Spanish colonisers' imposed culture:

> Submissive, and even consenting to their subjection, the Indians nevertheless often *made* of the rituals, representations, and laws imposed on them something quite different from what their conquerors had in mind; they subverted them not by rejecting or altering them, but by using them with respect to ends and references foreign to the system they had no choice but to accept. (ibid.)

In this way, 'their use of the dominant social order deflected its power, which they lacked the means to challenge'; and, as de Certeau observes, 'they escaped it without leaving it. The strength of their difference lay in procedures of "consumption" ' (ibid.). Another example of the same process of subversion from within can be seen in the experience of the Africans who were enslaved and transported to the USA to work on the cotton plantations. As part of the process of instilling submission, the slaves were taught Christianity. As in de Certeau's example of Indians resisting Spanish culture, the slaves consumed and *used* the new religion as a means to think the possibilities of their own freedom. In other words, a religion which should have reconciled them to their position as slaves was used in such a way as to enable them not only to think outside the brutal confines of slavery, but also to think through the challenges and confrontations of the Civil Rights movement and beyond.

For de Certeau, the terrain of culture is a site of continual conflict (silent and almost invisible) between the 'strategies' of cultural imposition (the power of production) and the 'tactics' of cultural use (cultural consumption or 'secondary production'). The difference between the two is that 'strategies are able to produce . . . and impose . . . whereas tactics can only use, manipulate' (30). What interests de Certeau is the 'multitude of "tactics" articulated in the details of everyday life' (xiv); what he also calls 'poetic ways of "making do" ' (xv). Moreover, 'The tactics of consumption, the ingenious ways in which the weak make use of the strong, thus lend a political dimension to everyday practices' (xvii).

> Many everyday practices (talking, reading, moving about, shopping, cooking, etc.) are tactical in character. And so are, more generally, many 'ways of operating': victories of the 'weak' over the 'strong' (whether the strength be that of powerful people or the violence of things or of an imposed order, etc.), clever tricks, knowing how to get away with things, 'hunter's cunning', manoeuvres. (xix)

Reading a text, according to de Certeau (he substitutes consumption and production for reading and writing) has 'all the characteristics of a silent production' as the reader 'insinuates into another person's text the ruses of pleasure and appropriation: he [or she] poaches on it' (xxi). In this way, he claims, the reader 'makes the text habitable, like a rented apartment' (ibid.). He describes reading as an "art" which is anything but passive', adding that 'the procedures of contemporary consumption appear to constitute a subtle art of "renters" who know how to insinuate their countless differences into the dominant text' (xxii). The cultural critic, therefore, must always be alert to 'the difference or similarity between . . . production . . . and . . . secondary production hidden in the process of . . . utilisation' (xiii). He characterises the active cultural consumption of texts as a form of 'textual poaching', in which 'readers are travellers; they move across lands belonging to someone else, like nomads poaching their way across the fields they did not write' (174).

The acts of textual poaching, or reader appropriation, are always in potential conflict with the 'scriptural economy' (131–76) of textual producers and those institutional voices (professional critics, academics, etc.) who work, through an insistence on the authority of authorial and/or textual meaning, to limit and confine the productive proliferation and circulation of 'unauthorised' meanings. His concept of 'textual poaching' is a rejection of this traditional model of reading, in which the purpose of reading a text is the passive reception of authorial and/or textual intent. It is a model in which reading is reduced to a question of being right or wrong. This model also informs another mode of thinking about cultural consumption, one which assumes that the 'message' of the text is always, in the act of reading, imposed on the reader. De Certeau argues that to assume this is to once again misunderstand the practice of cultural consumption: 'This misunderstanding assumes that "assimilating" necessarily means "becoming similar to" what one absorbs, and not 'making something similar' to what one is, making it one's own, appropriating or reappropriating it' (166).

Resistance

It is through rituals of consumption, the selective appropriation and group use of what the culture industries make available, that youth subcultures form meaningful identities. The cultural-studies engagement with youth subcultural consumption begins with Phil Cohen's foundational analysis of working-class culture and youth subcultures in the East End of London (first published in 1972). In this essay Cohen offers his now famous formulation that 'the latent function of subculture is this: to express and resolve, albeit "magically", the contradictions which remain hidden or unresolved in the parent culture' (1980: 82). From the mid-1950s onwards the working class had been confronted by two contradictory discourses: the new ideology of affluence and 'conspicuous consumption' and the traditional claims of working-class life. Changes in local manufacturing (resulting in 'de-skilling') and changes in the local environment (high-rise flats) had together undermined traditional working-class life without increasing access to the new 'affluent society'. As Cohen observes,

> Mods, parkas, skinheads, crombies all represent, in their different ways, an attempt to retrieve some of the socially cohesive elements destroyed in their parent culture and to combine these with elements selected from other class fractions, symbolising one or other of the options confronting it. (83)

In other words, in a symbolic response to the break-up of traditional working-class culture, a succession of youth subcultures attempted to hold together traditional notions of working-class community, whilst at the same time taking part (through acts of selective appropriation and cultural consumption) in the opportunities presented by the 'affluent society'. For example, although mods tended to be employed in low-paid work, with few career opportunities, the style of the mod could be seen to represent 'an attempt to realise, but in an imaginary relation, the conditions of existence of the socially mobile white collar worker' (ibid.). Similarly, although they shared many of the traditional values of their parent culture ('their argot and ritual forms'), 'their dress and music reflected the hedonistic image of the affluent consumer' (ibid.).

A key concept in the early cultural-studies work on youth subcultural consumption is 'homology'. Perhaps the classic cultural-studies statement of this process is made by Hall and Jefferson in the appropriately titled volume on youth subcultures, *Resistance through Rituals*:

> This involves members of a group in the appropriation of particular objects which are, or can be made, 'homologous' with their focal concerns, activities, group structure and collective self-image – objects in which they see their central values held and reflected. (1976: 56)

One such object is music. The cultural consumption of music is one of the principal means through which a youth subculture defines its sense of self and marks out its difference from other youth. Subcultural use of music was first noted by the American sociologist David Riesman. Writing in 1950, he noticed how the audience for popular music could be divided into two groups, 'a majority one, which accepts the adult picture of youth somewhat uncritically, and a minority one in which certain socially rebellious themes are encapsulated' (1990: 8). As he pointed out, the minority group is always small; its rebellion takes a symbolic form:

> an insistence on rigorous standards of judgement and taste . . .
> a preference for the uncommercialised, unadvertised small bands rather than name bands; the development of a private language and then a flight from it when the private language (the same is true of other aspects of private style) is taken over by the majority group. (9–10)

In this way, the cultural consumption of a particular type of music becomes a way of being in the world. Music consumption is used as a sign by which the *young* judge and are judged by others. To be part of a youth subculture is to display one's musical taste and to claim that its consumption is an act of communal creation. It does not matter, according to Riesman, whether the community is real or imagined. What is important is that the music provides a sense of community. It is a community created in the act of consumption: '[w]hen he [or she] listens to music, even if no one else is around, he listens in a context of imaginary "others" – his listening is indeed often an effort to establish connection with them' (10).

In his 1978 study of the music use of two subcultural groups, motorbike boys and hippies, Paul Willis explored the 'homologies' between musical selection and taste and other aspects of group lifestyle. As Willis explains it, homological analysis is essentially concerned with uncovering the extent to which particular texts and practices 'in their structure and content . . . parallel and reflect the structure, style, typical concerns, attitudes and feelings of the social group' (191). The purpose of homological analysis is to tease out the relationship between the particular cultural-consumption choices of a social group and how these are used to construct the cultural meaning of the social group.

Willis found that pop music was an integral part of the culture of the motorbike boys. The music of choice was the classic rock 'n' roll of the late 1950s (perceived by the motorbike boys as a 'golden age' of pop music). Their musical preference ('deliberate choice', not 'passive reception') had, Willis maintains, 'the dialectical capacity . . . to reflect, resonate and return something of real value to the motorbike boys' (62). What the music returned was a sense of 'security, authenticity and masculinity' (63). Willis identifies four homologies between the subculture and its cultural consumption of music. First, the historical unity of the music allowed its consumption to mark a difference and distinction from those who consumed contemporary pop music. This provided the group with a sense of authenticity. Second, the music, especially early Elvis Presley and Buddy Holly, was seen to validate aggressive masculinity in its celebration (mostly articulated through vocal delivery and the energy of the music, rather than in its lyrical content) of a tough and physical response to an uncertain and uncaring world. Thus the music was seen to have the capacity to make concrete and to authenticate the group's commitment to displays of aggressive masculinity. Third, classic rock 'n' roll was perceived as a music of movement (a music with beat) for a lifestyle of movement. Rock 'n' roll was seen to articulate the motorbike boys' sense of a life of endless physical movement. They valued its 'fastness and clarity of beat' (68). Dancing and fast bike-riding are at the heart of this relationship. The pounding rhythm of the music could both incite and supply an imaginary soundtrack to the fast bike-riding of the motorbike boys. Being fast on the road was both a consequence of the music's meaning and a living out of that meaning. Fourth, the motorbike boys preferred singles to albums. The fact a song was not available as a single amounted to a declaration of its worthlessness. For a culture which valued concrete experience over mental activity, listening to albums implied a level of seriousness and musical indulgence foreign to the motorbike boys. Singles put the listener in control; albums implied a commitment beyond the realm of the concrete now. In these ways, Willis argues, the motorbike boys demonstrated the 'profane' power of subordinate and marginal groups 'to sometimes take as their own, select and creatively develop particular artefacts to express their own meanings' (166).

Of all the early cultural-studies work on youth subcultures, Dick Hebdige's *Subculture: The Meaning of Style* (1979) is perhaps the most celebrated and most enduring. According to Hebdige, youth subcultures are 'concerned first and foremost with consumption' (94–5).

> They are . . . cultures of conspicuous consumption – even when, as with the skinheads and the punks, certain types of consumption are conspicuously refused – and it is through the distinctive rituals of consumption, through style, that the subculture at once reveals its 'secret' identity and communicates its forbidden meanings. It is basically the way in which commodities are used in a subculture which marks the subculture off from more orthodox cultural formations. (102–3)

Youth subcultural consumption is for Hebdige consumption at its most discriminating. Through a process of 'bricolage' they appropriate for their own purposes and meanings the commodities commercially provided by the culture industries. Through acts of 'bricolage' products are combined or transformed in ways not intended or envisaged by their producers; commodities are re-articulated to produce oppositional meanings. As Hebdige explains,

> Popular culture offers a rich iconography, a set of symbols, objects and artefacts, which can be assembled and reassembled by different groups in a literally limitless number of combinations. The meaning of each selection is transformed as individual objects are taken out of their original, historical and cultural contexts and juxtaposed against other objects and signs from other contexts. (104)

His examples include teddy boys wearing Saville Row Edwardian jackets; mods wearing Italian suits; punks using bin-liners and safety pins. In this way, through acts of cultural consumption (combined with patterns of behaviour, ways of speaking, taste in music, drug use, etc.) youth subcultures engage in symbolic forms of resistance to both dominant and parent cultures. According to Hebdige's now classic formulation, youth subcultures always move from originality and opposition to commercial incorporation and ideological defusion as the culture industries eventually succeed in marketing subcultural resistance for general consumption and profit. As Hebdige explains: 'Youth cultural styles may begin by issuing symbolic challenges, but they must end by establishing new sets of conventions; by creating new commodities, new industries or rejuvenating old ones' (96).[5]

Youth subcultural analysis has always tended to celebrate the extraordinary as against the ordinary. Subcultures represent youth in resistance, actively refusing to conform to the supposed passive commercial tastes in cultural consumption of the majority of youth. Once resistance has given way to incorporation, analysis stops, waiting for the next 'great refusal'. The move from youth subcultures to the cultural-consumption patterns of young people as a whole was developed around the recognition that all young people are active consumers of commodities and not the passive cultural dupes of much subcultural theory. Gary Clarke (in an essay first published by the Birmingham Centre for Contemporary Cultural Studies in 1981), rejects the 'dichotomy between subcultures and . . . the rest of society as being straight, incorporated in a consensus, and willing to scream undividedly loud in any moral panic' (1990: 84). He also objects to the London-centredness of much of the cultural-studies work on youth subcultures, with its implicit suggestion that the appearance of a given youth subculture in the provinces is a telling sign of the subculture's incorporation (86). At the core of Clarke's critique is a suspicion of the presence of an implicit cultural elitism structuring much subcultural theory. As he explains,

> I would argue generally that the subcultural literature's focus on the stylistic deviance of a few contains (albeit implicitly) a similar treatment of the rest of the working class as unproblematically incorporated. This is evident, for example, in the distaste felt for youth deemed as outside subcultural activity – even though most 'straight' working-class youths enjoy the same music, styles, and activities as the subcultures – and in the disdain for such cults as glam, disco, and the ted revival, which lack 'authenticity'. Indeed, there seems to be an underlying contempt for 'mass culture' (which stimulates the interest in those who deviate from it) which stems from the work of the Marxism of the Frankfurt School and, within the English tradition, to the fear of mass culture expressed in *The Uses of Literacy*. (90)

If youth subcultural consumption is to remain an area of concern in cultural studies, Clarke suggests that future analysis 'should take the breakthrough of a style as its starting point' (92), rather than seeing this as the moment of incorporation. Better still, cultural studies should focus on 'the activities of all youths to locate continuities and discontinuities in culture and social relations and to discover the meaning these activities have for the youths themselves' (95).

In recent years fan culture has come increasingly under the critical gaze of cultural studies. Traditionally, fans have been treated in one of two ways – ridiculed or pathologised. According to Joli Jenson, 'The literature on fandom is haunted by images of deviance. The fan is consistently characterized (referencing the term's origins) as a potential fanatic. This means that fandom is seen as excessive, bordering on deranged, behaviour' (1992: 9). Jenson suggests two typical types of fan pathology, 'the obsessed individual' (usually male) and 'the hysterical crowd' (usually female). She contends that both figures result from a particular reading and 'unacknowledged critique of modernity' in which fans are viewed 'as a psychological symptom of a presumed social dysfunction' (9). Fans are presented as one of the dangerous 'others' of modern life. They are conceived as the passive and pathological victims of the manipulations of the culture industries. Whereas 'you' and 'I' can discriminate and create distance between ourselves and the objects of our cultural consumption and our pleasure (and thus stay 'normal'), fans cannot.

The critical discourse on fan culture is a clear example of a discourse on other people. Fandom is what 'other people' do; 'we' always pursue interests, exhibit tastes and preferences. 'Furthermore,' as Jenson points out, 'what "they" do is deviant, and therefore dangerous, while what "we" do is normal, and therefore safe' (19). Similarly, in the ways outlined by Bourdieu, this is a discourse which seeks to secure and police distinctions between class cultures. This is clear in the way in which fandom is assigned to the cultural-consumption activities of popular audiences, while more sensible dominant groups are said to have cultural interests, more discriminating tastes and preferences in cultural consumption. This of course is confirmed by the object(s) of cultural consumption. Official or dominant culture produces aesthetic appreciation; fandom is only appropriate for the texts and practices of popular culture.[6] Moreover, distinction is not just established by the object of consumption but in how the object is said to be consumed. Fans are said to display their pleasure to emotional excess, whereas the audience for official or dominant culture are always able to maintain respectable aesthetic distance and control.

One of the most interesting recent accounts of fan culture from within cultural studies is Henry Jenkins's ethnographic investigation of a fan community (mostly, but not exclusively, white middle-class women). Jenkins, writing 'in active dialogue with the fan community', seeks to challenge the negative stereotypes of fans as figures of ridicule or concern, 'and to encourage a greater awareness of the richness of fan culture' (1992: 9). The study is written to increase academic knowledge of fan culture, but also with an insistence that academics 'can learn from fan culture' (8).

Fans, according to Jenkins, drawing on the work of Michel de Certeau, 'constitute a particularly active and vocal community of consumers whose activities direct attention onto this process of cultural appropriation. . . . Fans are not unique in their status as textual poachers, yet, they have developed poaching to an art form' (27). Unlike popular reading as described by de Certeau, which Jenkins characterises as 'transient meaning-production' (45), fan reading has an ongoing existence in discussions with other fan readers.

> Such discussions expand the experience of the text beyond its initial consumption. The produced meanings are thus more fully integrated into the readers' lives and are of a fundamentally different character from meanings generated through a casual and fleeting encounter with an otherwise unremarkable (and unremarked upon) text. For the fan, these previously 'poached' meanings provide a foundation for future encounters

with the fiction, shaping how it will be perceived, defining how it will be used. (ibid.)

According to Jenkins, there are three key features which mark fan culture's mode of appropriation of media texts: '[the] ways fans draw texts close to the realm of their lived experience; the role played by rereading within fan culture; and the process by which program information gets inserted into ongoing social interactions' (53).

First of all, then, fan reading is characterised by an intensity of intellectual and emotional involvement.

> The text is drawn close not so that the fan can be possessed by it but rather so that the fan may more fully possess it. Only by integrating media content back into their everyday lives, only by close engagement with its meanings and materials, can fans fully consume the fiction and make it an active resource. (62)

Arguing against textual determinism (the text determines how it will be read and in so doing positions the reader in a particular ideological discourse), Jenkins insists that 'The reader is drawn not into the preconstituted world of the fiction but rather into a world she has created from textual materials. Here, the reader's pre-established values are at least as important as those preferred by the narrative system' (63). Again, the difference between fan reader and other readers is a question of the intensity of intellectual and emotional involvement which constitutes 'the reader's pre-established values'. The ordinary reader reads in a context of shifting interests; the fan reads from within the realms of the 'lived experience' of fandom. The second feature highlights the fact that fans do not just read texts, they continually reread them. This profoundly changes the nature of the text–reader relationship. The rereading of texts alters a reader's experience of a text; it shifts the reader's attention from 'what will happen' to 'how things happen', to questions of character relations, narrative themes, the production of social knowledges and discourses. Finally, the third feature identified by Jenkins seeks to draw attention to the way in which whereas most reading is a solitary process, performed in private, fans consume texts as part of a community. Fan culture is about the public display and circulation of meaning production and reading practices. Fans make meanings to communicate with other fans. Without the public display and circulation of these meanings fandom would not be fandom. As Jenkins contends,

> Organised fandom is, perhaps first and foremost, an institution of theory and criticism, a semistructured space where

competing interpretations and evaluations of common texts are proposed, debated, and negotiated and where readers speculate about the nature of the mass media and their own relationship to it. (86)

Fan communities, as Jenkins points out, are not just bodies of enthusiastic readers, they are also cultural producers. Jenkins notes ten ways in which fans rewrite their favourite television shows. One form of cultural production is 'filking' (the writing and performing at conferences of songs – filk songs – about programmes, characters or fandom itself). In his discussion of filking, Jenkins draws attention to a common opposition within many filk songs between fandom and 'Mundania' (the world in which non-fans – 'mundane readers' or 'mundanes' – live). The difference between the two worlds is not simply one of intensity of response, 'they are also contrasted in terms of the shallowness and short-sightedness of mundane thinking' (264). As Jenkins explains, 'Fans are defined in opposition to the values and norms of everyday life, as people who live more richly, feel more intensely, play more freely, and think more deeply than "mundanes" ' (268). In this way, he argues, 'Fandom constitutes . . . a space . . . defined by its refusal of mundane values and practices, its celebration of deeply held emotions and passionately embraced pleasures. Fandom's very existence represents a critique of conventional forms of consumer culture' (283). What Jenkins finds particularly empowering about fandom is its struggle to create 'a more participatory culture' from 'the very forces that transform many Americans into spectators' (284). As he explains,

> I am not claiming that there is anything particularly empowering about the texts fans embrace. I am, however, claiming that there is something empowering about what fans do with those texts in the process of assimilating them to the particulars of their lives. Fandom celebrates not exceptional texts but rather exceptional readings (though its interpretive practices makes it impossible to maintain a clear or precise distinction between the two). (ibid.)

Like the early cultural-studies model of youth subcultural patterns of cultural consumption, Jenkins's community of fandom comes close to being situated in a heroic struggle to resist the demands of the ordinary and the ('Mundania') everyday. Lawrence Grossberg, in ways reminiscent of Clarke's early critique of work on youth subcultures, is critical of the 'subcultural' model of fandom, in which 'fans constitute an elite fraction of the larger audience of passive consumers' (1992: 52).

Thus, the fan is always in constant conflict, not only with the various structures of power, but also with the vast audience of media consumers. But such an elitist view of fandom does little to illuminate the complex relations that exist between forms of popular culture and their audiences. While we may all agree that there is a difference between the fan and the consumer, we are unlikely to understand the difference if we simply celebrate the former category and dismiss the latter one. (ibid.)

I think John Fiske is right in his assessment that the real difference between a fan and an 'ordinary' reader is 'excess' – the fan is an excessive consumer of popular culture (1992: 46).

Notes

1   Although they do agree that consumption in certain social contexts, 'with spontaneous sumptuary codes' (xxi), can operate as a means to exclude.
2   The class relations in what Bourdieu calls the cultural field are structured around two divisions: on the one hand, between the dominant classes and the subordinate classes, and on the other, within the dominant classes between those with high economic capital as opposed to high cultural capital, and those with high cultural capital as opposed to high economic capital.
3   Cultural capital is a social currency based on knowledge, familiarity and the ability to feel at ease with the texts and practices of 'legitimate' culture.
4   Although increased access to higher education, for example, would seem to be a move towards greater equality, the fact that it is always matched by a parallel inflation in qualifications demanded for particular types of employment works to undermine this possibility. Whereas in the past a school qualification would have secured a position in a particular type of employment, a university degree is now a requirement. Therefore although more people now go to university in the UK than ever before, the qualifications they leave with are worth much less in the employment market place than, say, 20 years ago when fewer people had degrees. In this way, the education system helps reproduce and legitimate a class hierarchy of social difference and social distinction.
5   Hebdige's model is remarkably similar to Simmel's thesis about the inevitable trajectory of fashion. As Simmel explains,

> As soon as an example has been universally adopted, that is, as soon as anything that was originally done only by a few has really come to be practised by all . . . we no longer speak of fashion. As fashion spreads, it gradually goes to its doom. (1957: 547)

6   Jenson (1992: 19–20) argues convincingly that is possible to be a fan of James Joyce in much the same way as it is possible to be a fan of Barry Manilow.

|4|

Reading as Production

In this chapter I consider a number of approaches in philosophy and literary theory which figure reading as a process which produces the text as read.[1] This is an approach to cultural consumption which maintains that the process of reading fictional texts is itself a form of cultural production. Putting this another way, the meaning of a novel by Thomas Hardy or a short story by Katherine Mansfield, or a poem by T.S. Eliot, cannot be separated from the meanings ascribed to these texts by actual readers who read them. Work on readers in literary theory and criticism is something which has developed over the past 20 to 25 years. Writing in 1980, in an introduction to a collection of essays on the relationship between the reader and the literary text, Susan Suleiman observed how 'The words *reader* and *audience*, once relegated to the status of the unproblematic and obvious, have acceded to a starring role' (1980: 3).

The chapter begins with a discussion of hermeneutics, the name given to the study and theory of interpretation. Although hermeneutics is a broad field of study, containing a range of positions on interpretation, I intend here to focus only on the work of the German philosopher Hans-Georg Gadamer. The next section considers the work of two German literary theorists, Wolfgang Iser and Hans Robert Jauss, who are both members of the so-called Constance School. The penultimate section focuses on the concept of 'interpretative communities' developed by the American literary critic Stanley Fish. The chapter concludes with an assessment of Tony Bennett and Janet Woollacott's model of the 'reading formation'.

Hermeneutics

In his major work, *Truth and Method*, Hans-Georg Gadamer argues that an understanding of a cultural text is always from the perspective of the person who understands. Authors may have intentions, and texts certainly have material structures, but meaning is not something inherent in a text (an unchanging essence); meaning is always something a person makes when he or she reads a text. Moreover, Gadamer is adamant that texts and readers always encounter each other in historical and social locations and that the situatedness of this encounter always informs the interaction between reader and text. In this way, he contends, a text is always read with preconceptions or prejudices; it is never encountered in a state of virginal purity, untouched by the knowledge with which, or the context in which, it is read. This is not, for Gadamer, something to regret, in a vain appeal to 'the ontological obstructions of the scientific concept of objectivity' (1979: 235), but is in fact the very conditions for understanding. It is through our preconceptions and prejudices that we organise our approach to a text. As Gadamer explains, 'the historicity of our existence entails that prejudices, in the literal sense of the word [pre-judgements], constitute the initial directedness of our whole ability to experience' (9). We always begin the task of understanding with 'our own fore-meanings . . . [our] own expectations of meaning' (238). This does not mean that our understanding of a text (its meaning)[2] is therefore a subjective event, leading to the suggestion that any meaning can be subjectively imposed upon a text. Preconceptions or prejudices, as Gadamer insists, are not the same as 'false judgments' (240). Furthermore, although we approach a text with preconceived ideas, what we always encounter is the materiality of the text itself (particular words ordered in particular ways, which allow the reader to recognise a difference between, say, Shakespeare's 'Sonnet 138' and 'Sailing to Byzantium' by W.B. Yeats). This is of course an encounter in which our preconceived ideas may well be modified. An understanding of a text (its meaning) is therefore always a process in which preconceived ideas are confronted (and perhaps modified) by the materiality of the text. He describes this process, what he calls the 'hermenuetic circle' (259), as working like a dialogue of questions and answers: we ask questions of a text, but if a satisfactory understanding is to be achieved we must always remain open to the answers it gives to the questions we ask. Both text and reader bring something to the encounter. In this way,

> meanings cannot be understood in an arbitrary way . . . we cannot hold blindly to our own fore-meaning . . . we [must] remain open to the meaning . . . of the text. But this openness always includes our placing the other meaning [the meaning of the text] in a relation with the whole of our own meanings. (238)

However, as Gadamer insists, 'Not occasionally only, but always, the meaning of a text goes beyond its author. That is why understanding is not merely . . . reproductive [simply activating the 'meaning' in the text], but [is] always . . . productive [producing a 'meaning' in the interaction between text and reader]' (264). He describes this process of dialogue between reader and text in which meaning is made as a 'fusion of horizons' (273). The 'horizon of understanding' (conceptual framework; the taken for granted) of the reader confronts the 'horizon of understanding' of the text. It is in the space opened up between the two that meaning is made in a 'fusion of horizons of understanding' (340). In this way, understanding is a process of 're-creation', which is 'both bound and free' (107). As he explains,

> the discovery of the true meaning of a text or a work of art is never finished; it is in fact an infinite process. Not only are fresh sources of error constantly excluded, so that the true meaning has filtered out of it all kinds of things that obscure it, but there emerge continually new sources of understanding, which reveal unsuspected elements of meaning. (266)

In other words, both text and reader are always historically situated, and therefore the encounter between the two is always a fusion of different historical horizons.[3]

To provide some sense of what Gadamer is arguing against, I will now consider briefly the theoretical position of the influential American literary critic E.D. Hirsch. Hirsch argues that the 'objective meaning' of a literary text (as opposed to the contingent and variable 'significances' ascribed by readers) is the author's intended meaning. The meaning of a text and its author's intention are one and the same. Aware of the difficulties entailed in knowing for certain the nature of such intentions, the work of interpretation must nevertheless remain focused on the task to reveal what the author intended:

> Even though we can never be certain that our interpretative guesses are correct, we know that they can be correct and that the goal of interpretation as a discipline is constantly to increase the probability that they are correct . . . Only one interpretative problem can be answered with objectivity: 'What, in all probability, did the author mean to convey?' (1967: 207)

Matters of cultural consumption (reduced by Hirsch to little more than questions of the extent to which authorial intention has been understood or misunderstood by readers) are of only secondary importance. It is of course possible to agree with Hirsch about there being a difference between authorial 'meaning' and the 'significances' discovered by readers in texts and yet draw conclusions very different from Hirsch's. One could argue that since authorial intentions are mostly unknowable (a point Hirsch concedes) and what we do have in abundance, and what in effect the institution of literature is largely made from, are readings of texts, we should take as our focus what readers take texts to mean, rather than what texts have supposedly been intended to mean. This would be to reverse Hirsch's logic of evaluation and to place cultural consumption above cultural production (knowing all the time that cultural consumption is only possible when there is production and that production would surely cease without cultural consumption).

The Constance School: Iser and Jauss

Wolfgang Iser is a German literary theorist, a member of the Constance School of reception theory. Like Gadamer, Iser insists that the act of reading is always an act of production. He maintains that

> As a literary text can only produce a response when it is read, it is virtually impossible to describe this response without also analysing the reading process . . . the text represents a potential effect that is realized in the reading process . . . the meaning of the text is something that [the reader] has to assemble. (1978: ix)[4]

The production of meaning, therefore, involves 'a dialectic relationship between text, reader, and their interaction' (x). Moreover, as Iser insists, 'meaning is [not] an object to be defined, but is an effect to be experienced' (10). It follows from this that the real focus of a literary critic should not be 'to teach the reader the meaning of the text, for without a subjective contribution and a context there is no such thing' (19). Rather, the object of study should be 'an analysis of what actually happens when one is reading a text, for that is when the text begins to unfold its potential; it is in the reader that the text comes to life' (ibid.). As he explains,

> Central to the reading of every literary work is the interaction between its structure and its recipient. [Therefore] . . . the study of a literary work should concern not only the actual text itself but also, and in equal measure, the actions involved in responding to that text. The text itself simply offers 'schematised aspects' through which the subject matter of the

work can be produced, while the actual production takes place through an act of concretization. (20–1)

Iser distinguishes between the text, the work and the reader. As he explains,

> The literary work has two poles, which we might call the artistic and the aesthetic: the artistic pole is the author's text and the aesthetic is the realization accomplished by the reader. In view of this polarity, it is clear that the work itself cannot be identical with the text or with the concretization, but must be situated somewhere between the two. (21)

As he contends, 'the meaning of a literary text is not a definable entity but, if anything, a dynamic happening' (22). The text in effect, he argues, offers itself for 'performance' by a reader. In this way, 'literary texts initiate "performances" of meaning rather than actually formulating meanings themselves . . . [and, moreover] without the participation of the individual reader there can be no performance' (27). In other words, although the text is produced by the author, it is the reader, according to Iser, who brings the text to life, and thus brings the work into existence. Therefore, it is in the act of reading that meaning is realised. However, although the text, in its potential as a performance script, offers to the reader 'certain conditions of actualisation' (34), or what he called in an earlier argument a range of 'polysemantic possibilities' (1974: 136), it still presents itself to the reader as a material structure, 'the repertoire of the text' (1978: 69), and thus limits the play of interpretation. There is always, therefore, 'the role offered by the text and the reader's own disposition, and as one can never be fully taken over by the other, there arises between the two [a] tension' (37).

Although in general terms, 'the role prescribed by the text will be the stronger . . . the reader's own disposition will never disappear totally' (ibid.). Performance of meaning always takes place in a context; the nature of the context both 'illuminates and stabilises the meaning' (62). Iser figures the literary text as an instruction manual for the performance of meaning. The repertoire of the text 'forms an organizational structure of meaning which must be optimised through the reading of the text. This optimisation will depend on the reader's own degree of awareness and on his willingness to open himself up to an unfamiliar experience' (85). However, the repertoire of the text cannot totally determine the performance of meaning: the repertoire of the text 'can only offer the reader *possibilities* of organization. Total organization would mean that there was nothing left for the reader to do' (86). Moreover, 'the reader's task is not simply to accept, but to assemble for himself [or herself] that which is to be accepted' (97). As he observes,

> Although the reader must participate in the assembly of meaning by realizing the structure inherent in the text, it must not be forgotten that he stands outside the text. His position must therefore be manipulated by the text if his [or her] viewpoint is to be properly guided. Clearly, this viewpoint cannot be determined exclusively by the individual reader's personal history of experience, but this history cannot be totally ignored either: only when the reader has been taken outside his own experience can his viewpoint be changed. The constitution of meaning, therefore, gains its full significance when something happens to the reader. The constituting of meaning and the constituting of the reading subject are therefore interacting operations that are both structured by the aspects of the text. (152)

As Iser contends, 'Reading is an activity that is guided by the text; this must be processed by the reader, who is then, in turn, affected by what he has processed' (163). In this way, reading can be seen as a creative process in which the text 'offers guidance as to what is to be produced, and therefore cannot itself be the product' (107). The difference he draws our attention to, between a text offering guidance on how it should be read and the text as the end product of reading, is an important theoretical distinction. It is a challenge to the many theoretical perspectives which advocate a view of meaning as something imposed on a reader by a text. As Iser maintains, 'Reading is not a direct "internalisation", because it is not a one-way process, . . . [it is] a dynamic *interaction* between text and reader' (ibid.).

Hans Robert Jauss, a former student of Gadamer's, is a literary historian and like Iser is a member of the Constance School. Although he shares Iser's view that the indeterminacy of the text requires a reader to realise its meaning, he also insists, against Iser's rather asocial/ahistorical reader, that readers and readings are always historically situated within specific conditions of reading. This is a rejection of the widespread 'belief in the timeless substance of a literary work and in the timeless point of view of the reader' (1982: 196). As he maintains,

> A literary work is not an object which stands by itself and that offers the same view to each reader in each period. It is not a monument that monologically reveals its timeless essence. It is much more like an orchestration that strikes ever new resonances among its readers and frees the text from the

material of the words and brings it to a contemporary existence. (21)

Therefore, if we are to fully understand the process of reading, he argues, readers and their readings must be located in specific historical conditions of reading. The reading of a text is always mediated by what Jauss calls an 'horizon of expectations' (22).

> A literary work, even when it appears to be new, does not present itself as something absolutely new in an informational vacuum, but predisposes its audience to a very specific kind of reception by announcements, overt and covert signals, familiar characteristics, or implicit allusions. It awakens memories of that which was already read, brings the reader to a specific emotional attitude, and with its beginning arouses expectations for the 'middle and end', which can then be maintained intact or altered, reoriented, or even fulfilled ironically in the course of the reading according to specific rules of the genre or type of text. (23)

In other words, texts are always read in the knowledge of other texts already read; information already stored, and available for use, in the cultural storehouse of the reader.

So far the theories we have considered are all predicated on the notion that literary texts place clear limits on their possible interpretation. Iser, for example, describes his work as a theory of 'aesthetic response' and not a theory of 'aesthetic reception' (1978: x). The distinction he is concerned to make is between an approach which begins with the text and one which starts with the reader. 'A theory of reception . . . always deals with existing readers, whose reactions testify to certain historically conditioned experiences of literature. A theory of response has its roots in the text; a theory of reception arises from a history of readers' judgments' (ibid.). The next example to be discussed is the work of the American literary critic Stanley Fish. As we shall see, he very definitely begins with the reader.

Interpretative Communities

Literature, as Stanley Fish contends, 'is an open category, not definable by fictionality, or by a disregard of propositional truth, or by a prominence of tropes and figures, but simply by what we decide to put into it' (1980: 11). This does not mean that what counts as literature is determined by the subjective will of individual readers; the 'we' Fish refers to is the 'literary community'. As he explains,

the act of recognising literature is not constrained by
something in the text, nor does it issue from an independent
and arbitrary will; rather, it proceeds from a collective decision
that will be in force only so long as a community of readers
or believers continues to abide by it. (ibid.)

It follows from this, Fish contends, that 'there is no single way of
reading that is correct or natural, only 'ways of seeing' that are
extensions of . . . [the] perspectives [of] interpretative communities'
(16). The literary community is thus divided into different interpretative communities, each with its own set of interests and
concerns, and each seeking to win support for their own particular 'set of interpretative assumptions' (ibid.). Moreover, Fish insists
that 'interpretation is the source of texts, facts, authors, and intentions'; all are 'the *products* of interpretation' (16–17).

Interpretative communities provide specific contexts for operating as a reader. In this way, the meaning of a text is always a
situated meaning, produced in a specific context. As Fish contends,
'meanings are the property neither of fixed and stable texts nor of
free and independent readers but of interpretative communities that
are responsible both for the shape of a reader's activities and for
the texts those activities produce' (322). Moreover, it is not possible for a text to have a meaning outside a specific situation. As
Fish explains,

> communication occurs within situations and . . . to be in a
> situation is already to be in possession of (or to be possessed
> by) a structure of assumptions, of practices understood to be
> relevant in relation to purposes and goals that are already in
> place; and it is within the assumption of these purposes and
> goals that any utterance is *immediately* heard. (318)[5]

Fish offers the example of what a group of poetry students were
able to do with the names of four linguists and one literary critic,
left on the blackboard from a previous class. When the poetry
students entered the room, he told them that what they saw on the
blackboard was a seventeenth-century English religious poem.
Armed with this information, the poetry students proceeded to
read, in a detailed and convincing manner, the five names on the
blackboard as a seventeenth-century English religious poem. What
allowed them to do this, according to Fish, is the fact that

> It is not that the presence of poetic qualities compels a certain
> kind of attention [the 'common sense' of literary criticism] but
> that the paying of a certain kind of attention results in the
> emergence of poetic qualities. As soon as my students were
> aware that it was poetry they were seeing, they began to look

with poetry-seeing eyes, that is, with eyes that saw everything
in relation to the properties they knew poems to possess. . . .
Thus the meanings of the words and the interpretation in
which those words were seen to be embedded emerged
together, as a consequence of the operations my students began
to perform once they were told that this was a poem. (326)

The example of this episode leads Fish to the conclusion that it is
not the properties of a text but the interpretative assumptions and
strategies performed by readers, situated in interpretative communities, which determine the outcomes of interpretation. In this way,
he argues, 'Interpretation is not the art of construing but the art of
constructing. Interpreters do not decode poems; they make them'
(327).

The interpretative strategies of interpretative communities are
always 'social and conventional' (331), therefore, as Fish explains,

while it is true to say that we create poetry . . . we create it
through interpretative strategies that are finally not our own
but have their source in a publicly available system of intelligibility. Insofar as the . . . literary system . . . constrains us,
it also fashions us, furnishing us with categories of understanding, with which we in turn fashion the entities to which
we can then point. (332)[6]

Reading Formations

Reading formations are, as Tony Bennett and Janet Woollacott
explain,

the product of definite social and ideological relations of
reading composed, in the main, of those apparatuses – schools,
the press, critical reviews, fanzines – within and between
which the socially dominant forms for the superintendence of
reading are both constructed and contested. (1987: 64–5)[7]

Reading formations are not simply the range of other texts which
come into play when one reads a specific text, but texts that carry
with them institutional power, directing specific reading strategies,
which seek to organise the conditions and relations of reading.
What Bennett and Woollacott refer to as

[the] specific determinations which bear in upon, mould and
configure the relations between texts and readers in determinant conditions of reading. [That is,] the inter-textual relations
which prevail in a particular context, thereby activating a

given body of texts by ordering the relations between them in a specific way such that their reading is always-already cued in specific directions that are not given by those 'texts themselves' as entities separable from such relations. (64)

In the politics of interpretation, as Bennett and Woollacott contend, 'Texts constitute sites around which the pre-eminently social affair of the struggle for meaning is conducted, principally in the form of a series of bids and counter-bids to determine which system of inter-textual co-ordinates should be granted an effective social role of organizing reading practices' (59–60).

Bennett and Woollacott reject the view that the texts of popular fiction are little more than containers of ideology, a convenient and always successful means to transmit dominant ideology from the culture industries to the duped and manipulated masses. The problem with such a view is that it leads to 'a politics of simple opposition and to a criticism which is little more than a constant unmasking of dominant ideologies at work' (4). Against this, they contend that popular fiction is a specific space, with its own ideological economy, making available a historically variable, complex and contradictory range of ideological discourses and counter-discourses to be activated in particular conditions of reading. While they accept that it may be possible to describe the Bond novels and films as racist, sexist and reactionary, to stop there is to fail to explore how these texts engage with a popular audience. That is, of course, 'Unless one subscribes to the view that the reading, cinema-going and television publics simply enjoy sexist, racist and reactionary texts' (ibid.). Rather than simply condemn these texts, Bennett and Woollacott seek to explore why and how they make their appeal.

. In *Bond and Beyond*, Bennett and Woollacott track the diverse and changing ways in which the figure of James Bond has been produced and reproduced through a range of different cultural texts and practices. Since his emergence in the 1950s the figure of Bond has, at different moments of his career as a popular hero, articulated (that is, expressed and been connected to) a series of ideological concerns. 'The ideological and cultural elements out of which the figure of Bond has been woven may have been constant, but these have been combined in different mixes and shifting permutations' (19). It is the ideological 'malleability' of the figure of Bond which has ensured his continuing popularity. As Bennett and Woollacott point out, 'it is not the popularity of *Bond* that has to be accounted for so much as the popularity of *different* Bonds, popular in different ways and for different reasons at different points in time' (20). They describe the figure of Bond as a 'mobile signifier' (42), and claim that the only thing that has remained constant throughout his career as a popular hero is the way in which he 'has functioned as a shifting focal point for the articulation of historically specific ideological concerns' (20).

A significant part of Bennett and Woollacott's discussion of Bond is taken up with the ways in which the films (and other 'texts of Bond'[8]) helped to organise and predispose 'readers to read the novels in certain ways, privileging some of their aspects at the expense of others' (43). At the centre of their argument is the claim that 'the conditions of Bond's existence have been *inter-textual*' (44). They use the hyphen to indicate the theoretical difference between their usage of the term and its usual employment (without the hyphen) within cultural studies to signify the way in which one text is marked by the signs of other texts. As Bennett and Woollacott make clear, their employment of the term is quite different: 'we intend the concept inter-textuality to refer to the social organisation of the relations between texts within specific conditions of reading' (45). Moreover, they argue that

> the latter overrides and overdetermines the former. *Intertextualities* . . . are the product of specific, socially organised *intertextualities*; it is the latter which, in providing the objective determinants of reading practices, provide the framework within which inter-textual references can be produced and operate. (86)

Thus, they argue,

> The figure of Bond has been produced in the constantly changing relations between the wide range of texts brought into association with one another via the functioning of Bond as the signifier which they have jointly constructed. In turn, it is this figure which, in floating between them, has thereby connected these texts into a related set in spite of their manifold differences in other aspects. (45)

In other words, what unites these texts is not an author (even the novels are written by a number of authors), but the figure of Bond. It is Bond who 'furnishes the operative principle of textual classification' (52). Moreover, when Bond changes, 'such changes form a part of the social and cultural determination which influence the way the texts concerned are available to be read' (52–3). An objection to this argument might be to claim that the novels (as the original source of Bond) have a privileged status over the other 'texts of Bond'. Bennett and Woollacott claim that such an argument 'is impossible to maintain' (53).

> The 'texts of Bond' have comprised a constantly accumulating
> and 'mutating' set of texts, 'mutating' in the sense that
> additions to the set have connected with the pre-existing 'texts
> of Bond' in such a way as to reorganise kaleidoscopically the
> relationships, transactions and exchanges between them. None
> of the texts in which the figure of Bond has been constructed
> can thus be regarded as privileged in relation to the others in
> any absolute or permanent sense. Rather, each region of this
> textual set occupies a privileged position in relation to the
> others, but in different ways depending on the part it has
> played in the circulation and expanded reproduction of the
> figure of Bond. (54)

Therefore, although Ian Fleming's novels came first and supplied
much of the material for the films that followed, once the films
were in circulation, it was the films which dominated imaginative
constructions of the figure of Bond. Moreover, it was the films
which produced the popular audience for the novels. But more than
this, Bennett and Woollacott would insist, it was the films which
provided the interpretative framework through which to read the
novels. Once this is acknowledged, the rather one-way relationship
(questions of difference and similarity, etc.) usually brought into
play in discussions of film adaptations of novels begins to look
unconvincing. As Bennett and Woollacott contend, the films 'have
culturally activated the novels in particular ways, selectively cueing
their reading, modifying the exchange between text and reader,
inflecting it in new directions by inserting the novels within an
expanded inter-textual set' (55). What makes this possible is the
way in which reading is always a process in which

> the inter-textually organised reader meets the inter-textually
> organised text. The exchange is never a pure one between two
> unsullied entities, existing separately from one another, but is
> rather 'muddied' by the cultural debris which attach to both
> texts and readers in the determinate conditions which regulate
> the specific forms of their encounter. (56)

Bennett and Woollacott reject both the view that the text determines its own reading (invites recognition of its objective properties) and the contrary view that it is the reader who produces the
meaning of the text. They accuse both approaches of working
with a 'metaphysical view of texts' (60), in that the first claims
that the meaning of a text pre-exists its conditions of reading,
while the second, although accepting the possibility of variable
readings, nonetheless insists that these are variable readings of the
same text. Against both of these positions, they argue for a

rethinking of the text–reader relationship, in which texts are 'conceived as having no existence prior to or independently of the varying "reading formations" in which they have been constituted as objects-to-be-read' (64). In other words, a text only becomes a text when read, just as a reader only becomes a reader in the act of reading; neither can exist outside this relationship. This of course exposes Bennett and Woollacott to the accusation that they are claiming that readers and texts have no objective existence. But, as they explain,

> This is not to suggest that texts have no determinate properties – such as a definite order of narrative progression – which may be analysed objectively. But it is to argue that such properties cannot, in themselves, validate certain received meanings above others; they do not provide a point of 'truth' in relation to which readings may be normatively and hierarchically ranked, or discounted. Nor are we suggesting that readers do not have determinate properties. They most certainly do, but complexly varying ones which, rather than being attributable to the reader as a subject independent of the text, are the product of the orders of inter-textuality which have marked the reader's formation. (65)

Regimes of inter-textuality organise how readers read texts. We never get access to texts 'in themselves', but always as situated within a network of inter-textual relations. In their approach to Bond, as they explain, they have 'stressed the degree to which these have always been variably produced – not as "the same text" but as different "texts-to-be-read" – as a result of their insertion within different regimes of inter-textuality' (260). In other words, text and context are not separate or separable moments available for analysis at different times. Text and context are always part of the same process, the same moment – they are inseparable: one cannot have a text without a context, or context without a text. Moreover, Bennett and Woollacott contend that all previous approaches to questions of meaning production have assumed that one can separate textual meaning from the meanings produced in actual acts of reading. The first supposedly approximates to the essential properties of the text (and can be determined without reference to factors outside the text); the second, influenced by extra-textual variables, may change through history and across cultures, but it is still a reading of (a variation on) the essential properties of the text (in other words, different readings of the same text). This is a mode of analysis which, despite its reference to the activities of readers, always ends up privileging the text. There is an objective structure and there is the endless flow of subjective responses.

Drawing on the work of the French linguist Michel Pecheux, Bennett and Woollacott argue that meaning (or reading) cannot exist prior to its articulation by a reader. It cannot pre-exist the encounter between reader and text. This is not an attempt to reduce text to context, but an insistence that context and text cannot be conceived of as separate entities. As they explain,

> The concept of reading formation . . . is an attempt to think of contexts of reception as sets of discursive and inter-textual determinations which, in operating on both texts and readers, mediate the relations between them and provide the mechanisms through which they can productively interact. (263)

Bennett and Woollacott offer the following summary of their contribution to the debate on reading as production,

> Much previous debate on the question of reading has deadlocked on the opposition between the view of the text as dictating its readings and the view that readers are able to mobilise cultural resources which enable them to read against the grain of the text or to negotiate its meanings in particular ways. Our purpose has been to displace the terms of this dispute by suggesting that neither approach takes sufficient account of the cultural and ideological forces which organise and reorganise the network of inter-textual relations within which texts are inserted as texts-to-be-read in certain ways by reading subjects organised to read in certain ways. The relations between texts and readers, we have suggested, are always profoundly mediated by the discursive and inter-textual determinations which, operating on both, structure the domain of their encounter so as to produce, always in specific and variable forms, texts and readers as the mutual supports of one another. (249)

Notes

1   Because my interest here is with theoretical and methodological perspectives in thinking about cultural consumption, my presentation of this work will not include any consideration of the way in which it engages with other issues in philosophy or literary studies.

2   As Gadamer points out, 'Interpretation is not an occasional additional act subsequent to understanding, but rather understanding is always an interpretation' (1979: 274). In this way, as he explains, 'all interpretation presumes a living relationship between the interpreter and the text' (295).

3   Hermeneutics and phenomenology have had very little influence on the study of popular culture. Tony Wilson's work is the rare exception to the rule, in that using 'the conceptual geography . . . derive[d] from phenomenology and

hermeneutics', it seeks to introduce a 'phenomenological revision of media analysis' (1993: 4).

4   As Karl Marx observed, 'Consumption produces production . . . because a product becomes a real product only by being consumed' (1973: 91). Terry Eagleton makes the similar point that 'Literary texts do not exist on bookshelves: they are processes of signification materialised only in the practice of reading. For literature to happen, the reader is quite as vital as the author' (1983: 74).

5   Fish is aware that this opens him up to the dreaded accusation of relativism. This is a charge he strongly refutes, arguing that

> everyone is situated somewhere, there is no one for whom the absence of an a situational norm would be of any practical consequence. . . . In other words, while relativism is a position one can entertain, it is not a position one can occupy. No one can *be* a relativist, because no one can achieve the distance from his own beliefs and assumptions which would result in their being no more authoritative *for him* than the beliefs and assumptions held by others, or, for that matter, the beliefs and assumptions he himself used to hold. . . . The point is that there is never a moment when one believes nothing, when consciousness is innocent of any and all categories of thought, and whatever categories of thought are operative at a given moment will serve as an undoubted ground. (319–20)

6   Janice Radway argues that readers of romantic fiction also operate in an 'interpretative community'. How the women read this genre of fiction, she argues, is governed by 'reading strategies and interpretative conventions that the reader has learnt to apply as a member of a particular interpretative community' (1984: 11). Radway's work on romance readers is discussed in the next chapter.

7   For other interesting work on reading formations, see Tony Bennett (1983), John Storey (1992), John Tulloch (1995).

8   Besides the novels and the films, Bennett and Woollacott include, as the 'other texts of Bond', academic criticism, showbiz journalism, fanzine articles, advertising copy and interviews with the actors and other film-makers involved in the production of the Bond films.

|5|

Cultural Consumption: Texts

In this chapter I critically assess a number of influential 'ethnographic' accounts (from Ien Ang, David Buckingham, Bob Hodge and David Tripp, Tamar Liebes and Elihu Katz, and John Tulloch and Albert Moran) of audiences watching television in Australia, Britain, Israel, Japan, the Netherlands and the USA. This is followed by an examination of Janice Radway's very influential exploration of romance reading in the USA. Finally, the chapter concludes with a discussion of Jackie Stacey's work on women going to the cinema in Britain in the 1940s and 1950s. The chapter begins with a discussion of the foundations of the cultural studies approach to the cultural consumption of media texts – the early work of Stuart Hall and David Morley.

From Encoding/Decoding to the 'Nationwide' Audience

The publication of Stuart Hall's 'Encoding and Decoding in the Television Discourse' (first published in 1973) is perhaps the moment when British cultural studies finally emerges from left-Leavisism, 'pessimistic' versions of Marxism, American mass-communication models, culturalism and structuralism, and begins to take on a recognisable form of its own. In Hall's model of televisual communication (*see* Fig 5.1), the circulation of 'meaning' in televisual discourse passes through three distinctive moments: 'each has its specific modality and conditions of existence' (1980: 128). First, media professionals put into meaningful televisual discourse their particular account of, for example, a 'raw' social event. At this moment in the circuit, a range of ways of looking at the world ('ideologies') are 'in dominance'. This is the moment of encoding,

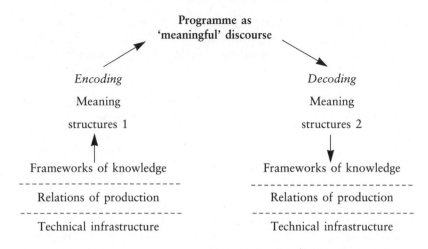

Fig. 5.1 Televisual communication. Source: Hall 1980: 130

when the media professionals involved determine how the 'raw' social event will be encoded in discourse. In the second moment, once the meanings and messages are in meaningful discourse, that is, once they have taken the form of televisual discourse, the formal rules of language and televisual discourse (for example, the play of polysemy) are now 'in dominance'. Finally, in the third moment, the moment of audience decoding, another range of ways of looking at the world ('ideologies') are 'in dominance'. The audience is confronted not by a 'raw' social event, but by a discursive translation of the event. If the event is to become 'meaningful' to the audience, it must now decode and make sense of this discourse.

As Hall explains, 'If no "meaning" is taken, there can be no "consumption". If the meaning is not articulated in practice, it has no effect' (ibid.). If an audience acts upon its decoding, this then itself becomes a social practice, a 'raw' social event, available to be encoded in another discourse. Thus, through the circulation of discourse, 'production' becomes 'consumption' to become 'production' again. The circuit starts in the 'social' and ends, to begin again, in the 'social'. In other words, meanings and messages are not simply 'transmitted', they are always produced: first by the encoder from the 'raw' material of everyday life; and then, second, by an audience situated in relation to other discourses. Each moment is 'determinate', operating in its own conditions of production and cultural consumption. Moreover, as Hall makes clear, the moments of encoding and decoding may not be perfectly symmetrical. There is nothing inevitable about the outcome of the process – what is intended and what is taken may not coincide. Media professionals may wish decoding to correspond with encoding, but they cannot prescribe or guarantee this. Governed by different conditions of existence, encoding and decoding are open to variable reciprocity. This may be simply the result of misunderstanding. Hall acknowledges this, but he is more interested in more deliberate strategies of understanding. Drawing on the work of sociologist Frank Parkin (1971), Hall develops 'three hypothetical positions from which decodings of a televisual discourse may be constructed' (Hall 1980: 136). The first position is 'the dominant-hegemonic position'. This position is occupied

> [w]hen the viewer takes the connoted meaning from, say, a television newscast or current affairs programme full and straight, and decodes the message in terms of the reference code in which it has been encoded, we might say that the viewer *is operating inside the dominant code*. (ibid.)

To decode a television discourse in this way is to decode in harmony with the 'professional code' of the broadcasters. The dominant code is always articulated through the professional code. As Hall explains,

> The professional code is 'relatively independent' of the dominant code, in that it applies criteria and transformational operations of its own, especially those of a technico-practical nature. The professional code, however, operates *within* the 'hegemony' of the dominant code. Indeed, it serves to reproduce the dominant definitions precisely by bracketing their hegemonic quality and operating instead with displaced professional codings which foreground such apparently neutral-technical questions as visual quality, news and presentational values, televisual quality, 'professionalism' and so on. (ibid.)

The second decoding position is 'the negotiated code or position' (137). Hall regards this as the position most likely to be adopted by the majority of viewers. Decoding from this position always involves 'a mixture of adaptive and oppositional elements' (ibid), in which the televisual discourse is negotiated through and in terms of the situated conditions of the viewer. An example of the negotiated code might be a worker who agrees in general terms with a news report's claim that increased wages cause inflation, while insisting on his or her own right to strike for better pay and conditions. The third decoding position identified by Hall is 'the oppositional code'. This is the position occupied by the viewer who recognises the preferred code of the televisual discourse but who none the less chooses to decode within an alternative frame of reference. 'This is the case [for example] of the viewer who listens to a debate on the need to limit wages but "reads" every mention of the "national interest" as "class interest" ' (138).

As Hall readily acknowledged, this hypothetical model would 'need to be empirically tested and refined' (136). This in part is the project of David Morley's *The 'Nationwide' Audience* – to test Hall's model, to see how individual interpretations of televisual texts relate to socio-cultural background. To accomplish this Morley arranged for 29 different groups of people to view two episodes (from 1976 and 1977) of the BBC's early evening magazine/news programme *Nationwide*. The first programme was shown to 18 groups, the second to 11. Each group consisted of between five and 10 people. The groups were selected on the grounds that they might be expected to differ in their decodings from 'dominant' to 'negotiated' to 'oppositional'.

Much of what Morley found seemed to confirm Hall's model For example, a group of university arts students and a group of teacher-training-college students produced readings which moved between 'negotiated' and 'dominant', while a group of shop stewards produced an 'oppositional reading'.[1] However, when both the middle-class bank managers and the working-class apprentices produced the same dominant readings, the correlation between class and reading position looked less secure, forcing Morley to acknowledge that decodings are not determined 'directly from social class position' (Morley 1980: 134). Rather, as he reformulates it: 'it is always a question of how social position *plus* particular discourse positions produce specific readings; readings which are structured because the structure of access to different discourses is determined by social position' (ibid.).

In this way, Morley is able to explain the similarity in decodings between the working-class apprentices and the middle-class bank managers in terms of the formulation: determination of class plus other discourses (bodies of ideas and shared socio-cultural practices which help constitute us as social subjects and thus shape how we see and think about the world). Thus when we are 'interpellated' by a text, this is always in a context of other interpellations (for discussion of this term, see Chapter 8 below). The text–reader encounter does not occur in a moment isolated from other discourses, but always in a field of many discourses, some in harmony with the text, some which are in contradiction with it. One reads, for example, as a student, a Catholic, a socialist and a member of a youth subculture. Each discourse may pull how we read in a different direction. Each may assume a different level of importance in any given social context. The response of the black further-education students and other predominantly black groups to *Nationwide* – their 'critique of silence' – is therefore not to be explained as a failure of communication (the technical inability of the encoders to get their 'message' across). Rather, what it demonstrates is the discourses of the text coming into conflict with the discourses of the reader. 'Here,' as Morley explains, 'the action of the cultures and discourses which these groups are involved in acts to block or inflect their interpellation by the discourse of *Nationwide*' (143). The converse is also evident in the decodings made by the working-class apprentices. 'Here it is not simply a case of the absence of "contradictory" discourses; rather it is the presence of other discourses which work in parallel with those of the programme – enabling these groups to produce "corresponding" representations' (ibid.). In the process of decoding other discourses (both supporting and contradicting) are always in play, 'although their action is more visible when it is a case of negative-contradictory rather than positive-reinforcing effect' (144).

Despite the impact of these other determinations (these other discourses), Morley still concludes that a person's social-class position is an important determinant of which decoding position a person is likely to occupy. Social class is still important because it determines access (or the nature of access) to different discourses. As he explains, 'the subject's position in the social formation structures his or her range of access to various discourses and ideological codes' (158). This then may explain the correlation between the readings made by the middle-class bank managers and the working-class apprentices. The bank managers produced a dominant reading because of their political commitment to the conservatism of *Nationwide*'s discourse, while the apprentices accepted this conservatism uncritically because of a lack (unlike the shop stewards) of an alternative political discourse. Class, he contends, is the key to both readings. The bank managers decoded on the basis of 'class interest', while the apprentices' decoding can be explained in terms of the 'class interest' of the British education system (the working-class apprentices were schooled to be politically uncritical).

In the Afterword to *The 'Nationwide' Audience*, Morley sums up (rather too modestly, in my opinion) the achievements of his research:

> I have been able to do no more than to indicate some of the ways in which social position and (sub)cultural frameworks may be related to individual readings. To claim more than that, on the basis of such a small sample, would be misleading. Similarly, I would claim only to have shown the viability of an approach which treats the audience as a set of cultural

groupings rather than as a mass of individuals or as a set of rigid socio-demographic categories. Clearly, more work needs to be done on the relation between group and individual readings. (163)

The early work of Hall and Morley is absolutely fundamental to the development of British cultural studies, and to the ongoing project of cultural studies more generally. Hall and Morley laid the foundations, by both example and provocation, of a way to understand cultural consumption as a structured and situated practice.

Cultural Consumption of Television

In this section I critically assess five different accounts of the cultural consumption of television. The first is Ien Ang's now classic study, *Watching Dallas* (first published in the Netherlands in 1982).

Ang's starting point is an attempt to understand the success of *Dallas* in the Netherlands, where it was regularly watched by 52 per cent of the population. It is in this context that Ang placed the following advertisement in *Viva*, a Dutch women's magazine: 'I like watching the TV serial *Dallas*, but often get odd reactions to it. Would anyone like to write and tell me why you like watching it too, or dislike it? I should like to assimilate these reactions in my university thesis. Please write to . . . ' (1985: 10). Following the advertisement she received 42 letters (39 from women or girls), from both lovers and haters of *Dallas*. Ang uses these letters as an empirical basis to construct an argument about the pleasures of *Dallas*. She is not concerned with pleasure understood as the satisfaction of an already pre-existent need, but 'the mechanisms by which pleasure is aroused' (9). Instead of the question: 'What are the effects of pleasure?' she poses the question: 'What is the mechanism of pleasure; how is it produced and how does it work?' (ibid.).

For Ang's letter-writers the pleasures or displeasures of *Dallas* are inextricably linked with questions of 'realism'. The extent to which a letter-writer finds the programme 'good' or 'bad' is determined by whether they find it 'realistic' (good) or 'unrealistic' (bad). Critical of both 'empiricist realism' (a text is considered realistic to the extent to which it adequately reflects that which exists outside itself) and 'classic realism' (the claim that realism is an illusion created by the extent to which a text can successfully conceal its constructedness), she contends that *Dallas* is best understood as an example of what she calls 'emotional realism' (34–41). *Dallas*, she argues (in an argument that draws on the early work of Roland Barthes; see Chapter 2 above), can be read on two levels: the level of denotation and the level of connotation. The level of denotation refers to the literal content of the programme, general storyline, character interactions, etc. The level of connotation refers to the associations, implications, which resonate from the storyline and character interactions, etc. As she observes,

> It is striking; the same things, people, relations and situations which are regarded at the denotative level as unrealistic, and unreal, are at the connotative level apparently not seen at all as unreal, but in fact as 'recognisable'. Clearly, in the connotative reading process the denotative level of the text is put in brackets. (42)

Viewing *Dallas*, like watching any other television programme, is a selective process, reading across the text from denotation to connotation; weaving our sense of self in and out of the narrative. As one letter-writer tells Ang: 'Do you know why I like watching it? I think it's because those problems and intrigues, the big and little pleasures and troubles occur in our own lives too. . . . In real life I know a horror like JR, but he's just an ordinary builder' (43). It is this ability to connect our own lives with the lives of a family of Texan millionaires which gives the programme its emotional realism. We may not be rich, but we have other fundamental things in common: relationships and broken relationships, happiness and sadness, illness and health. Those who find it realistic shift the focus of attention from the particularity of the narrative to the generality of its themes. Ang uses the term a 'tragic structure of feeling' (46) to describe the ways in which *Dallas* plays with the emotions in an endless musical chairs of happiness and misery. As one letter-writer told her: 'Sometimes I really enjoy having a good cry with them. And why not? In this way my other bottled up emotions find an outlet' (49). Viewers who 'escape' in this way, Ang argues, are not so much engaging in 'a denial of reality as playing with it . . . [in a] game that enables one to place the limits of the fictional and the real under discussion, to make them fluid. And in that game an imaginary participation in the fictional world is experienced as pleasurable' (ibid.).

However else it might be explained, or whatever else is involved, part of the pleasure(s) of *Dallas*, as revealed to Ang by her correspondents, is quite clearly connected to the amount of fluidity viewers are able or are willing to establish between its fictional world and the world of their own everyday lives. In order to activate *Dallas*'s tragic structure of feeling viewers must have the necessary cultural capital to occupy a 'reading formation' (see discussion of this in Chapter 4 above) informed by what she calls the 'melodramatic imagination'. The melodramatic imagination is the articulation of a way of seeing that finds in ordinary day-to-day existence, with its triumphs and its pains, its victories and defeats, a world as profoundly meaningful and significant as the world of classical tragedy. In a world increasingly freed since the nineteenth century from the certainties of religion, the melodramatic imagination offers a means of organising reality into meaningful contrasts and conflicts, and into the 'good' and the 'bad'. As a narrative form committed to melodrama's emphatic contrasts, conflicts and emotional excesses, *Dallas* is ideally placed to give sustenance to, and to make manifest, the melodramatic imagination. For those who see the world in this way (Ang claims that it demands a cultural competence most often shared by women), 'the pleasure of *Dallas* . . . is not a *compensation* for the presumed drabness of daily life, nor a flight from it, but a *dimension* of it' (83). The melodramatic imagination activates *Dallas*'s tragic structure of feeling, which in turn produces the pleasure of emotional realism. However, because the melodramatic imagination is an effect of a specific reading formation, it follows that not all viewers of *Dallas* will activate the text in quite this way.

On the basis of the views expressed in the letters, Ang separates her 42 correspondents into four viewing positions, the first three of which are connected to what she calls 'the ideology of mass culture' (15). The ideology of mass culture *articulates* (using the term in the Gramscian sense discussed in Chapter 8 below) the view that mass culture, as a product of capitalist commodity production, amounts to little more than the seemingly endless production and circulation of degraded commodities, whose only real significance is that they make a profit for their producers, and in doing so manipulate and dupe the gullible. This is a position she completely rejects. Against the claims of this ideology, she insists that it is not possible to read off the value of a product or how a product might be consumed from the means by which it was produced. The ideology of mass culture, like all other ideological discourses, works by interpellating individuals into specific subject positions (see discussion of Althusser in Chapter 8 below). The views expressed in the letters point to four reading positions from which one might consume and understand *Dallas*: (1) those who hate the programme, (2) ironical viewers, (3) fans, and (4) populists.

The letter-writers who claim to hate *Dallas* draw most clearly on the ideology of mass culture. They use the ideology in two ways: first, to locate the programme negatively as an example of mass culture; second, as a means to account for and support their own dislike of the programme. As Ang puts it, 'their reasoning boils down to this: "*Dallas* is obviously bad because it's mass culture, and that's why I dislike it"' (95–6). In this way, the ideology provides both comfort and reassurance. Moreover, 'it makes a search for more detailed and personal explanations superfluous, because it provides a finished explanatory model that convinces, sounds logical and radiates legitimacy' (96). This is not to say (and Ang does not say) that it is wrong to dislike *Dallas*, only (and this is Ang's position) that professions of dislike are often made without thinking; in fact, often made with a confidence born of uncritical thought.

From within the second viewing position she identifies, it is in fact possible to like *Dallas* and still subscribe to the ideology of mass culture. The contradiction is resolved by the deployment of 'mockery and irony' (97). In this way, *Dallas* is subjected to an ironising and mocking commentary in which it 'is transformed from a seriously intended melodrama to the reverse: a comedy to be laughed at. Ironising viewers therefore do not take the text as it presents itself, but invert its preferred meaning through ironic commentary' (98). From this perspective, the pleasure of *Dallas* derives in the main from the fact that it is *bad*. In this strategy, pleasure and bad mass culture are reconciled in an instant. As one of the letter-writers explains it: 'Of course *Dallas* is mass culture and therefore bad, but precisely because I am so well aware of that I can really enjoy watching it and poke fun at it' (100). For both the ironising viewer and the hater of *Dallas*, the ideology of mass culture operates as a bedrock position of common sense, making judgments obvious and self-evident. Although both operate within the normative standards of the ideology, the difference between the two positions is marked by the question of pleasure. On the one hand, the ironisers can have pleasure without guilt, in the sure and certain knowledge that they know mass culture is bad, and by knowing this, they are protected from its harmful effects. On the other hand, the haters of *Dallas*, although they also seek security in the same knowledge, can, nevertheless, suffer 'a conflict of feelings if, *in spite of this*, they cannot escape its seduction' (101).

The third viewing position is occupied by the letter-writers who declare themselves to be fans of *Dallas*. For the viewers in occupation of the previous two viewing positions, to actually love, or even like, *Dallas* without resort to the distancing strategy of irony is to be identified as someone who is completely and hopelessly duped by the manipulations of mass culture. As one letter-writer explains to Ang: 'The aim is simply to rake in money, lots of money. And people try to do that by means of all these things – sex, beautiful people, wealth. And you always have people who fall for it' (103). The claim of the letter-writer is presented with all the confidence of having the full weight of the ideology of mass culture's discursive support. Ang's next step is to analyse the different strategies the fans of *Dallas* must use to deal consciously and unconsciously with such condescension. The first strategy, she claims, is to 'internalise' the ideology; that is, to acknowledge the supposed dangers of *Dallas*, and then, in order to still derive pleasure from the programme, to consciously declare one's ability to deal with the dangers. It is a risky strategy, a little like the heroin user in the early 1990s' British drugs-awareness campaign, who, against all the warnings of impending addiction, declares: 'I can handle it.' A second strategy employed by fans is to confront and to challenge the credibility of the ideology of mass culture. As one letter-writer maintains: 'Many people find it worthless or without substance. But I think it does have substance' (105). But, as Ang points out, the writer remains firmly within the discursive constraints of the ideo-logy, even as she attempts to relocate *Dallas* in a different relation-ship to the binary oppositions – with substance/without substance, good/bad. According to Ang, 'This letter-writer "negotiates", as it were, within the discursive space created by the ideology of mass culture, she does not situate herself outside it and does not speak from an opposing ideological position' (106). A third strategy of defence deployed by fans against the normative standards of the ideology of mass culture is to use irony. These fans are different from the occupants of the second viewing position identified by Ang, the ironist, in that the strategy employed involves the use of 'surface irony' to justify what is in all other respects a form of non-ironic pleasure. Irony is used by this group of viewers to condemn the characters as 'horrible' people, whilst at the same time demon-strating an intimate knowledge of the programme and a tremend-ous involvement in its narrative development and character interactions. One letter-writer who uses this strategy is clearly caught between the dismissive power of the ideology of mass culture and the pleasure she herself obviously derives from watch-ing *Dallas*. Her letter seems to suggest that she adheres to the dictates of the ideology when viewing with friends, and to a strat-egy of surface irony when viewing alone (and perhaps secretly when viewing with friends). As Ang explains: 'irony is here a defence mechanism with which this letter-writer tries to fulfil the social norms set by the ideology of mass culture, while secretly she "really" likes *Dallas*' (109).

As Ang is able to show, the fans of *Dallas* find it necessary to locate their pleasure in relation to the ideology of mass culture; they 'internalise' it; they 'negotiate' with it; they use 'surface irony' to defend their pleasure in the programme against its withering dismissal. What all these strategies of defence reveal to Ang is that 'there is no clear cut ideological alternative which can be employed against the ideology of mass culture – at least no alternative that offsets the latter in power of conviction and coherence' (109–10). The struggle between those who like *Dallas* and those who dislike it is an unequal struggle between those arguing from within the discursive strength and ontological security of the ideology of mass culture and those resisting from within (for them) its inhospitable confines. 'In short, these fans do not seem to be able to take up an effective ideological position – an identity – from which they can say in a positive way and independently of the ideology of mass culture: "I like *Dallas* because . . .".' (ibid.).

The final viewing position revealed in the letters, one that might help the fans struggling in the third viewing position, is a point of view informed by the ideology of populism. At the core of the ideology of populism is the belief that one person's taste is of equal value to another person's taste. As one letter-writer explains to Ang: 'I find the people who react oddly rather ludicrous – they can't do anything about someone's taste. And anyway they might find things pleasant that you just can't stand seeing or listening to' (113). The ideology of populism insists that as taste is an autonomous category, continually open to individual inflection, it is absolutely pointless to pass aesthetic judgments on the cultural preferences of other people. Given that this would seem to be an ideal discourse from which to defend one's pleasure in *Dallas*, why is it that so few of the letter-writers take up this position? Ang's answer is to point to the ideology's extremely limited vocabulary. After one has repeated 'there's no accounting for taste' a few times, the argument begins to appear somewhat bankrupt. Compared to the ideology of populism, the ideology of mass culture has an extensive and elaborate range of arguments and theories at its disposal. It is little wonder, then, that when invited to explain why they like or dislike *Dallas*, the letter-writers find it difficult to escape the normative discourse of the ideology of mass culture. However, according to Ang, there are ways to escape its dampening and debilitating presence. She claims that the 'theoretical' nature of the discourse may well restrict its influence to a cognitive level: that is, 'to people's opinions and rational consciousness, to the discourse people use when *talking* about culture. These opinions and rationalisations need not, however, necessarily prescribe people's cultural *practices*' (115). If true, this might in part explain the troubling contradictions experienced by some letter-writers, when confronted by both 'the intellectual dominance of the ideology of mass culture and the "spontaneous", practical attraction of the populist ideology' (ibid.).

Ang accepts that there are many difficulties associated with adopting the ideology of populism for a radical perspective on cultural consumption. One problem is that it has already been appropriated by the culture industries in carefully planned strategies to maximise profits. However, drawing on the work of Bourdieu (see Chapter 3 above), Ang argues that populism can be mobilised to promote a 'popular aesthetic' in which the moral categories of middle-class taste are challenged and are replaced by an emphasis on contingency, on pluralism, but above all, on pleasure. Pleasure is for Ang the key term in a transformed feminist cultural politics. Feminism, she argues, must break with 'the paternalism of the ideology of mass culture . . . [in which w]omen are . . . seen as the passive victims of the deceptive messages of soap operas . . . [their] pleasure . . . totally disregarded' (118–19). Even when pleasure is considered, too often it is there only to be condemned as an obstruction to the feminist goal of women's liberation. The question Ang poses is: Can pleasure through identification with the women of 'women's weepies' or the emotionally masochistic women of soap operas 'have a meaning for women which is relatively indepen- dent of their political attitudes?' (133). Her answer is yes: fantasy and fiction do not

> function in place of, but beside, other dimensions of life (social practice, moral or political consciousness). It . . . is a source of pleasure because it puts 'reality' in parenthesis, because it constructs imaginary solutions for real contradictions which in their fictional simplicity and their simple fictionality step outside the tedious complexity of the existing social relations of dominance and subordination. (135)

This does not of course mean that cultural representations do not matter. They can still be condemned for being reactionary in an ongoing cultural politics. But to experience pleasure from them is a completely different issue: 'it need not imply that we are also bound to take up these positions and solutions in our relations to our loved ones and friends, our work, our political ideals, and so on' (ibid.).[2]

> Fiction and fantasy, then, function by making life in the present pleasurable, or at least livable, but this does not by any means exclude radical political activity or consciousness. It does not follow that feminists must not persevere in trying to produce new fantasies and fight for a place for them. . . . It does, however, mean that, where cultural consumption is concerned, no fixed standard exists for gauging the 'progress- iveness' of a fantasy. The personal may be political, but the personal and the political do not always go hand in hand. (135–6)

In a rather hostile review of *Watching Dallas*, Dana Polan accuses Ang of attacking 'an antiquarian and anachronistic approach to mass culture'. He also claims that she is out of touch with the new postmodern sensibility, still clinging, supposedly, 'to mythic notions of culture as tragedy, culture as meaning' (1988: 198). The idea that the ideology of mass culture is antiquated and anachronistic might be true in the fantasy realms of American academic psychoanalytic cultural criticism, but it is still very much alive in the conscious/unconscious lived cultures of everyday life.

Dallas is also the subject of a research project carried out by Tamar Liebes and Elihu Katz. Their starting point is very different from Ang's; their research begins with the concept of cultural imperialism, and with a question this perspective prompts; that is, whether or not television programmes, made in the United States, but successful worldwide, like *Dallas*, are more than just cultural commodities for sale in the global marketplace, 'but also agents [for the] subversion of indigenous values' (1993: viii). In other words, the question they set out to answer is, are *Dallas* and programmes like it the very substance of cultural imperialism? It is perhaps worth noting at the outset that Liebes and Katz are not convinced by the cultural-imperialism thesis. As they contend,

> To prove that *Dallas* is an imperialistic imposition, one would have to show (1) that there is a message incorporated in the program that is designed to profit American interests overseas, (2) that the message is decoded by the receiver in the way it was encoded by the sender, and (3) that it is accepted uncritically by the viewers and allowed to seep into their culture. . . . .
>
> Whatever the message in the text – if there is one – *our* interest is in what message reaches the viewers. We argue that ideology is not produced through a process of stimulus and response but rather through a process of negotiation between various types of senders and receivers. To understand the messages perceived by viewers of a television program, one cannot be satisfied with abstract generalisations derived from content analysis, however sophisticated. The actual interaction between the program and its viewers must be studied. In the case of *Dallas*, the challenge is to observe how the melodrama of a fictional family in Texas is viewed, interpreted, and discussed by real families throughout the world, in the light of the drama of their own lives and those of the fictional and real others whom they have come to know through symbolic culture and actual community. (4)

To fathom the cultural and political influence of *Dallas*, they decided to observe and to study the reception of *Dallas* in a number of Israeli homes. Rather than focus on Israelis in general, and in order to see the extent to which 'different ethnicities might "use" . . . *Dallas* to

explore and redefine their own identities and to compare themselves
not just with Americans but with other Israelis' (viii), they chose four
subcultural groups: veteran kibbutz members of Western origin, new
immigrants from Russia, Israeli Arabs and Moroccan Jews. For
further comparison, they also included in their study American
viewers in Los Angeles, part of the programme's original audience,
and Japanese viewers in Tokyo, one of the few places where *Dallas*
failed. From their Israeli sample they constructed 44 small groups of
family and friends. Added to this were 10 American groups and 11
Japanese.

When asked to retell an episode from *Dallas*,

> some groups chose to represent the story more sociologically,
> as if it were the story of a linear progress through a social
> obstacle course. Other groups retold the story more psycho-
> logically, emphasizing the motivations and personalities of the
> characters, while yet others retold the story in terms of themes
> and leitmotifs. (152)

When questioned about particular details in the narrative of an
episode, some groups (for example, Moroccan Jews and Israeli
Arabs) employed a referential frame (reading the programme in
relation to their own lives) to explain what had happened in terms
of 'real life'. Other groups, the American and kibbutz groups, for
example, used a critical frame (reading the text as text) and
explained what had happened in terms of genre.

One significant difference between the different groups concerned
the framing discourse chosen to interpret the programme. For the
Americans, kibbutzniks and Japanese, the framing discourse was
aesthetic; for the Moroccan Jews it was moral; and for the Russians
immigrants it was ideological. For example, one Russian respondent described *Dallas* as 'propaganda for the American way of life'
(76). On the other hand, an Israeli Arab condemned in more
general terms the life the programme supposedly depicts: 'When
materialism dominates, society falls apart, and the material begins
to be everything' (88). One Japanese viewer had difficulty taking
the programme seriously because of the way in which it violated
his sense of social realism: 'it is hard for me to believe that such a
marriage between Bobby and the girl, which is typical to the middle
class, happens in high society' (134).

The conclusion Liebes and Katz draw from their study is that a
programmes like *Dallas* 'may beam a homogeneous message to the
global village, but our study argues that there is pluralism in the
decoding' (152). In other words, although the different sub-groups
offered distinct ways in which to understand *Dallas*, they can all
be seen to clearly relate to the 'content' of the programme – the

programme is the same for all the sub-groups; what is different, and inflects how *Dallas* is understood, is the cultural mode of understanding that each different sub-group brings to their involvement with the programme.

John Tulloch and Albert Moran's research begins with the same question Ang had sought to answer; that is, how to account for the popularity of a particular television programme. In search of answers to the question of why *A Country Practice* was the most popular serial on Australian television in the mid-1980s, they, like Liebes and Katz, begin with the working assumption that there 'is not one product, *A Country Practice*, but a variety of *ACP* texts, each being "read" and "performed" in terms of the cultural experience of its audience' (1986: 10). The 'audience' for the serial, they contend, includes not only viewers in front of a television set, but children talking about it in school playgrounds, the television executives who first approved it, the actors who perform it, and the producers, writers, directors and other production workers who make it. Each of these different audiences read and perform the serial in specific ways. Moreover, as they explain, 'these different audiences are each involved in a struggle over questions of meaning and over media power – what is said, and who controls it' (11). Although they readily acknowledge that this is a struggle in which the different audiences are differently and unequally located in a hierarchy of power, they are very uneasy about arguments which place meaning and media power firmly with ownership and control. As they explain,

> we believe that meaning is contested and re-made by different production personnel and by different audiences. . . . On the one hand is the negotiation of meaning in production and performance among the different sources of information – writing, acting, directing, set design, lighting and so on. On the other is the general audience's active involvement in constructing meanings. (ibid.)

They argue for a mode of analysis which understands the text as 'a dramatic text', one that is 'performed' by its different audiences in 'a whole series of "theatrical" spaces where meaning is contested' (11, 12). Although there is clearly a hierarchy of power between each of these different performance spaces (from the producer's edit to schoolyard discussions), and each space will itself operate with a specific power hierarchy, they insist 'power is an active, negotiative process involving fluid relationships' (14). Nevertheless, the hierarchy of power (between those who make the serial and those who consume it) is made clear in a discussion of letters written by fans concerned over newspaper speculation that two of their favourite characters may be getting divorced. As one letter explains, 'I feel I write on behalf of a lot of viewers . . . we have watched Vicky and Simon's romance for two years and waited patiently for this wedding' (234).

> Her point [the letter writer's] is simple – the fans have *earned* the right, through their patient loyalty, to expect that the marriage will last. Their investment – of time and emotions – makes the program in so many ways *their* show. They feel this entitles them to say what should or should not happen. These fans are insisting explicitly (by the threat of withdrawing their viewing) as well as implicitly (in the courtliness of their compliments) on their right to have a say. They recognise of course that *ACP* is controlled by others, that it is not their property. But, at the same time, the characters are friends who have come into their living room week after week for years; they are really involved with them. They are right; *ACP* cannot go on without its audience, so in the public domain it is their program. (ibid.)

Tulloch and Moran discussed one particular episode – 'Unemployment – A Health Hazard' – with school students from nine different schools. Boys aged between 13 and 14 years, from a middle-class school, claimed that one of the main reasons they liked the programme was because of its education value (what the programme taught them about the world). As Tulloch and Moran comment, 'It is not surprising that students with qualified, professionally successful parents should rate the educational function of *ACP* highly' (261). They also note how this tendency may well have been reinforced by the fact that the interview had taken place in school, and that it had been conducted, inevitably, in a formal manner as if by a school teacher. In this context, it is not surprising, they suggest, that the boys read 'Unemployment – A Heath Hazard' in terms of education. Tulloch and Moran also offer another reason for this way of reading the programme. They point out how the *Sunday Telegraph* (a newspaper likely to be in the homes of the boys' families), featured, in the week the episode was broadcast, an article by the programme's producer, pointing to the educational aspects of *A Country Practice*. Specifically, the producer maintained, she hoped the episode would educate its audience to think more sympathetically about people who are unemployed. Tulloch and Moran argue that newspaper articles of this type act as 'a pre-text to an episode, directing interpretations in advance' (263). As they point out, 'We are suggesting that the "educational" focus of "Health Hazard" was called up by both the school situation of the interview and the

publicity circulated by JNP [the production company] – among
boys who had this kind of reading well within their competence'
(264). However, as Tulloch and Moran observe, although the
production company was able to activate an educational pre-text,
it was unable to dictate the educational meaning ascribed to the
programme by the boys. Instead of feeling sympathy for the
unemployed, the boys saw unemployment as a direct consequence
of not doing well at school, because of a wilful refusal to take
education seriously. According to one of the boys, the message
of the episode was absolutely clear: 'don't leave [school] when
you're fifteen' (266).

Tulloch and Moran found a very different response to the
programme when they interviewed a group of 13- to 14-year-old
girls from a school with 'a heavily migrant and working-class
population, and a significant number of parents unemployed'
(ibid.). The girls' reading of the episode was informed by a very
different discursive pre-text, one that 'had less to do with school-
type learning than with the experience of living through teenage
and family situations' (267). According to Tulloch and Moran,

> These girls had seen the daily hardship of parents struggling
> to pay the rent . . . they saw its relevance to their mothers and
> themselves *now* . . . Unlike [the reading made by] the boys,
> there was a total and *felt* sympathy for the lot of the
> unemployed, which was seen as a perennial, daily condition,
> not something temporary and to be avoided by gaining quali-
> fications. (268)

As one girl explained, commenting on what she understood as the
episode's realism, 'it was good because that's how people that I
know feel' (ibid.). As Tulloch and Moran explain,

> The girls . . . at no point mentioned schooling and qualifica-
> tions as a key to avoiding unemployment. Rather than dismiss-
> ing the unemployed as 'dole bludgers' as the boys did, the
> theme of unemployment helped the girls establish a feeling of
> solidarity with the workless, particularly within their families.
> For them a continuing motif of interpretation was the release
> of frustration when the exploited and inactive unemployed
> could take no more. (271)

David Buckingham's 'ethnographic' work on television audiences
also focuses on children and soap opera, in this case the very
successful British soap *EastEnders*. The aim of his study is to show
that the relationship between audience and programme 'is characterised by a considerable degree of diversity and contradiction'
(1987: 6). As he explains,

EastEnders was clearly designed to create, and to retain, a large audience. In this sense, it was the product of a series of quite specific calculations. Yet these calculations were based on an extremely limited amount of data about the audience itself – and it is for this reason that its eventual success was far from guaranteed. In order to explain its popularity, we therefore need to look beyond the intentions of the programme-makers, and to investigate the complex and ambiguous relationship between the programme and its audience. (33)

Therefore, he argues, 'The relationship between *EastEnders* and its audience cannot be regarded either as a dangerous process of "mass deception" or as a matter of "catering to the lowest common denominator" (6).[3] In making these points, Buckingham does not agree with the claim that the meanings made by audiences are therefore 'infinite in scope' (36).[4] Rather, he argues for a position of understanding in which the structure of a programme is confronted by the agency of a viewer. As he explains,

While I would agree that it is ultimately impossible to reduce a soap opera to a single 'meaning' – in effect to 'translate' it into a series of substantive propositions – it remains possible to specify the ways in which it invites its viewers to produce meaning. If one cannot say what *EastEnders* 'means' to its audience, one can at least say a good deal about how it *works* . . . Nevertheless, the text cannot be seen to 'contain' an ideology which it simply imposes on its viewers – even a 'hidden' ideology which viewers are not consciously aware of, but which can be recovered from the text by means of analysis. On the contrary, making sense of the text is an active and often self-conscious process, in which viewers draw on a whole variety of different types of prior knowledge. (36, 86)

As Buckingham points out, in order to ensure its popularity, a soap opera has to remain 'open' to a number of possible meanings: 'in this sense, the text may be seen to construct, not an ideological position, but an ideological *terrain*, on which a limited range of meanings may be negotiated' (86).

Buckingham's study is based on discussions he had about the television programme with small 'friendship groups' of children aged between 7 and 18. The average size of a group was five; in all he interviewed 60 young people. Although they were fans of the programme, they were not uncritical of it. He discovered, however, that their 'critical distance was not incompatible with their overall enjoyment of the programme' (160). Moreover, this confirmed for him that 'Laughing *at* television and questioning its representations of the world is one of the everyday pleasures of viewing' (ibid.).

A number of the children interviewed talked of the social or peer pressure to watch the programme; that is, they had started watching the programme in order not to be excluded from the conversations of their peers. In this way, talking about the programme formed 'part of a broader process of social interaction, through which friendships and enmities were constructed and reconstructed' (162).[5] Buckingham observed the way in which talking about television, in particular the re-staging of its narratives, often provided children with a pleasurable means to think through and to try to understand some of the more troubling details of adult life, which usually remain hidden from them.

> For younger children, this often has a particular fascination, akin to voyeurism. Television may provide them with representations of aspects of adult behaviour which are usually hidden from them, although they may well be aware of their existence. Discussing television may thus provide a relatively 'safe' way of acknowledging things which they are normally forbidden to talk about. (164)[6]

In discussions of the programme, Buckingham observed the way in which the children would constantly shift between judging the programme from 'outside' its fictional world (i.e. in terms of how this world is represented) and from 'inside' (i.e. in terms of how individual characters behaved in the constructed fictional narrative). For example, Michelle's teenage pregnancy was discussed by the children both in terms of the disputed realism of the family support she received (representation) and in terms of what many of the children regarded as her selfish behaviour (constructed fiction). Ultimately, what held these two positions in dynamic play was an overriding concern with the question of 'plausibility'. Occasionally 'inside' and 'outside' would merge. One 12-year-old boy, commenting on Angie's inability to really fight back against Den, observed: 'I know what my mum would do. She'd get a frying pan and knock him over the head with it' (175). Similarly, a 14-year-old boy told Buckingham:

> I like Lofty. Because he stands for Den having a go at him and all this, but in real life he's a martial arts expert. He's a karate expert, judo, all this. All he has to do is give Den one kick in the throat and he's dead. (190)

Buckingham's study is a rejection of all simplistic models of media reception, working, as such models do, with a cause-and-effect view of the relationship between programme and audience, seeing meaning as singular and as something which is imposed on a manipulated and duped viewer. As he observes,

> the text does not 'contain' a meaning which can simply be extracted and defined. Yet if we cannot say what the text *means*, we can at least begin to describe how it *works* – that is, *how it enables viewers to produce meaning.* (203)

Buckingham concludes his discussion of the relationship between programme and audience with the suggestion that

> Perhaps the most appropriate metaphor for soap opera is to regard it as a form of collective game, in which viewers themselves are the major participants. The programme itself provides a basis for the game, but viewers are constantly extending and redefining it. Far from being simply manipulated, they know they are playing a game, and derive considerable pleasure from crossing the boundaries between fiction and reality. Yet although the rules of the game are flexible, they are ultimately determined by the programme-makers: while viewers may seek to play by their rules, they must inevitably acknowledge those which are set for them. (204)

Another study which takes as its focus children's cultural consumption of television is Bob Hodge and David Tripp's *Children and Television*. Their research is driven by two principles:

> One was that children's response to television is typically a complex cognitive act, not the enemy of reading and thought as so widely feared, but so closely akin that it makes good sense to talk of 'reading' television. Allied to this is a conception of children as not solely passive and helpless in this transaction, but active as well, creating and using meanings in their lives, for their own purposes. (1986: 3)

As they point out, the influence of television is often exaggerated and misunderstood. Rather than something with a self-evident meaning imposed on isolated individuals, television is consumed actively within a complex web of social and cultural relationships. Moreover, 'Among the determinants of ideological formation, television plays an ambiguous and often passive role because it carries no sanctions, only gratifications, to enforce its meanings' (10). Similarly, they argue that watching television should not be understood as 'time-out from thinking' (92). Watching television, they claim,

> provides grist for the mills of thought, innumerable opportunities for normal cognitive growth. Without television, of

course, children's minds would be exercised on other things, but that does not alter the fact that today's children use television to think with, that thinking being limited by, and adapted to, their general powers at each stage. (ibid.)

Hodge and Tripp showed 42 children (23 boys, 19 girls), arranged in groups of five to six (all aged between 8 and 9, except one group aged 11 to 12), the first five minutes of the American cartoon *Fangface*. The discussions which followed were recorded on video tape so as to enable Hodge and Tripp to judge both verbal and non-verbal responses to the interviewer's questions, and to perhaps highlight the subtle differences between telling and showing. As they point out, 'A transcript of the words alone . . . will give a very impoverished record of the dynamics of an exchange, and its social meanings' (147). Inevitably, to rely solely on a typescript is to lose sight of the evidence of the way in which words are combined with gestures, and to forget, say, the physical way in which remarks are often directed to specific individuals in a group. For example, Hodge and Tripp observed how the boys addressed their remarks equally in the direction of both boys and girls, whereas the girls tended to direct their attention more often at the boys alone. In addition, when the boys were speaking, the girls paid closer attention than they did when the girls were speaking. However, when the girls were speaking, the boys paid them the same amount of attention as they did to the boys. Given the deeply embedded nature of patriarchal society, what Hodge and Tripp observed is perhaps not that surprising. Perhaps a more interesting observation, which a verbal transcript would have certainly missed, occurred when they observed how one boy in the group, Adrian, described Kim, a character in the cartoon who 'plays as humble and deferential a role as a male chauvinist could wish', as a '"smart person" who "knows all the answers" ' (152). Watching this pronouncement later on video tape, and noting the smiles and sideways glances exchanged between Adrian and two other boys in the group, they concluded that the real target of Adrian's description was not Kim (the cartoon character), but Kristie – a girl in the group described by Hodge and Tripp as 'talkative, norm-breaking female' (ibid.). As they point out, 'It seems likely that the three boys are establishing a connection between Kim (the cartoon character) and Kristie. The comment "A smart person" then would be directed at Kristie rather than Kim' (ibid.). What this reveals, they argue, is 'one rather surprising way in which media content can have social effects' (153).

The primary effect of the television show, here, is not as a direct influence – a version of the world which is uncritically repeated by its passive victims. What it does is to provide the pretext for a struggle in which Kristie is briefly and lightly punished for breaking sexist ideological norms. We can see that this is not merely a direct reflection of the content of the show from the fact that Adrian can administer his put-down more effectively by a desexist *misreading* of the show than by a correct reading of its actual sexist content. This is not to say, however, that the sexist content was irrelevant. Adrian needs it to establish the covert meaning of his comment and its application to Kristie. (ibid.)

They conclude that television should be seen 'as a kind of "catalyst", acting to enhance or inhibit the operation of other forces to produce a range of different, sometimes contradictory, effects' (211). As they point out, 'It is not helpful to see any aspect of television content as an autonomous cause with consistent effects irrespective of the social conditions of the viewer' (211–12). Moreover,

> television has too diffused and contradictory a content to have a single effect one way or another on its own: it has a social role to play, but only in conjunction with other forces and structures, and can never be singly and aberrantly determining. (218)

Reading the Romance

Although Janice Radway concedes that the growth in the popularity of romance reading may be explained as much by the increasingly sophisticated selling techniques of publishers, making romance titles more visible, more available, as by any simple notion of women's increased need for romantic fantasy, her primary interest is the cultural consumption of romantic fiction by women. As she contends,

> if we wish to explain why romances are selling so well, we must first know what a romance *is* for the woman who buys and reads it. To know that, we must know what romance readers make of the words they find on the page; we must know, in short, how they construct the plot and interpret the characters' intentions. (1987: 11)

At the core of Radway's study is research she carried out in 'Smithton' involving a group of 42 romance readers (women, mostly married with children). The women are all regular customers at the book shop where 'Dorothy Evans' works. It was in fact Dot's reputation which attracted Radway to Smithton. Out of her own enthusiasm for the genre, Dot publishes a newsletter ('Dorothy's diary of romance reading') in which romances are graded in terms of their romantic worth. The newsletter, and Dot's general advice to customers, have in effect created what amounts to a small but significant symbolic community of romance readers. It is this symbolic community which is the focus of Radway's research. Research material was compiled through individual questionnaires, open-ended group discussions, face-to-face interviews, some informal discussions, and by observing the interactions between Dot and her regular customers at the book shop. Radway supplemented the work with readers by reading the titles brought to her attention by the Smithton women.

The influence of Dot's newsletter, its suggested selections and rejections, on the purchasing patterns of readers, alerted Radway to the inadequacy of a methodology that attempts to draw conclusions about the genre from a sample of current titles. She discovered that in order to understand the cultural significance of romance reading, it is necessary to pay attention to popular discrimination – 'the singularity of readers' (53) – in the process of selection and rejection, in which some titles are found satisfying and others are not. She also discovered (to her surprise) the actual *extent* of romance reading. The majority of the women she interviewed claimed to read every day, spending between 11 and 15 hours a week on romance reading. At least a quarter of the women she interviewed informed her that, unless prevented by domestic and other family demands, they prefer to read a romance from start to finish in one sitting. Consumption of titles varies from one to 15 books a week. Four informants claimed to actually read between 15 and 25 romances a week (a figure Radway found implausible).

Radway was informed by the Smithton women that the ideal romance is one in which an intelligent and independent woman, with a good sense of humour, is overwhelmed, after much suspicion and distrust, and some cruelty and violence, by the love of an intelligent, tender and good-humoured man, who in the course of their relationship is transformed from an emotional pre-literate to someone who can *care* for her and *nurture* her in ways that traditionally we would expect only from a woman to a man. As Radway observes: 'The romantic fantasy is . . . not a fantasy about discovering a uniquely interesting life partner, but a ritual wish to be cared for, loved, and validated in a particular way' (83). It is a fantasy that is primarily about reciprocation; the wish to believe that men can bestow on women the care and attention women are expected regularly to bestow on men. But the romantic fantasy offers more than this; it recalls to the reader a time when she was herself in fact the recipient of an intense 'maternal' care.

Drawing on the work of Nancy Chodorow (1978), Radway claims that romantic fantasy is a form of regression in which the reader is imaginatively and emotionally transported to a time 'when she was the center of a profoundly nurturant individual's attention' (1987: 84). Romance reading, she argues, is a fantasy in which the hero of the narrative eventually becomes the source of a form of care and attention not experienced by the reader since she was an Oedipal child. Radway argues that romance reading is, by this mechanism, a means by which women can vicariously – through the hero–heroine relationship – experience the emotional succour and support which they themselves are expected to provide to others, without adequate reciprocation of such succour and support for themselves in their everyday existence.

Radway also takes from Chodorow the notion of the female self as a self-in-relation to others, and the male self as a self autonomous and independent. Chodorow argues that this results from the different relations that girls and boys have with their mothers. Radway sees a correlation between the psychological events described by Chodorow and the narrative pattern of the ideal romance. This is particularly clear, she maintains, in the journey from identity in crisis to identity restored, in which 'the heroine successfully establishes by the end of the ideal narrative . . . the now familiar female self, the self-in-relation' (139). Another theoretical claim she takes from Chodorow is the belief that women emerge from the Oedipus complex with a 'triangular psychic structure intact' (ibid.). The result of this is that 'not only do they need to connect themselves with a member of the opposite sex, but they also continue to require an intense emotional bond with someone who is reciprocally nurturant and protective in a maternal way' (140). In order to experience the pleasures of this regression to maternal emotional fulfilment, a woman has three options: (1) lesbianism; (2) a relationship with a man; or (3) to seek fulfilment by other means. Radway points out that the homophobic nature of our culture limits the first option; the nature of masculinity severely limits the second; and that romance reading may be an example of the third. As she argues,

> the fantasy that generates the romance originates in the oedipal desire to love and be loved by an individual of the opposite sex *and* in the continuing pre-oedipal wish that is part of a woman's inner-object configuration, the wish to regain the love of the mother and all that it implies – erotic pleasure, symbiotic completion, and identity confirmation. (146)

The resolution to the ideal romance provides perfect triangular satisfaction: 'fatherly protection, motherly care, and passionate adult love' (149).

The failed romance is unable to provide these satisfactions because, on the one hand, it is too violent, and on the other, it concludes sadly, or with an unconvincing happy ending. This highlights in an unpleasurable way the two structuring anxieties of all romances. The first is the fear of male violence. In the ideal romance, this is contained by revealing it to be not the fearful thing it appears to be; either an illusion or benign form of courtship. The second anxiety is the 'fear of an awakened female sexuality and its impact on men' (169). In the failed romance, female sexuality is not confined to a permanent and loving relationship; nor is male violence convincingly brought under control. Together these two deviations from the ideal find form and expression in the violent punishment inflicted on women who are seen as sexually promiscuous. In short, the failed romance is unable to produce a reading experience in which emotional fulfilment is satisfied through the vicarious sharing of the heroine's journey from a crisis of identity to an identity restored in the arms of a nurturing male. What this suggests to Radway is that the answer to the question of whether or not a romance is good or bad is ultimately determined by the kind of relationship the reader is enabled to establish with the heroine. As she explains,

> If the events of the heroine's story provoke too intense feelings such as anger at men, fear of rape and violence, worry about female sexuality, or worry about the need to live with an unexciting man, that romance will be discarded as a failure or judged to be very poor. If, on the other hand, those events call forth feelings of excitement, satisfaction, contentment, self-confidence, pride, and power, it matters less what events are used or how they are marshalled. In the end, what counts most is the reader's sense that for a short time she has become other and been elsewhere. She must close that book reassured that men and marriage really do mean good things for women. She must also turn back to her daily round of duties, emotionally reconstituted and replenished, feeling confident of her worth and convinced of her ability and power to deal with the problems she knows she must confront. (184)

Radway claims that by engaging in this process of discrimination, the Smithton women are producing emotional benefits for themselves. In this way, they are able to 'partially reclaim the patriarchal form of the romance for their own use' (ibid.). The fact that 60 per cent of the Smithton women said that they find it occasionally necessary to read the ending of a novel first, to ensure that the experience of the novel will not deny the satisfactions to be gained from an encounter with romance fiction's underlying myth of the nurturing male, suggests quite strongly that it is the underlying myth that is, ultimately, of most importance in the women's experience of romance reading.

Following a series of comments from the Smithton women, Radway was forced to concede that if she really wished to fully understand the pleasures of romance reading she must relinquish her preoccupation with the text, and consider also the very *act* of romance reading itself; that is, cultural consumption as actual social event. In conversations with the women, it became clear that when they used the term 'escape' to describe the pleasure of romance reading, the term was being deployed to operate in a double but related sense. As we have seen, it can be used to describe the process of identification between the reader and the relationship between the heroine and the hero in the fictional narrative. However, the women made it clear to Radway that the term was also used quite 'literally to describe the act of denying the present, which they believe they accomplish each time they begin to read a book and are drawn into its story' (90). Dot revealed to Radway that men often found the very act of women reading (regardless of the reading matter) as something threatening in itself. The very act of reading was regarded by many of the Smithton women as the creation of a private space; as time and space reclaimed from the demands of domestic and other family duties. Many of the Smithton women describe romance reading as 'a special gift' that they are able to give themselves. To explain this, Radway again draws on Chodorow's view that the patriarchal family is an institution in which 'There is a fundamental asymmetry in daily reproduction . . . men are socially and psychologically reproduced by women, but women are reproduced (or not) largely by themselves' (91, 94). Romance reading, therefore, makes a small but not insignificant contribution to the emotional reproduction of the Smithton women. It offers 'a temporary but literal denial of the demands women recognise as an integral part of their roles as nurturing wives and mothers' (97). Moreover, as Radway maintains, 'Although this experience is vicarious, the pleasure it induces is nonetheless real' (100).

> I think it is logical to conclude that romance reading is valued by the Smithton women because the experience itself is *different* from ordinary existence. Not only is it a relaxing release from the tension produced by daily problems and responsibilities, but it creates a time or a space within which a woman can be entirely on her own, preoccupied with her personal needs, desires, and pleasure. It is also a means of transportation or escape to the exotic or, again, to that which is different. (61)

The conclusion Radway finally comes to is that it is at present very difficult to draw absolute conclusions about the cultural significance of romance reading. To focus on the act of reading or to focus on the narrative fantasy of the texts produces different, contradictory answers. The first suggests that 'romance reading is oppositional because it allows the women to refuse momentarily their self abnegating social role' (210), while the second suggests that 'the romance's narrative structure embodies a simple recapitulation and recommendation of patriarchy and its constituent social practices and ideologies' (ibid.). It is this difference, 'between the meaning of the act and the meaning of the text as read' (ibid.), that must be brought into tight focus, she contends, if we are to understand the full meaning of romance reading. One thing Radway is clear about is that women do not read romances out of a sense of contentment with the structural inequalities of patriarchal society. Romance reading quite clearly contains an element of utopian protest, a longing for a better world. But in contradiction to this, the narrative structure of the romance appears to suggest that male violence and male indifference are really expressions of love waiting to be decoded by the right woman. This in turn seems to suggest that patriarchy is only a problem until women learn how to read the signs properly. It is these complexities and these contradictions which Radway refuses to ignore or to pretend to have resolved. Her only certainty is that it is too soon to know if romance reading can be cited simply as an ideological agent of the patriarchal social order. As she explains,

> I feel compelled to point out . . . that neither this study nor any other to date provides enough evidence to corroborate this argument fully. We simply do not know what practical effects the repetitive reading of romances has on the way women behave after they have closed their books and returned to their normal, ordinary round of daily activities. (217)

Therefore we must continue to acknowledge the activity of readers – their selections, purchases, interpretations, appropriations, uses, etc. – as an essential part of the cultural processes and complex practices of cultural consumption. By paying attention in this way we increase the possibility of 'articulating the differences between the repressive imposition of ideology and oppositional practices that, though limited in their scope and effect, at least dispute or contest the control of ideological forms' (221–2). The ideological power of romances may be great, but where there is power there is always resistance. The resistance may be confined to selective acts of cultural consumption – dissatisfactions momentarily satisfied by the articulation of limited protest and utopian longing – but as feminists,

We should seek it out not only to understand its origins and its utopian longing but also to learn how best to encourage it and bring it to fruition. If we do not, we have already conceded the fight and, in the case of the romance at least, admitted the impossibility of creating a world where the vicarious pleasure supplied by its reading would be unnecessary. (222)

In a generally sympathetic review of the British edition of *Reading the Romance*, Ien Ang makes a number of criticisms of Radway's approach. She is unhappy with the way in which Radway makes a clear distinction between feminism and romance reading: 'Radway, the researcher, is a feminist and *not* a romance fan, the Smithton women, the researched, are romance readers and *not* feminists' (1998: 526). Ang sees this as producing a feminist politics of 'them' and 'us' in which non-feminist women play the role of an alien 'them' to be recruited to the cause. In her view, feminists should not set themselves up as guardians of the true path. This is what Radway does in her insistence, as Ang sees it, that ' "real" social change can only be brought about . . . if romance readers would stop reading romances and become feminist activists instead' (ibid.). Ang simply does not believe that one (romance reading) excludes the other (feminism). Radway's 'vanguardist . . . feminist politics' leads only to 'a form of political moralism, propelled by a desire to make "them" more like "us" '(527). What is missing from Radway's analysis, according to Ang, is a discussion of 'pleasure as pleasure'. Pleasure is discussed, but always in terms of its unreality – its vicariousness, its function as compensation, its falseness. Ang's complaint is that such an approach focuses too much on the effects, rather than the mechanisms of pleasure. Ultimately, for Radway, it always becomes a question of 'the *ideological function* of pleasure' (528). Against this, Ang argues for seeing pleasure as something which can 'empower' women and not as something which always works 'against their own "real" interests' (530). Radway has reviewed this aspect of her work and concluded,

Although I tried very hard not to dismiss the activities of the Smithton women and made an effort to understand the act of romance reading as a positive response to the conditions of everyday life, my account unwittingly repeated the sexist assumption that has warranted a large portion of the commentary on romance. It was still motivated, that is, by the assumption that someone ought to worry responsibly about the effect of fantasy on women readers. . . . [Repeating] the familiar pattern whereby the commentator distances herself as knowing analyst from those who, engrossed and entranced by fantasy, cannot know. . . . Despite the fact that I wanted to

claim the romance for feminism, this familiar opposition
between blind fantasy and perspicacious knowing continued to
operate within my account. Thus I would now link it [*Reading
the Romance*] . . . with the first early efforts to understand the
changing genre, a stage in the debate that was characterised
most fundamentally, I believe, by suspicions about fantasy,
daydream, and play. (1994: 19)

Radway cites with approval Alison Light's (1984) point that
feminist 'cultural politics must not become "a book-burning legis-
lature" ', nor should feminists fall into the traps of moralism or
dictatorship when discussing romances. 'It is conceivable . . . that
Barbara Cartland could turn you into a feminist. Reading is never
simply a linear con job but a . . .process which therefore remains
dynamic and open to change' (Radway 1994: 20).

Going to the Cinema: 'Escapism' as Social Practice

Jackie Stacey's analysis begins with the audience in the cinema,
rather than the audience as constructed by the text. Her approach
takes her from the traditions of film studies, especially psychoanalytic accounts of spectatorship,[7] to the theoretical concerns of
cultural studies. She offers the following diagram to mark the differences between the two traditions (Stacey 1994: 24):

Film studies	*Cultural studies*
spectatorship positioning	audience readings
textual analysis	ethnographic methods
meaning as production-led	meaning as consumption-led
passive viewer	active viewer
unconscious	conscious
pessimistic	optimistic

Stacey's study is based on an analysis of responses she received from
a group of white British women, mostly aged over 60, and mostly
working-class, who had been keen cinema-goers in the 1940s and
1950s. Escapism is one of the most frequently cited reasons given
by the women in Stacey's sample for going to the cinema. Seeking
to resist its pejorative connotations, Stacey deploys Richard Dyer's
(1981) argument that there is a utopian sensibility in many forms
of popular entertainment, to construct an account of the utopian
possibilities of Hollywood cinema for British women in the 1940
and 1950s. Dyer deploys a set of binary oppositions to reveal the
relationship between the social problems experienced by audiences

and the textual solutions played out in the texts of popular entertainment.

Social problems	*Textual solutions*
scarcity	abundance
exhaustion	energy
dreariness	intensity
manipulation	transparency
fragmentation	community

For Dyer, entertainment's utopian sensibility is a textual property.
It can be characterised, with specific reference to film, as the way
a film might work to give pleasurable resolutions to the social
problems an audience may bring with it into the cinema. Stacey
extends this argument beyond the textual to include the social
context in which entertainment is actually experienced. The letters
and questionnaires completed by the women made it clear to her
that the pleasures of cinema were always more than the visual and
aural pleasures of the cinema text – they included: (1) the actual
ritual of attending a screening, (2) the shared experience and
imagined community of being there in the audience, and (3) the
comfort and comparative luxury of the cinema building. It was
never a simple a matter of enjoying the glamour of Hollywood. As
Stacey explains,

> The physical space of the cinema provided a transitional space
> between everyday life outside the cinema and the fantasy
> world of the Hollywood film about to be shown. Its design
> and decor facilitated the processes of escapism enjoyed by
> these female spectators. As such, cinemas were dream palaces
> not only in so far as they housed the screening of Hollywood
> fantasies, but also because of their design and decor which
> provided a feminised and glamorised space suitable for the
> cultural consumption of Hollywood films .(99)

Escapism is always a historically specific two-way event. Stacey's
women were not only escaping *into* the luxury of the cinema and
the glamour of Hollywood film, they were also escaping *from* the
hardships, the dangers and the restrictions of wartime and post-war
Britain. It is this mix of Hollywood glamour, the relative luxury of
the cinema interiors, experienced in a context of war and its after-
math of shortages and sacrifice, which generates 'the multi-layered
meanings of escapism' (97).

A second category she uses to organise her account is 'cultural consumption'. Again, she rejects the rather monolithic position which
figures cultural consumption as always irredeemably entangled in an

always successful relationship of domination, exploitation and control. She insists instead that cultural 'consumption is a site of negotiated meanings, of resistance and of appropriation as well as of subjection and exploitation' (187). Much work in film studies, she claims, has tended to be production-led, fixing its critical gaze on 'the ways in which the film industry produces cinema spectators as consumers of both the film and the [associated] products of other industries' (188). Such analysis is never quite able to pose theoretically (let alone discuss in concrete detail) how audiences actually use, understand and make meanings from the commodities they consume. She argues that her respondents' accounts reveal a more contradictory relationship between audiences and what they consume. For example, she highlights the ways in which 'American feminine ideals are clearly remembered as transgressing restrictive British femininity and thus employed as strategies of resistance' (198). Many of the letters and completed questionnaires reveal the extent to which Hollywood stars were seen to represent an alternative femininity, one that was welcomed as exciting and transgressive. In this way, Hollywood stars, and the cultural commodities associated with them, could be used as a means to negotiate with and extend the boundaries of what was perceived as a very restrictive British femininity. She is careful not to argue that these women were totally free to construct through cultural consumption entirely new feminine identities. Similarly, she does not deny that such forms of cultural consumption may at times pander to the libidinous satisfactions of patriarchal gaze. The key to her position is the question of excess. As she explains, 'the consumption of Hollywood stars and other [associated] commodities for the transformation of self-image produces something in excess of the needs of dominant culture' (223). As she contends,

> Paradoxically, whilst commodity consumption for female spectators in mid to late 1950s Britain concerns producing oneself as a desirable object, it also offers an escape from what is perceived as the drudgery of domesticity and motherhood which increasingly comes to define femininity at this time. Thus, consumption may signify an assertion of self in opposition to the self-sacrifice associated with marriage and motherhood in 1950s Britain. (238)

Stacey's study represents something of a rebuke to the universalistic claims of much cine-psychoanalysis. By studying the audience, 'female spectatorship might be seen as a process of negotiating the dominant meanings of Hollywood cinema, rather than one of being passively positioned by it' (12). From the perspective of her research, women enjoying Hollywood films cease to be the cultural dupes and unproblematic occupants of subject positions they are often taken to be. Similarly, Hollywood's power to impose patriarchal ideology begins to look less plausible, its success far from guaranteed.

Notes

1   Richard Dyer (1977) notes an interesting problem with the way the model seems to always assume that encoding will be from a dominant or hegemonic position. What happens to the clarity of the model when the encoded 'message' is 'radical' or 'progressive'? See Morley (1992) for a response to this and other problems and criticisms.

2   As the German playwright Bertolt Brecht remarked, in a discussion of one of his own plays, *Mother Courage*, 'Even if Courage learns nothing else at least the audience can, in my view, learn something by observing her' (1978: 229).

3   As Buckingham points out,

> Popular Television is often accused by its critics of 'catering to the lowest common denominator', which implies that success is comparatively easy to achieve. In fact, as television producers know only too well, the whole process is highly unpredictable, not least because broadcasting institutions are very isolated from their audiences: broadcasters have few reliable and systematic ways of discovering 'what the public wants' and – perhaps more crucially – why it wants it. For this reason, they are often unwilling or unable to explain the success of their own programmes, relying instead on what amounts to 'professional intuition'. (1987: 4)

4   Buckingham cites Dorothy Hobson's study of the British soap opera *Crossroads* (discussed in the next chapter) as an example of this approach.

5   Television talk is discussed in the next chapter.

6   Bruno Bettelheim (1991) makes a similar point with regard to children's uses of fairy tales.

7   For a sympathetic review of this approach, see Sue Thornham (1997).

6

Cultural Consumption in Contexts of Everyday Life

In this chapter I consider a number of approaches to cultural consumption which, in contrast to the work discussed in the previous chapter, begin with the context of the audience in the routines of everyday life, rather than with a specific text or practice that an audience may appropriate and use. The chapter discusses work by Dorothy Hobson, David Morley, Hermann Bausinger, Mary Ellen Brown, Ann Gray, Shaun Moores, Marie Gillespie and Joke Hermes. The chapter concludes with a discussion of some theoretical work on the question of 'nomadic audiences'.

Television Talk and Everyday Life

In the introduction to *Crossroads: The Drama of a Soap Opera*, Dorothy Hobson observes

> it is only by long and relaxed talks and viewing with the audience that any understanding of how people watch television can be achieved. The effort is well worth while for it reveals the important contribution which viewers make to any television programme which they watch. (1982: 12)

Hobson's account of the consumption of the British soap opera *Crossroads* forms only a small part of her study of the production of the programme. Nevertheless, her observations have a formative place in the development of 'ethnographic' work in (British) cultural studies. Hobson conducted a series of unstructured interviews with viewers of the programme, mostly women, after watching episodes with them in their homes. As she explains, 'It is important to stress that the interviews were unstructured because I wanted the viewers to determine what was interesting or what they noticed, or liked, or disliked about the programme and specifically about the episodes which we had watched' (105).

Although her book does not seek to articulate a precise theoretical position, the research which informs it is nonetheless structured by clear underlying assumptions about the productive work of audiences. As she explains,

> Different people watch television programmes for different reasons, and make different 'readings' of those programmes, and much of what they say is determined by preconceived ideas and opinions which they bring to a programme. The message is not solely in the 'text' but can be changed or 'worked on' by the audience as they make their own interpretation of a programme. (105–6)

Watching *Crossroads* with its audience allowed Hobson to understand the extent to which 'Watching television is part of the everyday life of viewers. It is not, as is sometimes suggested, a separate activity undertaken in perfect quiet in comfortable surroundings' (110). Television is usually watched in the midst of other everyday activities. As Hobson discovered, domestic routines and responsibilities and the expectations of other family members ensured that many of the women with whom she watched *Crossroads* were not allowed the luxury of the detailed concentration expected and enjoyed by staff and students watching in darkened rooms on media-studies courses. As she quickly was made aware, domestic circumstances impact on both the level of concentration with which, and the perspective from which, a programme is viewed. As she explains, 'To watch a programme at meal time with the mother of young children is an entirely different experience from watching with a seventy-two-year-old widow whose day is largely structured around television programmes' (111).

Meaning is not, as Hobson discovered, something which happens only once, in the first moment of cultural consumption as one sits in front of the television screen. The making of meaning is an ongoing process which may reach well beyond the first moment of consumption. New contexts will bring about the enactment of new significances; a narrative seemingly discarded seems suddenly to have a new relevance and a new utility. Travelling on a train back from London, Hobson discovered how viewers can integrate and reintegrate the world of soap opera, for example, into their own lives: playing a 'fantastical' game in which the fictional and the real are allowed to merge. She recounts how she overheard, during the course of that train journey, a conversation between four pensioners in which they talked about their respective children and grandchildren, and then without comment, the conversation switched to a discussion about the current problems of a character in the British soap opera *Coronation Street* (125). She listened as the four women discussed recent happenings in the soap opera and interwove these with a discussion of recent narratives in their own family lives; family narratives then in turn provoked further discussion of soap-opera narratives; soap-opera narratives then provoked more discussion of family narratives. And so it went on.[1]

Hobson's research also reveals the extent to which viewers use their own experience to measure and judge the events happening in television programmes like *Crossroads*. On the basis of these findings, she dismisses as 'invalid' the common claim that the appeal of soap opera is escapism. Soap operas, she maintains, 'are precisely a way of understanding and coping with problems which are recognised as "shared" by other women, both in the programme and in "real life" ' (131). What is important, what the women she interviewed sought to relate to, is the raising of social problems, regardless of the adequacy or the supposed progressiveness of the programme's narrative solutions. As one woman told Hobson, in response to a question about *Crossroads*'s failure to pursue an issue to a radical conclusion, 'you can make your own conclusions' (132). Hobson insists that viewers 'work with the text and add their own experiences and opinions to the stories in the programme' (135). People

> do not sit there watching and taking it all in without any mental activity or creativity . . . they expect to contribute to the production which they are watching and bring their own knowledge to augment the text. Stories which seem too fantastic for an everyday serial are transformed through a sympathetic audience reading whereby they strip the storyline to the idea behind it and construct an understanding on the skeleton that is left. (135–6)

I think Hobson is absolutely correct to point to the creativity of the audience for *Crossroads*; where I disagree with her is about the extent of its creativity. She claims, 'To try to say what *Crossroads* means to its audience is impossible for there is no single *Crossroads*, there are as many different *Crossroads* as there are viewers' (136). Later, she adds,

> there can be as many interpretations of a programme as the individual viewers bring to it. There is no overall intrinsic message or meaning in the work, but it comes alive and communicates when the viewers add their own interpretation and understanding to the programme. (170)

Against these claims, I would want to insist on two points of objection. First, it is undoubtedly the case that programmes have material structures, which must set definite limits on the range and possibilities of interpretation. Second, viewers always view in contexts, both social and discursive (see discussion of Morley in previous chapter), and these must set definite limits on the range and possibilities of interpretation. For these reasons, I think Hobson is wrong to propose what is in effect an entirely subjective theory of interpretation. Moreover, I think it is the case that her own excellent study of women watching *Crossroads* contradicts this theoretical claim.

In another interesting piece of work based on interviews with a woman working as a sales manager in a telephone sales office, Hobson develops the ideas she had first formulated on the the train journey back from London. On the basis of this new research she argues that 'women use television programmes as part of their general discourse on their own lives, the lives of their families and friends and to add interest to their working lives' (1990: 62). Her research highlights how quickly a conversation about a television programme can become a conversation about the lives and interests of the women involved. For example, discussion of events in a soap opera can produce a discussion about events in the real lives of viewers. In this way, Hobson maintains, viewers are able to use events within television narratives to explore issues in their own lives; issues that might otherwise remain too painful to speak about openly in public. She argues that recognition of how women use television in this way should

> disprove the theory that watching television is a mindless, passive event in the lives of the viewers. On the contrary, the events and subjects covered in television programmes often acted as the catalyst for wide-ranging and open discussions. The communication was extended far beyond the moment of viewing. (1990: 66)

As she concludes, 'It is the interweaving of the narratives of fiction with the narratives of their reality that formed the basis for sharing their experiences and opinions and *creating their own culture* within their workplace' (71; my italics). Making a similar point, Mary Ellen Brown argues that such conversations illustrate what she calls 'a carnivalesque sense of play in the crossing of the boundary between fiction and reality' (1990: 195). Furthermore, Brown maintains that women's talk about soap operas is best understood as a fundamental part of the long tradition of women's oral culture – a 'feminine discourse' (183). As she explains,

> As consumers of soap operas and the products they advertise, women do participate in the process of consumption,

but the extent to which women can be said to be the passive objects or 'victims' of dominant discursive practices by watching and enjoying soap operas is limited by the women's use of these same cultural forms to affirm their own positions of subjectivity in a women's discursive tradition. This breaking of the rules is a source of pleasure, and the act of taking that pleasure entails defiance of dominant reading practices which attempt to shape the construction of meaning in our culture. Because the hierarchy of dominant values is either ignored or parodied in some of the reading practices around soaps, these practices may open up new possibilities for ways of thinking about culture from the subordinate's point of view. (198)

As both Hobson and Brown remind us, what we might call 'television talk' is not just talk about what is on, has been on or is coming on television, it is also talk provoked by television. Liebes and Katz provide the example of a Russian who had recently emigrated to Israel and said that 'viewing [the American soap opera] *Dallas* is like doing homework for other conversations' (1993: 92). As Liebes and Katz also observe,

Viewing escapist programs is not as escapist as it seems. In fact, viewers typically use television fiction as a forum for discussing their own lives. Concern over family, social issues, women's status, etc. are activated in response to these programs . . . and there is good reason to believe that an agenda is set for discussion as a result of the negotiation between the culture of the viewers and of the producers. (154)

One obvious example of this is the way in which discussion of the relationship difficulties of a particular fictional character can quickly provide the pretext and the context for revelations about real difficulties in real relationships. Talking about the problems of a character can be a rather less painless or less embarrassing way of talking about one's own problems or a relatively easy means to introduce these problems into a discussion. Moreover, as John Fiske observes, television talk provides cultural-studies researchers with an important bridge between the social and the textual, replete with 'clues about which meanings offered by the text are being mobilised' in people's everyday lived cultures (1989c: 66). Marie Gillespie suggests that 'One of the most tangible examples of the way that the discourses of TV and everyday life are intermeshed is when jingles, catch-phrases and humorous storylines of favourite ads are incorporated into everyday speech' (1995: 178). I recently witnessed an example of this practice. On the small estate where I live, a group of girls who normally play together had a rather acrimonious disagreement over what they should play. One group (the majority) wanted to play with dolls and prams, the other (the minority) wanted to play football. The two groups separated, and very soon the separation grew more acrimonious, with the minority group feeling increasingly victimised by the majority group. The minority group responded to the treatment they felt they were receiving from the other group by rewriting (and recording in one of the girl's bedrooms) their own version of the Chumbawamba song 'Tub-thumping', changing the lyrics to both reflect and comment on the majority group's activities. Part of the lyric is as follows:

> You push a fat doll, you push a thin doll
> You push an ugly doll, you push a hairy doll
> You push dolls that remind of the good times
> You push dolls that remind of the best times
> You're pushing your lives away
> Pushing your lives away [repeated]

Cultural Consumption in Domestic Contexts

David Morley makes the point that

> Once one takes seriously the fact that television is a domestic medium (and is characterised by programme forms specifically designed for that purpose), it becomes clear that the domestic context of television viewing is not some secondary factor, which can subsequently be sketched in. Rather, the domestic context of TV viewing, it becomes clear, is constitutive of its meaning. (1995: 321)

This is the focus of Morley's *Family Television*.

It had originally been Morley's intention to follow up his investigation of the *Nationwide* audience by conducting further interviews with the interviewees in the more 'natural' environment of their families and the home. Limitations of time and a lack of funding combined to ensure that this did not happen. In a way, then, it could be argued that *Family Television* represents to a certain extent the 'completion' of the *Nationwide* research project. Specifically, what Morley seeks to accomplish in this research is to bring into a critical and fruitful relationship questions which until then had generally been kept apart, seen as the separate provinces of different disciplinary approaches – how television is interpreted (literary/semiological approaches) and how television is used (sociological approaches). Combining 'the respective strengths of these two different perspectives' enabled him, he argues, 'to consider problems of audience decoding/choice in the context of family leisure' (1986: 13). Moreover, by locating the audience in a domestic context, he is able to demonstrate the ways in which the cultural consumption of television always involves so much more than isolated individuals making particular interpretations of specific programmes. As he explains,

> 'Watching television' cannot be assumed to be a one-dimensional activity which has equivalent meaning or significance at all times for all who perform it. I was concerned to identify and investigate the differences hidden behind the catch-all description 'watching television'; both the differences between the choices made by different kinds of viewers in relation to different viewing options, and the differences (of attention and comprehension) between different viewers' responses to the same viewing materials – differences which are masked by the finding that they all 'watched' a given programme. (ibid.)

Watching television is always so much more than a series of acts of interpretation; it is above all else a social practice. That is, it can be a means both to isolate oneself (Don't talk to me, I'm watching this), or to make contact with other family members (watching a programme you are indifferent about, or worse, in order to make contact with a particular member of the family or the family as a whole). It can also be a means to reward or punish children (You cannot watch Y until you've done X). In these ways, the cultural consumption of television is as much about social relationships as it is about interpretations of individual programmes. The German media theorist Hermann Bausinger provides an example of a woman's account of her husband's behaviour:

> 'Early in the evening we watch very little TV. Only when my husband is in a real rage. He comes home, hardly says anything and switches on the TV.' Although [as Bausinger observes] this is a direct expression of his psychic state, which is . . . habitualized and routinized, the specific semantic of the everyday comes in: pushing the button doesn't signify, 'I would like to watch this', but rather, 'I would like to hear and see nothing'. (1984: 344)

Furthermore, contrary to the myth, which this example might seem to support, that watching television kills conversation, Bausinger in fact argues that 'Media contents are materials for conversation' (350). As we have already noted, watching television actually generates a common currency (television talk) to be exchanged in the cultural economy of everyday life (this is also true where other media are concerned). Television talk is not just a currency which operates in the family, it is also important in most of the everyday interactions between people. As one respondent told Morley about television talk at work: 'We haven't got much else in common, so we talk a lot about TV' (1986: 79). In this way, rather than an alternative to a social life, the cultural consumption of television may play an integral part in its success. In certain instances, not being able to deal in the currency of television talk (i.e. not having seen particular programmes) may put a person at a distinct social disadvantage in the workplace or with a specific peer group. As Morley maintains,

> television can be seen to provide in one sense an alibi, in another sense a context, for encounters between family members, where the content of the television programme they are watching together may often simply serve as a common experiential ground for conversation. In this kind of instance, television is being used as a focus, as a method for engaging in social interaction with others. So, far from simply disrupting family interaction, television is being used purposefully by family members to construct the occasions of their interactions, and to construct the context within which they can interact. It is being used to provide the reference points, the ground, the material, the stuff of conversation. (22)[2]

In the course of his study Morley interviewed 18 white working-class/lower-middle-class families from an inner-city area in South London. One key finding, supported by the research of, for example, Ann Gray (see below), was the contrasting styles of viewing described by men and women. Men claimed to view attentively, while women said they view distractedly. These findings are not too surprising when one considers the nature of gender relations in most homes. Put simply, for men home is a site of leisure (an escape from work), whereas for women it is a site of work (regardless of whether or not they are also employed outside the home). Therefore an investigation of the cultural consumption of television in the home is an investigation of an activity 'which men are better placed to do wholeheartedly, and which women seem only to be able to do distractedly and guiltily, because of their continuing sense of their domestic responsibilities' (147). A second finding was that men tend to watch factual and sports programmes, whereas women watch fictional programmes. Based on interviews, and not on participant observation, Morley is only too aware that he is dealing with respondents' own accounts of how and what they watch. Nevertheless, as he points out with reference to the enactment of specific gender stereotypes by the male interviewees,

Even if it could be successfully argued that my results misrepresent the actual viewing behaviour of these men, it would remain a social fact of considerable interest that these were the particular accounts of their behaviour that these viewers felt constrained to give. (52)

In *Video Playtime: The Gendering of a Leisure Technology*, Ann Gray examines how women in a domestic setting use the video cassette recorder (VCR). Building both theoretically and empirically on Morley's research on family television, Gray's excellent study brings together four areas of research which until very recently have tended to be kept apart: home-based leisure, audience studies, textual analysis and domestic technology. The fact, as she sees it, that she is concerned with a item of domestic technology, rather than a text or group of texts,[3] and is therefore not tempted to produce her own reading or to infer the position of the reader on the basis of such a reading, means that she is free, she claims, 'to attend to how respondents themselves accounted for their own use, choices and preferences' (1992: 17).

Gray's study is based on the use of 'a loosely structured but open-ended conversational interview, which [she] recorded in the women's homes, lasting for a minimum of one and a half hours' (32). She is aware that her method, together with other similar methods already widely employed in cultural-studies research, cannot be accurately described as 'ethnography'. In awareness of this, she prefers to use the term 'audience-led research' to describe work like her own in cultural studies which is driven by 'ethnographic intentions' (ibid.). She is also aware of the need to think of cultural consumption as a situated practice: that is, we make culture and we are made by culture. Therefore, while recognising the 'agency' of the women she interviews, she nonetheless insists on the necessity to locate them in a 'structure'; that is, in social and historical conditions which are not of their making. Moreover, she is careful not to read their statements as given, as if they provided a direct reflection of the women's experiences, giving an immediate access to the reality of their experience of using the VCR. As she is fully aware, what she is given access to 'is their way of articulating that experience' (33). Gray is admirably clear on what this means:

The interview data upon which this project is based has therefore been subjected to a double interpretation: the first is the interpretation which the women bring to their own experience, and the one they share with me, whilst the second is the interpretation I make of what they say. Their interpretations depend on their subject position and the discourses to which they have access and through which their subjectivities are constructed. My interpretation depends on these things also, with the important addition of a theoretical and conceptual discourse, which constitutes the framework of my analysis. (33–4)

Gray insists, as we noted earlier, that in order to understand women's use of the VCR, their use of this technology must be situated in the domestic context of the home. As she observes, regardless of whether or not women engage in paid employment outside the home, the home is not for most women, as it is in fact for most men, an unproblematic site of leisure. As she explains,

> In order to explore women's use of the VCR, we must set our understanding within the context of her work, both outside and inside the home; her responsibilities and obligations to others; and the amount of spare time that she is able to organize for herself. (4)

Moreover, as she observes, the fact that this division of labour has become so embedded in the 'common sense' of the everyday practices of many homes makes it very difficult to critically problematise it sufficiently to generate a meaningful discussion. She developed, however, an ingenious strategy with which to overcome the problem. In an effort to make visible the gendered power relations of the home, she asked the women to colour code (pink or blue) the different items of domestic technology in terms of gender use. This simple procedure both quickly and starkly revealed, in most of the homes she visited, a clear gendered division of labour. As she observes,

> For the majority of women the home is first and foremost a work place and it is therefore often difficult for them to find the time and space within their domestic environment to pursue leisure or non-work activities. They therefore consider going out as a more direct route to leisure and relaxation. (54)

Gray was soon made aware by the women of how in practice the gender inequalities of the domestic setting can have a direct influence on the conditions of the women's use of the VCR. For example, she found that some of the women often used watching programmes recorded on the VCR as a personal reward for work done in the home. As one woman put it, 'I can be working, and I've got that to look forward to [watching *Falcon Crest*], that hour, to sit down and relax and that hour's mine' (63). Even when the women watched television in the evening, after a day of domestic and family duties, they reported they rarely did so without the accompaniment of something else: mending, knitting, ironing, reading. As one woman told Gray, this way of viewing is often driven by guilt:

> Now my husband . . . he just seems to be able to turn himself off, I wish I could, because I think that's the way to keep yourself sane. . . . You see, men can sit down and do their thing and they don't feel guilty. (108)

In the hope of reaching a fuller understanding of how the women she interviewed used the VCR, Gray began to reconceptualise the domestic setting, not as one monolithic 'determining' context, but as the site of many sub-contexts. For example, she discovered that use varied (especially women's control over use), depending on whether viewing occurred with the whole family together, or with the male partner, or the woman on her own. Predictably, it was only in the last sub-context of viewing that women had any real control over use of the VCR. Gray concludes from this 'that very often women are watching television programmes or movies which they do not enjoy and would not choose to watch themselves' (120).

Gray concludes her study by observing,

> The implications of this study are that new entertainment technology enters the existing household structures and familial ideology, and these structures and traditions, particularly in relation to gender, become encoded in the new technology both in terms of its physical use and choice of software. (252)

It is, however, worth noting that she does not see the gender encoding of the VCR as an articulation of an 'essential' masculinity or femininity. Rather, as is also the case with the different modes of viewing by men and women reported by the women interviewed (supporting Morley's account discussed earlier in this chapter), it is the articulation of domestic power relations. Referring specifically to modes of viewing, she argues,

> This would seem to suggest that there is a masculine mode of viewing which is concentrated and single-minded and a feminine mode of viewing which is distracted and lacking in concentration. Unless we situate these viewing modes within the domestic context and the social relations of power which appear to prevail, there is a tendency to fall into an essentialist explanation of male and female behaviour. (126)

Against such an 'essentialist' explanation, she argues that the different modes of viewing can be explained by the different positions traditionally occupied by men and women in the domestic sphere.

Moreover, these are social positions, and not essential or natural categories. It is possible, and it is in fact the case (as Gray discovered) that, given a particular set circumstances, women can adopt the 'masculine' mode of viewing, because, as Charlotte Brunsdon points out, this is a way of viewing which is 'not so much a masculine mode, but a mode of power' (quoted in Gray 1992: 126). Gray concludes, 'We cannot therefore speak of a "masculine" mode of viewing which is only practised by men. Rather, we must see particular modes of behaviour as being contingent upon the specific social dynamics which are in operation at the time' (Gray 1992: 126).

Cultural Consumption in Other Contexts

Like the work of Morley and Gray, Shaun Moores's study *Satellite Television and Everyday Life* is focused, not so much on the texts of cultural consumption as on the contexts in which it takes place. The specific focus of Moores's research is the ways in which 'a new media technology can get "embedded" in the activities and structures of households, neighbourhoods and broader cultural communities' (1996: 1). Using Stuart Hall's concept of 'articulation' (for discussion of this term, see Chapter 8 below), Moores sought to tease out how the placing of a satellite dish on the side of a house can both express and connect to a particular mode of cultural being.

Moores's findings are derived from 'ethnographic' research he carried out between 1990 and 1992, in which he interviewed members of 18 households in three quite different urban neighbourhoods in a city in South Wales. What they had in common was the recent acquisition of a domestic satellite dish. Perhaps the most surprising result of his research concerns the relationship he discovered between the channels a satellite dish gives access to and the user's sense of identity. One respondent told Moores that owning a satellite dish allowed him access to European television and that being able to watch television from other European countries had brought about a significant shift in his sense of national identity. 'I very much get the sense of being a European,' he said, adding, 'you do get the feeling of not being restricted in the good old British way' (41).

The relationship between media use and identity formation is also the subject of Marie Gillespie's *Television, Ethnicity and Cultural Change*, which presents a fascinating account of 'the role of television in the formation and transformation of identity among young Punjabi Londoners' (1995: 1). Gillespie's study is based on ethnographic fieldwork carried out between 1988 and 1991, including a survey of 333 Southall youths. Throughout the work she details and explores the relationship between media consumption and the lived everyday cultures of migrant and diasporic communities, demonstrating the ways in which the young (mainly in the 12 to 18 age group) Punjabi Londoners are 'shaped by but [are] at the same time reshaping the images and meanings circulated in the media and in the market' (2) – what she calls 're-creative consumption' (3). As she points out, she does not wish 'to celebrate consumer creativity any more than consumer culture itself' (13), but she is nonetheless insistent that cultural 'consumption, despite its overdetermination by the market and the unequal distribution of access to economic and cultural capital, is not a passive process but an expressive and productive activity' (ibid.). Therefore, she contends, it is never enough to study the images and narratives of television, or of other media; we must also examine how these are appropriated and used by viewers. Underpinning her analysis is the insistence that 'London Punjabi youth are engaged in constructing a viable culture through negotiations around the diverse resources available to them both in "real life" and on screen' (28).

Gillespie's critical focus on appropriation and use, rather than on the structural properties of texts, is a way of working that is also advocated by the Dutch media theorist Joke Hermes. She begins her study of women reading magazines with an observation about previous feminist work on women's magazines:

> I have always felt strongly that the feminist struggle in general should be aimed at claiming respect. It is probably for that reason that I have never felt comfortable with the majority of (feminist) work that has been done on women's magazines. Almost all of these studies show *concern* rather than *respect* for those who read women's magazines. (1995: 1)

This kind of approach generates a form of media criticism, she argues, in which the feminist scholar is both 'prophet and exorcist'. As she explains,

> Feminists using modernity discourse speak on behalf of others who are, implicitly, thought to be unable to see for themselves how bad such media texts as women's magazines are. They need to be enlightened; they need good feminist texts in order to be saved from their false consciousness and to live a life free of false depictions as mediated by women's magazines, of where a woman might find happiness. (ibid.)

Against this way of thinking and working, Hermes advocates what she calls 'a more postmodern view, in which respect rather than concern – or, for that matter, celebration, a term often seen as the hallmark of a postmodern perspective – would have a central place' (ibid.). She is aware 'that readers of all kinds (including we critics) enjoy texts in some contexts that we are critical of in other contexts' (2). The focus of her study, therefore, is to 'understand how women's magazines are read while accepting the preferences of [the women she interviewed]' (ibid.). Working from the perspective of 'a postmodern feminist position', she advocates an

> appreciation that readers are producers of meaning rather than the cultural dupes of the media institutions. Appreciation too of the local and specific meanings we give to media texts and the different identities any one person may bring to bear on living our multi-faceted lives in societies saturated with media images and texts of which women's magazines are a part. (5)

More specifically, she seeks to situate her work in a middle ground between a focus on how meanings are made of specific texts (Ang 1985, Radway 1987, for example), and a focus on the contexts of media consumption (Gray 1992, Morley 1986). In other words, rather than begin with a cultural text and show how people appropriate it and make it meaningful, or begin with the contexts of cultural consumption and show how these constrain the ways in which appropriation and the making of meaning can take place, she has 'tried to reconstruct the diffuse genre or set of genres that is called women's magazines and [to demonstrate] how they become meaningful exclusively through the perception of their readers' (6). She calls this approach 'the theorisation of meaning production in everyday contexts' (ibid.). In working in this way, she is able to avoid the deployment of textual analysis, with its implied notion of an identifiably correct meaning, or limited set of meanings, which a reader may or may not activate. 'My perspective,' she explains, 'is that texts acquire meaning only in the interaction between readers and texts and that analysis of the text on its own is never enough to reconstruct these meanings' (10). To enable this way of working she introduces the concept of 'repertoires', which she explains as follows: 'Repertoires are the cultural resources that speakers fall back on and refer to. Which repertoires are used depends on the cultural capital of an individual reader' (8). Moreover, 'Texts do not directly have meaning. The various repertoires readers use make texts meaningful' (40).

Hermes conducted 80 interviews with both women and men. She was initially disappointed at the fact that her interviewees seemed reluctant to talk about how they made meanings from the women's magazines they read; and when they did discuss this issue, they often suggested instead, against the common sense of much media and cultural theory, that their encounters with these magazines were hardly meaningful at all. After the initial disappointment, these discussions gradually prompted Hermes to recognise what she calls 'the fallacy of meaningfulness' (16). What this phrase is intended to convey is her rejection of a way of working in media and cultural analysis which is premised on the view that the encounter between reader and text should always be understood *solely* in terms of the production of meaning. This general preoccupation with meaning, she claims, has resulted from an influential body of work which concentrated on fans (and, I would add, youth subcultures), rather than on the cultural-consumption practices of ordinary people; and, moreover, it resulted from a conspicuous failure to situate cultural consumption in the routines of everyday life. Against the influence of this body of work, she argues for a critical perspective in which 'the media text has to be displaced in favour of readers' reports of their everyday lives' (148). As she explains, 'To understand and theorize everyday media use a more sophisticated view of meaning production is required than one that does not recognise different levels of psychological investment or emotional commitment and reflection' (16).

By a detailed and critical analysis of recurrent themes and repeated issues which arise in the interview material she collected, Hermes attempts to reconstruct the various repertoires employed by the interviewees in the cultural consumption of women's magazines. She identifies four repertoires: 'easily put down', 'relaxation', 'emotional learning and connected knowing' and 'practical knowledge' (31). The first of these repertoires, perhaps the most straightforward to understand, identifies women's magazines as a genre that makes limited demands on its readers. It is a genre that can be easily picked up and easily put down, and because of this, it can be easily accommodated into the routines of everyday life. The second repertoire, clearly related to the first, and perhaps as expected as the first repertoire, identifies reading women's magazines as a form of relaxation. But, as Hermes points out, 'relaxation' (like 'escapism' discussed in Chapter 5 above) should not be understood as an innocent or a self-evident term – it is, as she maintains, 'ideologically loaded' (36). On the one hand, the term can be employed simply as a valid description of a particular activity, and, on the other, it can be used as a blocking mechanism in defence against personal intrusion. Given the low cultural status of women's magazines, as Hermes reminds us, using the term 'relaxation' as a means to block further entry into a private realm is perhaps understandable. The third repertoire, the repertoire of practical knowledge, can range from tips on cooking to film and book reviews. But its apparently secure anchorage in practical application is deceptive. The repertoire of practical knowledge may offer much more than practical hints on how to become adept at making Indian cuisine or culturally knowing about which films are worth going to the cinema to see. Readers can use these practical tips, Hermes claims, to fantasise an 'ideal self . . . [who] is pragmatic and solution-oriented, and a person who can take decisions and is an emancipated consumer; but above all she is a person in control' (39). The final repertoire, the repertoire of emotional learning and connected knowing, is also about learning, but rather than being about the collection of practical tips, it is learning through the recognition of oneself, one's lifestyle and one's potential problems, in the problems of others as represented in the pages of magazine stories and articles. As one interviewee told Hermes, she likes to read 'short pieces about people who have had certain problems . . . [and] how such a problem can be solved' (41). Or as another interviewee told her, 'I like to read about how people deal with things' (42). With specific reference to problem pages, another interviewee observed, 'you learn a lot from other people's problems . . . and the advice they [the magazine] give' (43). As with the repertoire of practical knowledge, the repertoire of emotional and connected learning may also involve the production of an ideal self, a self who is prepared for all the potential emotional dangers and human crises that might need to be confronted in the social practices of everyday life. As Hermes explains,

> Both the repertoire of practical knowledge and the repertoire of connected knowing may help readers to gain (an imaginary and temporary) sense of identity and confidence, of being in control or feeling at peace with life, that lasts while they are reading and dissipates quickly [unlike the practical tips] when the magazine is put down. (48)

Hermes's originality is to have broken decisively with an approach to cultural analysis in which the researcher insists on the need to establish first the substantive meaning of a text or texts and then how an audience may or may not read the text to make this meaning. Against this way of working, as she observes,

> the repertoires that readers use give meaning to women's magazine genres in a way that to a quite remarkable extent is independent of the women's magazine text. Readers construct new texts in the form of fantasies and imagined 'new' selves. This leads to the conclusion that a genre study can be based entirely on how women's magazines are read and that it does not need to address the (narrative) structure or content of the text itself at all. (146)

Against more celebratory accounts of women and cultural consumption, Hermes's investigation of the role of repertoires makes her reluctant to see in the practices of women reading magazines an unproblematical form of empowerment. Instead, she argues, we should think of the cultural consumption of women's magazines as providing temporary 'moments of empowerment' (51).

Nomadic Audiences

Janice Radway is critical of work on audiences, like her own work on romance readers (discussed in the previous chapter), which begin with a particular text and then seek to demonstrate how this text is consumed. Research projects which are formulated along these lines will 'inevitably begin by assuming that individuals in the audience are already stitched into a particular kind of relation with the [text in question]' (1988: 361). As she explains,

> Audiences . . . are set in relation to a single set of isolated texts which qualify already as categorically distinct objects. No matter how extensive the effort to dissolve the boundaries of the textual object or the audience, most recent studies of reception, including my own, continue to begin with the 'factual' existence of a particular kind of text which is understood to be received by some set of individuals. . . . Users are cordoned off for study and therefore defined as particular kinds of subjects by virtue of their use not only of a single medium but of a single genre as well. No matter how intense our interest in the subsequent, more dispersed cultural use to which such forms are put in daily life by historical subjects infinitely more complex than our representations of them, our practical and analytical starting-point is still always within the producer-product-receiver circuit. (363)

Conducting research in this way, the audience, 'rarely if ever presented as active subjects, let alone as producers of culture' (362), are situated as receivers of whatever 'messages' the text, as the privileged object, has to offer. Radway proposes that we should 'rethink the process of cultural circulation from a new point of view . . . [that is,] from the point of view of the active, producing cultural worker who fashions narratives, stories, objects, and practices from myriad bits and pieces of prior cultural production' (ibid.). This would produce a mode of research 'which would focus on the complexities of everyday cultural use' (ibid.). Just as texts are marked by multiple discourses, so are individual members of an audience. Subjectivity (as we shall see in the next chapter) is not something fixed and unchanging; it is always on the move, constantly being addressed by, and always taking up, a range of different subject positions. This is subjectivity as nomadic and dispersed.[4] Radway, as a consequence of this recognition, advocates a different research strategy for thinking the relationship between texts and audiences:

> Instead of segmenting a social formation automatically by construing it precisely as a set of audiences for specific media and/or genre, I have been wondering whether it might not be more fruitful to start with the habits and practices of everyday life as they are actively, discontinuously, even contradictorily pieced together by historical subjects themselves as they move nomadically via disparate associations and relations through day-to-day existence. In effect, I have begun to wonder whether our theories do not impress upon us a new object of analysis, one more difficult to analyse because it can't be so easily pinned down – that is, the endlessly shifting, ever-evolving kaleidoscope of daily life and the way in which the media are integrated and implicated within it. (366)

This would produce a research practice which, rather than starting with the text, would begin with the lived cultures of people's everyday lives. Therefore, instead of the focus being on, say, the cultural consumption of one specific genre, it would pay attention to how this practice operates in relation to other practices which may in turn, for example, reinforce it or undermine it.

Radway's argument leads to a recognition that cultural consumption is a practice of everyday life. Cultural commodities are not appropriated or used in a social vacuum; such usage and appropriation always take place in the context of other forms of appropriation and use, themselves connected to the other routines, which together form the shifting fabric of everyday life. Roger Silverstone makes a similar point (with specific reference to television viewing, but applicable to other forms of cultural consumption), that we must acknowledge

> the complexity of the social and cultural relations in and through which audiences are embedded. In this sense an enquiry into the audience should be an enquiry, not into a set of preconstituted individuals or rigidly defined social groups, but into a set of daily practices and discourses within which the complex act of watching television is placed alongside others, and through which that complex act is itself constituted. (1994: 133)

Moreover, as Ien Ang argues, ethnographic research of the kind advocated by Radway and Silverstone has the potential to free research of monolithic notions of the 'audience'. It will allow researchers, she maintains, to see audiences not as an unproblematic given, 'but as a discursive construct, a moving resultant of the power-laden ways in which it is known' (1990: x).

Notes

1 Another example of how meaning continues beyond the initial moment of cultural consumption is the experience of Rose Cohen, a Russian Jew who emigrated to the United States in the 1880s. She writes in her autobiography of the moment she read her first book in English, a love story whose name she cannot recall: 'I felt so proud that I could read an English book that I carried it about with me in the street' (quoted in Denning 1987: 36).

2 Similar points can be made about 'going shopping'. Going shopping is always more than an economic activity. We may visit a shopping centre, for example, for a range of different, often contradictory, reasons. We may go to purchase a special gift or to buy the weekly groceries. We may go to look or to be looked at. Shopping centres, as Meaghan Morris points out, are used by different groups differently:

> there are different practices of use in one centre on any one day: some people may be there for the one and only time in their lives; there are occasional users choosing that centre rather than this on that day for particular, or quite arbitrary reasons; people may shop at one centre and go to another to socialise or hang around. The use of centres as meeting places (and sometimes for free warmth and shelter) by young people, pensioners, the unemployed and the homeless is a familiar part of their social function – often planned for, now, by centre management (distribution of benches, video games, security guards). (1988a: 200)

Morris's observations are confirmed by Mike Pressdee's (1986) research on the way unemployed youth in the South Australian town of Elizabeth use the local shopping centre. Shopping for the young people of Elizabeth means congregating at the local shopping centre not to buy what is on sale but to consume the public space of the mall. Pressdee invents the term 'proletarian shopping' to describe this practice. Young people are not alone in engaging in similar forms of shopping. They are frequently joined by tourists, escapees from bad weather, window shoppers and others who avail themselves of the facilities without necessarily contributing to the profit made by the shopping centre. Fiske (1989b: 18) cites a boutique owner in an Australian shopping centre who estimated that for every 30 people who visited her shop only one made a purchase.

3 It could be argued that Gray is working here with a rather limited notion of 'text'. John Frow and Meaghan Morris offer this very useful definition,

> There is a precise sense in which cultural studies uses the concept of text as its fundamental model . . . . Rather than designating a place where meanings are constructed in a single level of inscription (writing, speech, film, dress . . .), it works as an interleaving of 'levels'. If a shopping mall [for example] is conceived on the model of textuality, then this 'text' involves practices, institutional structures and the complex forms of agency they entail, legal, political, and financial conditions of existence, and particular flows of power and knowledge, as well as a particular multilayered

semantic organisation; it is an ontologically mixed entity, and one for which there can be no privileged or 'correct' reading. It is this, more than anything else, that forces cultural studies' attention to the diversity of audiences for or users of the structures of textuality it analyses – that is, to the open-ended social life of texts – and that forces it, thereby, to question the authority or finality of its own readings. (1996: 355–6)

Frow and Morris make clear that texts exist only within networks of inter-textual relations. To study a 'text' means to locate it across a range of competing moments of inscription, representation and struggle. In other words, cultural studies seeks to keep in equilibrium the different moments of cultural production – material production, symbolic production, textual production and the 'production in use' of cultural consumption.

4   See Lawrence Grossberg (1997) for a critique and an extension of Radway's argument.

|7|

Cultural Consumption, Postmodernism and Identities

When we meet someone for the first time, in order to get to know the kind of person they are, we ask certain questions. An obvious question is what kind of work they do. But sooner or later, in order to get to know them better, we will ask questions about matters of cultural consumption: What books do they like? What films do they like? Do they have favourite television programmes? To what kinds of music do they listen? Which football team do they support? These, and many more like them, are all questions which connect cultural consumption with questions of cultural identity. On knowing the answer to enough of these questions, we feel able to construct a cultural and social pattern and thus to begin to locate the person in a particular cultural and social space – we begin, in other words, to think we know who they are.

In this chapter I discuss ways of thinking about the relationship between cultural consumption and cultural identity. This will include a critical assessment of the legacy of Louis Althusser, a consideration of postmodernism and popular culture in order to introduce a discussion of postmodern identity, and accounts of both 'displaced meaning' and the historical role played by the department store in the process of learning to make identities in the practice of cultural consumption.

The Althusserian Inheritance

Identity first became an issue in (British) cultural studies in the 1970s, as a result of the enormous influence exerted on British intellectual life by the work of the French Marxist philosopher Louis Althusser. As Hall suggests, 'Althusser's interventions and their consequent development are enormously formative for the field of

cultural studies' (1978: 21). Here I will consider only the contribution his ideas made to work in cultural studies on identity and
subjectivity.

Althusser argues that it is through ideology that men and women
live their relations to the real conditions of existence. He maintains
that ideology is best understood as a practice. As he explains, 'By
practice in general I shall mean any process of transformation of a
determinate given raw material into a determinate product, a transformation effected by a determinate human labour, using determinate means (of "production")' (1969: 166). Ideological practice is
the transformation of an individual's lived relations to the social
formation. In this definition, ideology exists to dispel contradictions
in lived experience. It accomplishes this by offering false, but
seemingly true, resolutions to real problems. This is not a
'conscious' process; ideology 'is profoundly unconscious' (233) in
its mode of operation.

> In ideology men [and women] . . . express, not the relation
> between them and their conditions of existence, but the way
> they live the relation between them and their conditions of
> existence: this presupposes both a real relation and an 'imagin-
> ary', 'lived' relation. Ideology . . . is the expression of the
> relation between men and their 'world', that is, the (over-
> determined) unity of the real relation and the imaginary relation
> between them and their real conditions of existence. (233–4)

The relationship is both real and imaginary in the sense that ideology is the way we live our relationship to the real conditions of
existence at the level of representations (myths, concepts, ideas,
images, discourses): that is, there are real conditions and there are
the ways we represent these conditions to ourselves and to others.

As a lived material practice, ideology is always more than a body
of ideas – it consists of rituals, customs, patterns of behaviour, ways
of thinking which take practical form. Althusser claims that ideology
as a material practice is produced and reproduced through the
practices and productions of the Ideological State Apparatuses (ISAs):
for example, the education system, organised religion, the family,
organised politics, the media, the culture industries. As a material
practice, 'all ideology', as Althusser argues, 'has the function (which
defines it) of "constituting" concrete individuals as subjects' (1998:
161). Ideological subjects are produced by acts of 'hailing' or 'interpellation'. Althusser uses the analogy of a police officer hailing an
individual: 'Hey, you there!' When the individual hailed turns in
response, he or she has been interpellated, has become a subject of
the police officer's discourse. In this way, ideology is the creation of
subjects who are thus subjected to the material practices of ideology.

Throughout the 1970s, it became commonplace for academic work to seek to demonstrate how specific texts and practices interpellated individuals into subject positions – fixed their identity in relation to the cultural consumption of a specific text or practice. In perhaps the best of this work, Judith Williamson deploys Althusser's approach in her influential study of advertising, *Decoding Advertisements* (1978). She argues that advertising is ideological in the sense that it represents an imaginary relationship to our real conditions of existence. Instead of class distinctions based on our role in the process of production, advertising continually suggests that what really matters are distinctions based on the cultural consumption of particular goods. Thus social identity becomes a question of what we consume rather than what we produce. Like all ideology, advertising functions by interpellation: it creates subjects who in turn are subjected to its meanings and its patterns of cultural consumption. The consumer is interpellated to make meaning and ultimately to purchase and consume and purchase and consume again.

For example, when I am addressed by an advertisement in terms such as, 'people like you' are turning to this or that product, I am interpellated in two ways: first, as a member of a group ('people like you'); and second, as an individual 'you' of that group. I am addressed as an individual who can recognise myself in the imaginary space opened up by the pronoun 'you'. In this way, I am invited to become the imaginary 'you' spoken to in the advertisement. But such a process is for Althusser a double act of ideological 'misrecognition'. First, in order for the advert to work it must attract many others who also recognise themselves in the space opened up by the pronoun 'you' (each one thinking they are the real 'you' of its discourse). Second, the 'you' I recognise in the advert is in fact a 'you' created by the advertisement – it has no other existence except in this process of interpellation. The advertisement that seeks my attention, according to this perspective, attempts to flatter me into thinking that I am the special 'you' of its discourse and in so doing – if the process works – I am drawn in and become a subject in and thus subjected to its invidious material intent: an act of cultural consumption.

It is not difficult to think of other ways in which Althusser's concept of interpellation might be used to explain the means by which cultural commodities seek to locate us in specific subject positions. For example, consider the different modes of address at work in, say, a news programme (we are addressed as a citizen), a football programme (we are addressed as a fan) and a television commercial (we are addressed as a consumer). It is of course possible to be addressed as all three within a couple of hours of television viewing. Although this is true, and it points to the multiplicity of subject positions and identities we may be invited to occupy, the problem with the Althusserian approach to identity and subjectivity is the assumption that interpellation is always successful; that people are the passive victims of its invidious processes. Another way of seeing this is to note that the major problem with Althusser's model of subjectivity, and its application in cultural analysis, is that paradoxically it seems to work too well. Men and women are always successfully interpellated; always successfully positioned to be reproduced with all the necessary ideological habits required by the capitalist mode of production; there is no sense of failure, let alone any notion of conflict, struggle or resistance. In other words, these successes were the model's downfall: it has no sense of agency. Although cultural studies gradually turned to the more complex account of consumption and identity promised by the work of the Italian Marxist Antonio Gramsci (see next chapter), this model was itself overtaken by the debate on postmodernism.

An Introduction to Postmodernism and Popular Culture

Whether postmodernism is seen as a new historical moment, a new sensibility or a new cultural style, popular culture is usually cited as a terrain on which these changes are to be most readily found. Postmodernism begins in the late 1950s and early 1960s. The American cultural critic Susan Sontag coined the term the 'new sensibility' to describe and to celebrate a developing attitude to culture in early 1960s' New York. As she explains, 'One important consequence of the new sensibility [is] that the distinction between "high" and "low" culture seems less and less meaningful' (1966: 302). The postmodern 'new sensibility' rejected the cultural elitism of modernism. Although it often 'quoted' popular culture, modernism was marked by a deep suspicion of all things popular. Its entry into the museum and the academy as official culture was undoubtedly made easier (despite its declared antagonism to 'bourgeois philistinism') by its appeal to, and homologous relationship with, the elitism of class society. The response of the postmodern 'new sensibility' to modernism's canonisation was a re-evaluation of popular culture. The postmodernism of the 1960s was therefore in part a populist attack on the elitism of modernism. It signalled a refusal of what Andreas Huyssen calls 'the great divide . . . [a] discourse which insists on the categorical distinction between high art and mass culture'. Moreover, according to Huyssen, 'To a large extent, it is by the distance we have travelled from this "great divide" between mass culture and modernism that we can measure our own cultural postmodernity' (1986: 57).

The American and British Pop Art movement of the 1950s and the 1960s, with its rejection of the distinction between popular and high culture, is generally regarded as postmodernism's first cultural flowering. As Pop Art's first theorist, Lawrence Alloway, explains,

> The area of contact was mass produced urban culture: movies, advertising, science fiction, pop music. We felt none of the dislike of commercial culture standard among most intellectuals, but accepted it as a fact, discussed it in detail, and consumed it enthusiastically. One result of our discussions was to take Pop culture out of the realm of 'escapism', 'sheer entertainment', 'relaxation', and to treat it with the seriousness of art. (quoted in Storey 1997: 172)

The debate about postmodernism has increasingly disturbed many of the old certainties surrounding questions of cultural value. Perhaps the most significant thing about postmodernism for the student of popular culture is the growing recognition that there is no absolute categorical difference between high and popular culture. There are no longer any easy reference points from which to judge cultural texts and practices. In fact, the collapse of the distinction (if this is the case) between high and popular culture may signify that at last it may be possible to use the term popular culture and mean nothing more than culture liked by many people. But is this is the end of standards? On the contrary, without easy recourse to fixed categories of value, it calls for rigorous, if always contingent, standards, if our task is to separate the good from the bad, the usable from the obsolete, the progressive from the reactionary. As John Fekete points out,

> the prospect of learning to be at ease with limited warranties, and with the responsibility for issuing them, without the false security of inherited guarantees, is promising for a livelier, more colourful, more alert, and, one hopes, more tolerant culture that draws enjoyment from the dappled relations between meaning and value. (1987: 17)

Fekete's point brings us back to the argument made by Susan Sontag at the birth of the postmodern 'new sensibility'. As she explains,

> The new sensibility is defiantly pluralistic. . . . From [its] vantage point . . . the beauty of a machine or of the solution to a mathematical problem, of a painting by Jasper Johns, of a film by Jean-Luc Godard, and of the personalities and music of the Beatles is equally accessible. (1966: 304)

Sontag's explanation draws attention to a crucial but too often overlooked aspect of the debate about postmodernism; that is, that postmodernism is in part (and perhaps the main part) a way of seeing culture. As Simon Frith and Howard Horne observe,

> In the end the postmodern debate concerns the source of meaning – not just its relationship to pleasure (and, in turn, to the source of that pleasure) but its relationship to power and authority. Who now determines significance? Who has the right to interpret? For pessimists and rationalists like Jameson the answer is multinational capital – records, clothes, films, TV shows, etc. are simply the results of decisions about markets and marketing. For pessimists and irrationalists, like Baudrillard, the answer is nobody at all – the signs that surround us are arbitrary. For optimists like Iain Chambers and Larry Grossberg the answer is consumers themselves, stylists and subculturalists, who take the goods on offer and make their own marks with them. (1987: 169)

By the mid-1980s, the postmodern 'new sensibility' had travelled from New York to Paris and in the process had become a 'condition' (Lyotard 1984), and, for many, a reason to despair. According to Iain Chambers, much of this despair in the debate over postmodernism can in part be understood as

> the symptom of the disruptive ingression of popular culture, its aesthetics and intimate possibilities, into a previously privileged domain. Theory and academic discourses are confronted by the wider, unsystemized, popular networks of cultural production and knowledge. The intellectual's privilege to explain and distribute knowledge is threatened. (1986: 216)

Angela McRobbie makes a similar point, welcoming postmodernism, seeing it as 'the coming into being of those whose voices were historically drowned out by the (modernist) metanarratives of mastery, which were in turn both patriarchal and imperialist' (1994: 23). Postmodernism, she argues, has enfranchised a new body of intellectuals, voices from the margins speaking from positions of difference: ethnic, gender, class, sexual preference; those whom she refers to as 'the new generation of intellectuals (often black, female, or working class)' (ibid.). Kobena Mercer supports this view, seeing postmodernism as in part an unacknowledged response to 'the emerging voices, practices and identities of dispersed African, Caribbean and Asian peoples [who have] crept in from the margins of postimperial Britain to dislocate commonplace certainties and consensual "truths" and thus open up new ways of seeing, and understanding' (1990: 2) . Parts of these new ways of seeing and understanding, as Mercer makes clear, are concerned with questions of cultural identity.

Before we consider the question of a postmodern cultural identity, it is worth noting another development that parallels the emergence of postmodernism – the moment of so-called 'mass consumption'. In the late 1950s and early 1960s, the nature and the social extent of cultural consumption changed radically. During this period there was for the first time sufficient relative affluence for working people in Europe and North America to consume on the basis of 'desire' rather than 'need' – televisions, fridges, cars, vacuum cleaners, foreign holidays become increasingly common-place items of consumption. Moreover, this period marks the emergence of working people (first noticed in working-class youth subcultures) using patterns of cultural consumption to articulate a sense of identity in much the same way as the urban elites of the late nineteenth century (as identified by Veblen and Simmel; see Chapter 2 above). What I think is particularly significant about this development is that it is only in this period that cultural consumption emerges as a cultural concern in debates about the development of a so-called 'consumer society'. This is also, as we noted earlier, the moment of the first flowerings of what is now called postmodernism. One aspect of postmodernism (and especially anxieties about cultural consumption and postmodernism) may well be the proliferation 'downwards' of the use of consumption to articulate a sense of cultural identity.

Postmodern Cultural Identities

Traditionally, identity has usually been understood as something coherent and fixed; an essential quality of a person that is guaranteed by nature, especially human biology ('human nature'). This traditional view is sometimes modified to produce a second view of identity in which it is still something fixed and determined, but in this formulation biology is said to combine with social variables such as class, 'race' or gender, to produce and guarantee (what is still) a coherent and fixed identity.

Over the course of the nineteenth century and the early part of the twentieth a number of major intellectual assaults were made on these ways of seeing identity, each in its different way making a successful challenge to the idea of a fixed and coherent self. In different ways, Charles Darwin's theory of evolution (the evolving self), Karl Marx's concept of history (the conditioned self), Sigmund Freud's theory of psychoanalysis (the unconscious self) and Ferdinand de Saussure's theory of language (the self enabled and

Traditional identity	Modern identity	Postmodern identity
Fixed or limited self	Being into becoming	Performative self
Unfolding without change		Self as process of change
Singular		Multiple
Centred		Decentred
Complete		Incomplete
Constituted outside culture		Constituted in culture
Universal		Historical

Fig. 7.1 Postmodernism and cultural identity

constrained in and through language) all helped to 'decentre' the traditional self. Out of these challenges, and more recently out of the theoretical work of post-structuralism and postmodernism, a third way to understand identity emerged. This view posits identity, not as something fixed and coherent, but as something constructed and always in a process of becoming, but never complete, as much about the future as the past (see Hall 1990, 1996a, 1996c, 1996d). This is identity as 'production' rather than inheritance and/or the result of circumstance. It is identity constituted in, not outside, history and culture. Moreover, according to this model, the concept of identity is itself replaced by the concept of identities; that is, multiple and mobile identities (*see* Fig. 7.1). Whereas Althusser (as we noted earlier) talks of being interpellated into a subject position, postmodern identities are said to be positions we occupy and we vacate, in a never-ending journey of self-formation.

According to Stuart Hall, 'identities are about questions of using the resources of history, language and culture in the process of becoming rather than being' (1996a: 4). Although identities are clearly about 'who we think we are' and 'where we think we came from', they are also about 'where we are going'. Identities are always a narrative of the self *becoming*. If you ask who I am, I will tell you a story. In this sense, as Hall points out, identities are increasingly less about 'roots' and more about 'routes' (ibid.). So, for example, I may be in one moment a supporter of Manchester United, at another a university lecturer, at another a father and in another a friend. Each of these moments has an appropriate context of articulation. That is, depending on context, our identities form particular hierarchies of the self. In particular contexts, the identity 'in dominance' may be one thing, in another context it might be something quite different. But these other non-dominant identities are always present, always waiting ready to play a part in the changing formation of the self. Therefore, in a situation where being a Manchester United supporter is my most important identity, how I might perform this identity may well be limited by the fact that I am still a university lecturer.

Michel Foucault's comment on the nineteenth-century French poet Charles Baudelaire's view of the modern individual provides an interesting link to postmodern notions of identity:

> Modern man [sic], for Baudelaire, is not the man who goes off to discover himself, his secrets and his hidden truth; he is the man who tries to invent himself. This modernity does not 'liberate man in his being'; it compels him to face the task of producing himself. (1982: 41)

The task of producing the self in the mid-nineteenth century may have been only the privileged labour of the modern middle-class male artists; in the late twentieth century it is now seen as a practice engaged in by all of postmodernity's shifting subjectivities.

Our identities (rather than our identity) are formed out of our everyday social being – our actions and interaction in the social. This is why it is important to include cultural consumption in a discussion of identities. As Madan Sarup observes, cultural '[c]onsumption is [now] a mode of being, a way of gaining identity' (1996: 105). Our identities are in part constructed out of the things we consume – what we listen to, what we watch, what we read, what we wear, etc. In this way, as Sarup observes, 'the market . . . offers tools of identity-making' (125). Our identities are in part a result of what we consume. Or to put it another way, what we consume and how we consume it says a great deal about who we are, who we want to be, and how others see us. Cultural consumption is perhaps one of the most significant ways we perform our sense of self. This does not mean that we are what we consume, that our cultural-consumption practices *determine* our social being; but it does mean that what we consume provides us with a script with which we can stage and perform in a variety of ways the drama of who we are.[1]

Of course identity formations are not freely chosen or freely performed. We cannot, for example, determine what cultural commodities the culture industries make available to practices of cultural consumption. Nor can we escape the fact that our current patterns of cultural consumption are always likely to be informed by past cultural consumption and, more generally, by our own personal histories and our location in the social formation. Moreover, although it may be true that our biology is less important than it was once thought to be in debates about identity, who we are still has a certain biological basis, which clearly shapes many of our practices of cultural consumption. But it still remains the case that how our biology is understood and how it is performed, and the determining power it can wield, are open to the powerful flow of social and historical change. To put it more simply, being a man or a woman (how these cultural identities are performed) is not the same in all historical periods and in all societies – it has changed and it changes. Or to take a different example: in *Imagined Communities* Benedict Anderson demonstrates how nationality or nation-ness 'are cultural artefacts of a particular kind' (1983: 13). He argues that nations are imagined political communities. '[A nation] is *imagined* because the members of even the smallest nation will never know most of their fellow-members, meet them, or even hear of them, yet in the minds of each lives the image of their communion' (15). What distinguishes all communities is 'the style in which they are imagined' (ibid.). Furthermore, a nation 'is imagined as a community, because, regardless of the actual inequality and exploitation that may prevail in each, the nation is always conceived as a deep, horizontal comradeship' (16). Anderson sees the emergence of the nation with the emergence of two nation-enabling cultural forms, the novel and the newspaper: 'for these forms', as he explains, 'provided the technical means for "re-presenting" the kind of imagined community that is the nation' (30). The daily newspaper, with its juxtaposition of news stories, presents its own imagined community, inviting the reader to make coherent sense of what might appear an arbitrary array of items. In this way, it mimics and reinforces the type of imagination necessary in order to figure oneself as belonging in an imagined community. In addition, the very act of reading a daily newspaper reinforces and reproduces a sense of communal belonging.

> We know that particular morning and evening editions will overwhelmingly be consumed between this hour and that, only on this day, not that. The . . . ceremony . . . is performed in silent privacy, in the lair of the skull. Yet each communicant is well aware that the ceremony he [or she] performs is being replicated simultaneously by thousands (or millions) of others of whose existence he is confident, yet of whose identity he has not the slightest notion. Furthermore, this ceremony is incessantly repeated at daily or half-daily intervals throughout the calendar. What more vivid figure for the secular, histor-ically-clocked, imagined community can be envisioned? At the same time, the newspaper reader, observing exact replicas of his own paper being consumed by his subway, barbershop, or residential neighbours, is continually reassured that the imagined world is visibly rooted in everyday life. (39–40)

As Anderson's example demonstrates, a cultural text expresses a reality which pre-exists it, contributes to the reality in which it is consumed, and, most importantly for our present discussion, contributes to the reality of the subjectivity of the person who consumes it.

In the previous chapter, in the discussion of Ann Gray's research on how women use the VCR, it was noted how she seeks to avoid seeing the gender encoding of the VCR, and the different modes of viewing by men and women as reported by the women interviewed, as an articulation of an 'essential' masculinity or femininity. Instead she sees these differences as the articulation of domestic power relations, and argues that the different modes of viewing can be explained by the different positions traditionally occupied by men and women in the domestic sphere. Traditional these positions may be, but they are certainly not positions determined or guaranteed by nature; rather they are social positions. It is possible, and it is in fact the case (as Gray discovered) that, given a particular set of circumstances, women can adopt the 'masculine' mode of viewing and men the 'feminine' mode. This is possible because, as Charlotte Brunsdon points out, this is a way of viewing which is 'not so much a masculine mode, but a mode of power' (quoted in Gray 1992: 126). What this points to is a particular way of seeing identity, not as something fixed and guaranteed by nature, but as a series of subject positions.

It is not difficult to see the ways in which the clothes we wear articulate for ourselves and others who we are or would like to be. Although this is obviously true in the case of spectacular youth subcultures, similar forms of speaking through what we wear are also evident in recent attempts by William Hague, the leader of the British Conservative Party, to persuade other party members of the need to dress, on appropriate occasions, in a more casual fashion ('wear sweaters').

Identities are also formed by the kind of music to which we listen. Paul Gilroy draws attention to the way in which the recent fusion of popular music genres – Asian bhangra and black hip hop, for example – have produced new hybrid forms of music, remarking that 'much of their power resides in their capacity to circulate a new sense of what it means to be British' (1993b: 61). Simon Frith, again using music as an example, argues that '[postmodern] identity comes from the outside not the inside; it is something we put or try on, not something we reveal or discover' (1996: 122). He contends that

> social groups [do not] agree on values which are then expressed in their cultural activities but that they only get to know themselves as *groups* (as a particular organization of individual and social interests, of sameness and difference) *through* cultural activity. . . . Making music isn't a way of expressing ideas; it is a way of living them. (111)

He argues that, 'Music constructs our sense of identity through the direct experiences it offers of the body, time and sociability, experiences which enable us to place ourselves in imaginative cultural narratives' (124). Therefore, music which becomes popular, according to Frith, does so

> because it places us in the social world in a particular way.
> . . . The experience of pop music is an experience of identity:
> in responding to a song, we are drawn, haphazardly, into
> emotional alliances with performers and with the performers'
> other fans. . . . Music . . . symbolises and offers the immedi-
> ate experience of collective identity. (121)

Frith's position, especially his reference to emotional alliances, is remarkably close to Michel Maffesoli's theory of 'postmodern tribes'. What interests Maffesoli is the surfeit of groups, situated between the individual and the mass, of which we are temporary members throughout the course of our everyday lives. He argues that such groups – postmodern tribes – signal the end of mass culture which in turn points to 'the tendency for a rationalised "social" to be replaced by an emphatic "sociality", which is expressed by a succession of ambiences, feelings and emotions' (1996: 11). It is in the ordinary rituals of everyday life – 'which leads to an organic sense of commitment between individuals' (27) – that the postmodern tribes are made visible: 'Having a few drinks; chatting with friends; the anodyne conversations punctuating everyday life enable an exteriorization of the self and thus create the specific aura which binds us together within tribalism' (25). In this way, the life of postmodern tribes is 'characterized by fluidity, occasional gatherings and dispersal' (76). Maffesoli sees cultural consumption as a specific organizing feature of the ritual practices of postmodern tribes, who 'are perceptible in the various sporting gatherings . . . We can see them . . . in . . . department stores, supermarkets and shopping centres . . . in . . . the rituals of . . . summer holidays' (98). Moreover, advertisers have begun to target them as consumer groups, seeking to supply 'the products, goods, services and ways of being that constitute them as groups' (138). Postmodern tribes 'define themselves in terms both of territory and of an affectual sharing – cultural pursuits, sexual tastes, clothing habits, religious representations, intellectual motivations, political commitments' (135). It is through an engagement in these and other practices – 'rituals of belonging' (140) – that a postmodern tribe 'declares itself, delineates its territory and thus confirms its existence' (137).

Marie Gillespie's ethnographic fieldwork in Southall (discussed in the previous chapter) provides some empirical evidence for Maffesoli's theoretical position, while at the same time supporting

's concept of the imagined community. She points out that
g people in Southall, the regular viewing of soaps encour-
nse of participating in a daily activity shared simultan-
ᴐusly with youth audiences nationally and internationally' (1995:
95). More than this, she claims, Southall's Punjabi youth 'draw on
the soap [*Neighbours*] as a cultural resource in their everyday interactions both in the peer culture and with parents and other adults,
as they endeavour to construct new modes of identity for
themselves' (143). Shaun Moores's research into the cultural meanings of satellite dishes (also discussed in the previous chapter)
uncovered a similar deployment of television as a way of becoming a member of an (imagined) community.

Cultural Consumption, Identities and Displaced Meaning

In Chapter 1 I discussed Colin Campbell's argument that the
consumer revolution required a shift from traditional to modern
hedonism. As he maintains,

> The capacity to gain pleasure from self-constructed, imagin-
> ative experience crucially alters the essential nature of all
> hedonistic activity. . . . In modern hedonism . . . if a product
> is capable of being represented as possessing unknown charac-
> teristics then it is open to the pleasure-seeker to imagine the
> nature of its gratifications and it thus becomes an occasion for
> day-dreaming. Although employing material from memory, the
> hedonist can now imaginatively speculate upon what grati-
> fications and enjoyments are in store, and thus attach his
> favoured day-dream to this real object of desire. In this way,
> imagined pleasures are added to those already encountered
> and greater desire is experienced for the unknown than the
> known. (1987: 85–6)

Campbell also claims that it is generally the case that the 'real'
experience of consumption will fail to match the experience
imagined in anticipation. In this way, 'The consummation of desire
is thus a necessarily disillusioning experience', in that the gap
between anticipation and reality will always produce, regardless of
the pleasures actual experience of consumption may bring, a 'resultant recognition that something is missing' (86). Although his
argument is that consumers are driven from object to object, from
anticipatory day-dreaming to disillusioning reality, longing for an
object of desire which can be experienced in actuality as it is experienced in imaginative anticipation, his 'central insight [however]

. . . is the realization that individuals do not so much seek satisfaction from products, as pleasures from self-illusory experiences which they construct from their associated meanings' (89). In this way,

> The essential activity of consumption is thus not the actual selection, purchase or use of products, but the imaginative pleasure-seeking to which the product image lends itself, 'real' consumption being largely a resultant of this 'mentalistic' hedonism. Viewed in this way, the emphasis upon novelty as well as that upon insatiability both become comprehensible. (89)

Working with a similar model, the Canadian anthropologist Grant McCracken claims to have detected a way in which cultural consumption can 'cultivate hopes and ideals'. As he explains,

> Consumer goods are bridges to these hopes and ideals. We use them to recover this displaced cultural meaning, to cultivate what is otherwise beyond our grasp. In this capacity, consumer goods are also a way of perpetually renewing our consumer expectations. The dark side of this aspect of consumption also helps to enlarge our consumer appetites so that we can never reach a 'sufficiency' of goods and declare 'I have enough'. This aspect of consumption also helps to illuminate some of the irrational, fantastic, escapist attachments we have to consumer goods. (1990: 104)

McCracken uses the term 'displaced meaning' to indicate that the process he seeks to describe is one which 'consists in cultural meaning that has deliberately been removed from the daily life of a community and relocated in a distant cultural domain' (104). According to this perspective, cultural consumption 'is one of the means by which a culture reestablishes access to the cultural meaning it has displaced' (ibid.). Cultural consumption, in other words, acts as a 'bridge' to cultural meanings that would otherwise remain lost.

McCracken claims that the process of displaced meaning is propelled by a growing awareness of the fact that we live in a world in which the real and the ideal rarely exist in close proximity. Therefore, he argues,

> Confronted with the recognition that reality is impervious to cultural ideals, a community may displace these ideals. It will remove them from daily life and transport them to another cultural universe, there to be kept within reach but out of danger. The displaced meaning strategy allows a culture to remove its ideals from harm's way. (106)

This strategy not only safeguards ideals, it also allows them to be demonstrated with safety. Ideals may be located temporally in a past golden age (the Leavisite 'organic community') or in a perfect future (God's other kingdom), or they may be located spatially in an existing place in another part of the world (what used to be called 'actually existing socialism'). These locations can be called upon to demonstrate what has been possible, what is possible, or what will be possible when the local difficulties of the here and now are overcome.

McCracken argues that what is true of cultures and communities is also true for individuals:

> Like cultures, individuals display a characteristic refusal to attribute the failure of ideals to the ideals themselves. Like cultures, individuals prefer to displace their ideals, removing them from the 'here and now' to the relative safety of another time or space. Individuals, like cultures, find the displaced-meaning strategy a useful sleight of hand, one that sustains hope in the face of impressive grounds for optimism. (108)

In this way, individuals, like cultures, will seek out suitable locations in other times or other spaces for the safe-keeping of their ideals. We may each have our own particular golden age in the past (memories of a carefree childhood) or we may locate our hopes in a possible golden age in the future (when I do this . . . when I get that . . . things will be . . .) or in a special geographic location (when I go to . . . things will be . . .). Displacing hopes and ideals in this way may well keep them safe, but how do we remain in contact with them? McCracken argues that part of the answer lies in cultural consumption. The texts and practices we consume 'serve both individuals and cultures as bridges to displaced meaning' (109). As he observes,

> The question of recovery is a delicate one. The process of meaning displacement is undertaken in the first place in order to establish a kind of epistemological immunity for ideas. When an attempt is made to recover this meaning, care must be taken to see that this immunity is not compromised. Recovery must be accomplished in such a way that displaced meaning is brought into the 'here and now' without having to take up all of the responsibilities of full residence. When displaced meaning is recovered from its temporal or spatial location, it must not be exposed to the possibility of disproof. In other words, access must not be allowed to undo the work of displacement. (109–10)

It is possible to construct a similar model for thinking critically about cultural consumption and strategies of displacement from the work of the post-structuralist psychoanalyst Jacques Lacan (1977). Lacan argues that a child's sense of self first emerges during what he calls the 'mirror phase'. Looking in the mirror (real or imagined), the child begins to see itself as a separate being (i.e. separate from its mother). For Lacan this is a process (which continues throughout the child's lifetime) of *misrecognition* (not the self, but an image of the self). The 'mirror phase' heralds the moment of entry into an order of subjectivity Lacan calls the imaginary. The imaginary is a domain of images and identifications. As the child grows older, it will proceed to make identifications with a range of different images and objects, and by so doing will construct its sense of self (ego). As Eagleton explains it, 'For Lacan, the ego is just this narcissistic process whereby we bolster up a fictive sense of unitary selfhood by finding something in the world with which we can identify' (1983: 165).

The child's entry into language (following transition through the Oedipus crisis), marks for Lacan its entry into the symbolic. Language allows the child to communicate with others, but it also intensifies its experience of 'lack'. Although demands can now be articulated through language, they cannot make good the child's experience of 'lack' – in fact, they intensify it. On entry into the symbolic realm of language, the child becomes a subject (subject in, subject of, and ultimately subjected to, language). Although language allows the child to articulate itself as 'I', it also draws attention to the fragility of this speaking self. Lacan distinguishes between the subject of the enunciation and the subject of the enounced. What he means is this: when the child says 'I', it is always different from the 'I' of whom it speaks. Moreover, the symbolic order of language is an impersonal structure available to all, and a structure which pre-exists the child's birth. The child is 'I' when it speaks to 'you', and 'you' when you speak to it. In this way its sense of being a unique individual is increasingly recognised as something very fragile. Therefore, although the child's subjectivity is made possible by language (without the symbolic realm of language the child would be unable to articulate its sense of self), it is also undermined by being articulated in language; language remains a structure for ever outside the child's sense of being, belonging to others in the same way as it belongs to it. It is language which enables us to think ourselves as subjects; without language we would have no sense of self, and yet within language our sense of self is always slipping away – fragile and threatening to fragment. The transition from the imaginary to the symbolic locks the child into the mechanisms of 'desire'. Desire is constituted and driven by 'lack' – the impossibility of closing the gap (and the continual need to try) between the child's 'self' and that which would make it whole again (the lost moment of plenitude/separation from the mother's body). As Eagleton explains,

> after the Oedipus crisis, we will never again be able to attain this precious object [the mother's body], even though we will spend all our lives hunting for it. We have to make do instead with substitute objects . . . with which we try vainly to plug the gap at the very centre of our being. We move among substitutes . . . never able to recover the pure (if fictive) self-identity and self-completion which we knew in the imaginary.
> . . . [I]t is an original lost object – the mother's body which drives forward the narrative of our lives, impelling us to pursue substitutes for this lost paradise in the endless metonymic movement of desire. (1983: 167, 168, 185)

It is not difficult to think of examples of the Lacanian notion of desire driven by lack. For example, we in the West live in a world in which romantic love is held up as the ultimate solution to all our problems. Love is a narrative compelled by lack. If we find love it will make us whole; finding the ideal partner completes our being. Love in effect promises to return us to the blissful state of the moment of plenitude, warm and secure against the body of the mother. Like the narrative search for love, it could be argued that what we might call the 'discourse of consumerism' also implies an incompleteness; something missing. The discourse of consumerism can be seen as a Lacanian displacement strategy; one example of the continual quest for fulfilment, the endless metonymic movement of desire. The promise it holds out is that cultural consumption, or the right kind of cultural consumption (this jacket, that coat), is the answer to all our problems; cultural consumption will make us whole again; cultural consumption will return us to the blissful state of the 'imaginary'. This perhaps makes some sense of the appeal of a card John Fiske found whilst browsing in a gift shop in Australia. The inscription read: 'Work to Live, Live to Love, and Love to Shop, so you see . . . if I can buy enough things I'll never have to work at love again' (1989b: 18).

Thinking Cultural Consumption and Identities Historically

Although the relationship between identity and consumption is said to be a key feature of postmodernism, it is certainly not something that is entirely new to the world, as was indicated above in the brief discussion of Anderson's concept of the 'imagined community'. Writing in 1747, Richard Campbell, for example, mocked those who sought to hide their true selves behind their chosen patterns of cultural consumption.

> There are Numbers of Beings in about this Metropolis who have no other identical Existence than what the Taylor, Milliner, and Perriwig-Maker bestow upon them. Strip them of these Distinctions, and they are quite a different Species of Beings; have no more Relation to their dressed selves, than they have to the Great *Mogul*, and are insignificant in Society as Punch, deprived of his moving Wires, and hung up upon a Peg. (quoted in McKendrick 1982b: 51)

What makes this different from the postmodern position, of course, is the very idea of a true self that can be disguised and concealed. Postmodern accounts of identity and cultural consumption argue, as we have already noted, that we are in part what we consume; identity is not an essence to be dressed in particular ways, it is something we become and continue to become; identity is not what we are but what we are becoming, and dressing in a particular way may form part of this process. Stuart Ewen quotes the psychologist Henry Floyd Allport (writing in 1924), who argues that 'our consciousness of ourselves is largely a reflection of the consciousness which others have of us. . . . My idea of myself is rather my own idea of my neighbor's view of me' (quoted in Ewen 1976: 34). Advertising plays on this notion of the self by locating the products it advertises in a world where self is continually under the watchful gaze of other; and the only way to be sure that we can successfully withstand such scrutiny is by using one of the products advertising offers to us to purchase. In similar fashion, the psychologist William James observed in 1890, 'There is a blurred line between what I think of as mine and what I think of as me. It is clear that between what a man calls me and what he simply calls mine, the line is difficult to draw, (quoted in Silverstone and Hirsch 1992: 56). A key moment in this connection between commerce and identity occurs with the development of the department store in the nineteenth century. The Swiss historian Philippe Perrot describes the impact of the department store in France as dramatic: it 'brought about the psychological "take off" of the desire for consumption in the modern sense, the extended socialisation of needs' (quoted in Laermans 1993: 80).

By the close of the nineteenth century the department store was a familiar feature of city shopping; for example, the Bon Marché in Paris, Harrods in London, Bainbridge in Newcastle upon Tyne, Macy's in New York, Wanamaker's in Philadelphia. As Rachel Bowlby explains,

Within a very short period, department stores had been established as one of the outstanding institutions in the economic and social life of the late nineteenth century; and together with advertising, which was also expanding rapidly, they marked the beginning of present-day consumer society. (1985: 3)

The department store brought into being many of the aspects of shopping we now take for granted. For example, as Bowlby also points out,

The principle of *entrée libre* or open entry did away with what had previously been a moral equation between entering a shop and making a purchase. At the same time, a fixed price policy, supported by clear labelling, put an end to the convention of bargaining which focused attention on shopping as paying. Assistants in department stores received commissions on sales, so were inclined to be flattering rather than argumentative: the customer was now to be waited on rather than negotiated with and money, in appearance, was not part of the exchange (particularly since paying in fact took place in a separate part of the store). People could now come and go, to look and dream, perchance to buy, and shopping became a new bourgeois leisure activity – a way of pleasantly passing the time, like going to a play or visiting a museum. (3–4)

In this way, the discourse of commerce had shifted from an insistence on the 'immediate purchase of particular items' to an attempt to generate and provoke the 'arousal of free-floating desire' (Williams 1982: 67). In other words, with the advent of the department store shopping became detached from buying and with this development came the pleasure of looking, with 'just looking' entering for the first the vocabulary of shopping.[2] As Rudi Laermans observes, 'The early department stores pioneered the transformation of traditional customers into modern consumers and of "just merchandise" into spectacular "commodity signs" or "symbolic goods". Thus they laid the cornerstones of a culture we still inhabit' (1993: 94).

But what do these developments in the practice of shopping have to do with questions of cultural identity? The answer is that articulating identities through the cultural consumption of commodities is a social practice that has had to be learned (see discussion in Chapter 1 above). This is not to suggest that it is a practice that was imposed on people by capitalist entrepreneurs, which certainly was not the case; but it is a practice with a history. As Michael B. Miller makes clear, with specific reference to France, but generalisable to other areas of Western Europe and North America, the department store did not simply reflect changing consumer practices, it actively and powerfully contributed to them. 'Far more than a mirror of bourgeois culture in France, the Bon Marché gave shape and definition to the very meaning of the concept of a bourgeois way of life' (1981: 182). The department store gave embodiment to this way of life; its catalogues operated as a 'cultural primer', telling readers who wanted this way of life, and these specific cultural identities, 'how they should dress, how they should furnish their home, and how they should spend their leisure time' (183). In this way, the department store promoted the idea that a middle-class self was something that could be purchased. Stuart Ewen and Elizabeth Ewen call this possibility 'the commercialization of the self' (1982: 215).

John B. Thompson makes the very important point that 'with the development of modern societies, the process of self-formation . . . is increasingly nourished by mediated symbolic materials, greatly expanding the range of options available to individuals and loosening – without destroying – the connection between self-formation and shared locale' (1995: 207). In other words, the relationship between self-formation (the making of identities) and shared locale (a particular social context) is clearly a relationship of 'structure' and 'agency'. Again to paraphrase Marx, we make our identities from materials and in conditions not of our making. Therefore, although the expansion of goods for cultural consumption, made available by the emergence of the department store, massively increases the repertoire of materials from which identities can be made, identities are always made from the position of a shared locale, a particular social context, with its tradition, its history, its routines of everyday life. I am in complete agreement with Thompson when he argues for a position in which the self is envisaged as

> neither . . . the product of an external symbolic system, nor as a fixed entity which the individual can immediately and directly grasp; rather the self is a symbolic project that the individual actively constructs . . . out of the symbolic matersials which are available to him or her, materials which the individual weaves into a coherent account of who he or she is, a narrative of self-identity. This is a narrative which for most people will change over time as they draw on new symbolic materials, encounter new experiences and gradually redefine their identity in the course of a life trajectory. (210)

Therefore, while we can recognise that using cultural consumption to articulate multiple and mobile identities has a history, and the early days of the department store constitute a key moment in this history, this is not the same as saying that it is something that capitalist entrepreneurs have imposed on an easily manipulated body of consumers.

Notes

1   It should not be forgotten that undoubtedly the least attractive aspect of this drama is to do with the fact that identities are always the result, not only of identifications through sameness, but also the marking out and maintaining of difference. Identity as difference can take us a long way beyond discussions of cultural consumption, to bring us face to face with the brutal corners of history where racial hatred and ethnic cleansing, rather than 'conspicuous consumption', are the vicious mechanisms of identity formation.
2   Like most popular pleasures, especially those practised by women, shopping soon attracted its cultural critics. For example, a critic writing in the *New York Times* (June 1881) complained about 'the awful prevalence of the *vice* of shopping among women . . . [an addiction] every bit as bad as male drinking or smoking' (quoted in Laermans 1993: 88; my italics).

8

Gramscian Cultural Studies, Popular Culture and Cultural Consumption

In this, the final chapter, I first outline a Gramscian cultural-studies perspective on popular culture. This is followed by a discussion of the place of cultural consumption (in terms of production, textual analysis and consumption) in Gramscian cultural studies. The argument throughout the chapter, and explicitly made in the final section, is that Gramscian cultural studies provides the most convincing means for thinking fruitfully about questions of cultural consumption.

Gramscian Cultural Studies and Popular Culture

The introduction of Antonio Gramsci's concept of hegemony into British cultural studies in the early 1970s brought about a rethinking of popular culture. It did this in two ways. First, it produced a rethinking of the *politics* of popular culture; popular culture was now seen as a key site for the production and reproduction of hegemony (see, for example, Hall *et al.* 1978). In this new formulation, popular culture was understood as a field of struggle and negotiation between the interests of dominant groups and the interests of subordinate groups; between the imposition of dominant interests and the resistance of subordinate interests. Second, the introduction of hegemony theory into cultural studies produced a rethinking of the *concept* of popular culture itself. This rethinking involved bringing into *active relationship* two previously dominant, but antagonistic, ways of thinking about popular culture. The first viewed popular culture as imposed by the culture industries; a culture provided for profit and ideological manipulation, establishing subject positions and imposing meanings (i.e. the Frankfurt School, structuralism, some versions of post-structuralism, political economy; see Chapter 2 above). This is popular culture as 'structure'. The second saw popular culture as a culture emerging spontaneously from below; an 'authentic' working-class culture – the 'voice' of the people (i.e. some versions of culturalism, social history/'history from below'). This is popular culture as 'agency'.

According to cultural studies, now informed by hegemony theory, popular culture is neither an 'authentic' working-class culture nor a culture imposed by the culture industries, but what Gramsci would call a 'compromise equilibrium' (1998: 211) between the two; a contradictory mix of forces from both 'below' and 'above'; both 'commercial' and 'authentic', marked by both 'resistance' and 'incorporation', 'structure' and 'agency'. Looking at popular culture as a 'compromise equilibrium', what has always interested cultural studies is not so much the cultural commodities provided by the culture industries, but the way these cultural commodities are appropriated and *made* meaningful in acts of cultural consumption; often in ways not intended or even envisaged by their producers. A key moment in this way of thinking about popular culture in cultural studies is the early work on the cultural-consumption practices of spectacular youth subcultures (see Hall and Jefferson 1976, Hebdige 1979).

Cultural Consumption: Production, Textual Analysis, Consumption

Production

There is a standard argument in circulation in some sections of the social sciences which claims that the growing significance of the study of cultural consumption in cultural studies points to nothing less than a 'paradigm crisis'. For example, Jim McGuigan claims that cultural studies has narrowed its focus to questions of interpretation, without situating such questions within a context of the material relations of power. To reverse this trend, he advocates a dialogue between cultural studies and the political economy of culture. As he contends,

> In my view, the separation of contemporary cultural studies from the political economy of culture has been one of the most disabling features of the field of study. The core problematic was virtually premised on a terror of economic reductionism.

In consequence, the economic aspects of media institutions and the broader economic dynamics of consumer culture were rarely investigated, simply bracketed off, thereby severely undermining the explanatory and, in effect, critical capacities of cultural studies. (1992: 40–1)

The point is repeated by Nicholas Garnham: 'cultural studies now needs to rebuild the bridges with political economy that it burnt in its headlong rush towards the pleasures and differences of postmodernism' (1997: 56). Work on cultural consumption in cultural studies has, or so the argument goes, vastly overestimated the power of consumers by failing to keep in view the 'determining' role of production on cultural consumption. According to Garnham,

These conditions ['the core structural characteristics of the capitalist mode of production'] shape in determinate ways the terrain upon which cultural practices take place – the physical environment, the available material and symbolic resources, the time rhythms and spatial relations. They also pose the questions to which people's cultural practices are a response; they set the cultural agenda. (71)

Moreover, as Peter Golding and Marjorie Ferguson contend, 'the shaping and packaging of most urban popular culture today results from sophisticated celebrity and product marketing on the part of media organisations before any element of consumer choice enters the marketplace' (1997: xxiv).[1] Even if this is true, it is only the beginning of the process. What McGuigan, Golding and Ferguson are describing is better understood, to borrow Stuart Hall's phrase, as 'determination by the economic in the first instance' (1996e: 45). There are economic conditions and fear of economic reductionism cannot just will them away. However, the point is not simply to recognise these conditions, and it is certainly not to fall down before them in abject submission; what is required is not just an understanding of how these conditions produce a repertoire of commodities, but also an understanding of the many ways in which people select, appropriate and use these commodities, and make them into culture; in other words, an understanding of the relationship between 'structure' and 'agency'.

Capitalism is more than an economic system, it is also a social and cultural formation. Furthermore, as Bourdieu makes clear, although power is ultimately economic, how it is lived is always cultural, which includes, at a fundamental level, the practice of cultural consumption. It is in culture – what Marx called the 'ideological forms in which men [and women] *become conscious of*

. . . conflict and *fight it out*' (Marx 1998: 193; my italics) – that we live our relations to power. After Marx's death, Frederick Engels found himself having to explain, through a series of letters, many of the subtleties of Marxism to younger Marxists who, in their revolutionary enthusiasm, threatened to reduce it to little more than a form of economic determinism. In a famous letter to Joseph Bloch, Engels explains:

> According to the materialist conception of history, the *ultimately* determining element in history is the production and reproduction of real life. Neither Marx nor I have ever asserted more than this. Therefore if somebody twists this into saying that the economic factor is the *only* determining one, he is transforming that proposition into a meaningless, abstract, absurd phrase. The economic situation is the basis, but the various components of the superstructure . . . also exercise their influence upon the course of the historical struggles and in many cases determine their *form*. . . . We make our own history, but, first of all, under very definite assumptions and conditions. Among these the economic ones are ultimately decisive. But the political ones, etc., and indeed even the traditions which haunt human minds also play a part, although not the decisive one. (1998: 194)

What Engels is claiming is that the economic base produces the superstructural terrain (this terrain, not that), but that the form of activity (the lived culture) which takes place there is conditioned, not just by the fact that the terrain was produced and is reproduced by the economic base (although this clearly sets limits and influences outcomes), but also by the (cultural) interactions of people and institutions as they occupy, and struggle over, the terrain. Gramsci makes much the same point:

> It may be ruled out that immediate economic crises of themselves produce fundamental historical events; they can simply create a terrain more favourable to the dissemination of certain modes of thought, and certain ways of posing and resolving questions involving the entire subsequent development of national life. (1971: 184)

As Raymond Williams maintains, 'we have to discover the nature of a practice and then its conditions' (1980: 47). Working with this idea from Williams, I would suggest, leads to a critical perspective in which production is seen to provide, not a mechanistically determining factor, but the conditions of existence for the practice of cultural consumption. But we will not understand this practice by pretending that all the answers can be found in its conditions of existence, nor will we understand it by pretending that its conditions of existence are unimportant; it is the relationship between the two that needs to be adequately understood. However, while it is clearly important to locate the commodities people consume within the field of the economic conditions of their existence, it is clearly insufficient to do this and think you have also already analysed important questions of audience appropriation and use. It seems to me that Gramscian hegemony theory still promises to do both, and even more import-antly, to keep both in an active relationship, whereas the political-economy-of-culture approach threatens, despite its admirable intentions, to collapse everything back into the economic. Until the political-economy-of-culture approach regards the cultural (the 'ideological forms') as a serious terrain for agency, struggle and study, it will deserve to bear the charge of 'reductionism' and 'functionalism' that Garnham so desperately seeks to defend it against (1997: 58).

Against the limited perspective of such forms of economic reduc-tionism, I think John Fiske is right to reject the view that 'the capitalist culture industries produce only an apparent variety of products whose variety is finally illusory for they all promote the same capitalist ideology' (1987: 309).[2] Similarly, I share his rejec-tion of the view 'that "the people" are "cultural dopes" . . . a passive, helpless mass incapable of discrimination and thus at the economic, cultural, and political mercy of the barons of the [culture] industry' (ibid.). He argues persuasively, I think, the case for a mode of analysis in which the commodities from which culture is made can be seen to circulate in two simultaneous economies, the financial and the cultural. Although there is contin-ual interaction between these separate, but related, economies, the financial economy is primarily concerned with exchange value and profit, while the cultural economy is primarily focused on appro-priation and use – 'meanings, pleasures, and social identities' (311). The power of consumers, Fiske contends,

> derives from the fact that meanings do not circulate in the cultural economy in the same way that wealth does in the financial. They are harder to possess (and thus to exclude others from possessing), they are harder to control because the production of meaning and pleasure is not the same as the production of the cultural commodity, or of other goods, for in the cultural economy the role of consumer does not exist as the end point of a linear economic transaction. Meanings and pleasures circulate within it without any real distinction between producers and consumers. (313)

In this way, influenced by both Gramsci and de Certeau, Fiske maintains that culture must always be seen as a site of struggle, not as something simply imposed from above to secure economic and ideological ends. As he explains,

> while accepting the power of the forces of dominance, it [Fiske's critical perspective] focuses rather upon the popular tactics by which these forces are coped with, are evaded or are resisted. Instead of tracing exclusively the processes of incorporation, it investigates rather that popular vitality and creativity that makes incorporation such a constant necessity. Instead of concentrating on the omnipresent, insidious practices of the dominant ideology, it attempts to understand the everyday resistances and evasions that make that ideology work so hard and insistently to maintain itself and its values. (1989a: 8)

Moreover, as Paul Willis perceptively and persuasively argues, the capitalist drive for profit produces contradictions in the market, 'supplying materials for its own critique' (1990: 139).

> People find on the market incentives and possibilities not simply for their own confinement but also for their own development and growth. Though turned inside out, alienated and working through exploitation at every turn, these incentives and possibilities promise more than any visible alternative. . . . Nor will it suffice any longer . . . to say that modern 'consumer identities' simply repeat 'inscribed positions' within market provided texts and artifacts. Of course the market does not provide cultural empowerment in anything like a full sense. There are choices, but not choices over choices – the power to set the cultural agenda. Nevertheless the market offers a contradictory empowerment which has not been offered elsewhere. It may not be the best way to cultural emancipation for the majority, but *it may open up the way to a better way*. (160; my italics)

It is simplistic, and, moreover, it is analytically disabling, to assume that practices of cultural consumption must mirror the intentions of production. The capitalist commodity has a double existence, as both use value and exchange value. Crucial to Willis's argument is the fact that 'the use value of a commodity cannot be known in advance of investigation of actual use of the commodity' (Lovell 1998: 477). As Marx observed, how a commodity is used 'may spring from the stomach or from the fancy' (quoted in Lovell 1998: 476). Too often supposedly radical attacks on capitalism are in reality little more than elitist and reactionary arguments about the *extent* of consumer choice made available by the market. Furthermore, as Terry Lovell points out, the commodities from which people make culture have different use values for the individuals who use and purchase them than they have for the capitalists who produce and sell them, and in turn, for capitalism as a whole. We may assume that people do not purchase these cultural artifacts in *order* to expose themselves to bourgeois ideology . . . but to satisfy a variety of different wants which can only be guessed at in the absence of analysis and investigation. There is no guarantee that the use-value of the cultural object for its purchaser will even be compatible with its utility to capitalism as bourgeois ideology. (Lovell 1998: 479)

As Lovell's comments suggest, it is important to distinguish between the power of the culture industries and the power of their influence. Too often the two are conflated, but they are not necessarily the same. The trouble with the political-economy-of-culture approach is that it too often assumes that they are the same. To explore the extent of their influence requires specific and detailed focus on cultural consumption as it is actually lived in particular social and economic conditions. Moreover, if our focus is cultural consumption, then our focus must be cultural consumption as it is experienced and not as it should be experienced as already determined in a prior analysis of the relations of production.

There is a real sense in which the insistence on 'structure' as the only valid object of study in the political economy of culture is really a rejection of 'agency'. At times their complaints about work in cultural studies on cultural consumption amount to little more than an argument in which if it can be shown that people make their own culture from the productions of the culture industries, this then invalidates the purposes of ideological critique. This sometimes seems to amount to a position in which in order to justify the theoretical methodology of the political economy of culture as political, it is essential to see 'ordinary people' as cultural dupes, hopelessly manipulated by the ruthless barons of the culture industries. As Angela McRobbie observes,

It is as though 'letting the people in' to the field of analysis rocks the boat of left consensus. The people are too difficult in their diversity, too unpredictable in their tastes, too likely to stray from the path of class politics, that it is better and perhaps safer to run the risk of being seen as elitist and have them safely suffering from either 'false consciousness' or ideological seduction. (1996: 252)

Stuart Hall is undoubtedly right to suggest that a number of people working in cultural studies have at times turned away from 'economic' explanations:

What has resulted from the abandonment of deterministic economism has been, not alternative ways of thinking questions about the economic relations and their effects, as the 'conditions of existence' of other practices . . . but instead a massive, gigantic, and eloquent *disavowal*. As if, since the economic in the broadest sense, definitely does *not*, as it was once supposed to do, 'determine' the real movement of history 'in the last instance', it does not exist at all! (1996: 258)

Hall describes this as 'a failure of theorisation so profound, and . . . so disabling, that . . . it has enabled much weaker and less conceptually rich paradigms to continue to flourish and dominate the field' (ibid.). A return there must be, but it cannot be a return to the kind of analysis canvassed by the political economy of culture approach, in which it is assumed that 'access' is the same as appropriation and use, and that production tells us all we need to know about cultural consumption. Nor does this mean the urgent necessity to build bridges to the political-economy-of-culture approach, but rather the need for a return to what has been, since the 1970s, the most convincing and coherent theoretical focus of (British) cultural studies – hegemony theory.

Textual Analysis

The problems with some forms of textual analysis are of a different nature. The fundamental problem is the assumption that the patterns of meaning discovered in close textual analysis will automatically produce predictable meaning-effects in readers. Approaches of this kind work with an assumption that meaning is something hidden in a text. The purpose of textual analysis in this model is to make visible what is hidden.[3] Moreover, this way of working is often informed (sometimes unconsciously) by a view in which 'other' meanings, as made by other readers, are seen as a 'contamination of the real meaning' (Hodge and Tripp 1986: 142) – ill-informed, irrelevant and easily dismissed. But, as I hope this book has made clear, reading is not the diving down into a text to find hidden treasure (the better the diver, the better the treasure); we do not read *into* a text, we read *with* it and *across* it. In this way, to read a text is to mobilise and make something out of its *specific materiality*. Although it is the case that the materiality of a text results from a process of production, meanings are always made in cultural consumption. Too often cultural critics confuse the difference between meaning and materiality; confusing a text's specific (and yet polysemic) materiality with its meaning – how it can be performed using a range of different 'accents' (Volosinov 1973). Think of a novel, for example: the author makes the text material in a specific way (these words, in this order, etc.), but it is the novel's readers (including the author her- or himself) who make it meaningful in actual practices of cultural consumption, and this of course always opens up the possibility of difference and disagreement. As Hodge and Tripp point out with reference to the cultural consumption of televisual texts,

> a television show is not a single stimulus, it is a vast meaning-potential complex, an interrelated set of verbal and visual meanings. But this potential is only abstract until there is someone to realise it. Interpretation is an intensely active process. Meaning is always constructed, or reconstructed, by the interaction of a set of signs with an overall code. (Hodge and Tripp 1986: 7)

Texts may be characterised by 'structured polysemy', organised to generate 'preferred readings', to offer to readers specific positions of understanding and intelligibility, but what they cannot do is to guarantee that particular meanings or specific reading positions will be taken up. To know how a text is activated requires the study of actual audiences. Culture is not a body of 'predigested' meanings, imposed on the duped by the culture industries; it is an active, social practice of making meanings. Cultural consumption is an encounter (as we noted in Chapter 5 above) between the discourses of the text and the discourses of the reader. Analysis

> must aim to lay bare the structural factors which determine the relative power of different discursive formations in the struggle over the necessary multi-accentuality of the sign – for it is in this struggle over the construction and interpretation of signs that meaning . . . is produced. (Morley 1980: 156)

For these reasons cultural studies is not concerned with the 'pure' or 'sacred' *meaning* of a text, discovered in the splendid isolation of an academic study. What interests cultural studies is the 'profane' meanings (see Willis 1978) which circulate in the varied practices of making culture in everyday life. With reference to television, Hodge and Tripp make the crucial point,

> Much to the regret of those who wish to deal with television meanings as if they were pure and uncontaminated, we must be prepared to find that non-television meanings are powerful enough to swamp television meanings. If that is how television works in practice, then it is that process that we must study, and which is important for us to understand. (1986: 144)

Hodge and Tripp's comments, point to the way in which cultural consumption must be seen as a practice of the lived cultures of everyday life. John Fiske, for example, makes this claim:

> Everyday life is constituted by the practices of popular culture, and is characterised by the creativity of the weak in using the resources provided by a disempowering system while refusing to submit to that power. The culture of everyday life is best described through metaphors of struggle or antagonism . . . These antagonisms, these clashes of social interest . . . are motivated primarily by pleasure: the pleasure of producing one's own meanings of social experience and the pleasure of avoiding the social discipline of the power-bloc. (1989a: 47)

As David Buckingham points out,

> Ultimately, textual analysis has distinct limitations: while it may provide a useful means of generating hypotheses, it is clearly incapable of accounting for the ways in which real audiences actually make sense of television. Viewers are not merely 'positioned' by television: they are also positioned in society and in history, and will therefore bring different kinds of prior knowledge to the text. As a result, they may refuse to accept, or indeed fail to perceive, the 'invitations' which the text offers. (1987: 115)

Janice Radway makes a similar point:

> Commodities like mass-produced . . . texts are selected, purchased, constructed, and used by real people with previously existing needs, desires, intentions, and interpretative strategies. By reinstating those active individuals and their creative, constructive activities at the heart of our interpretative enterprise, we avoid blinding ourselves to the fact that the essentially human practice of making meaning goes on even in a world dominated by things and by consumption. In thus recalling the interactive character of operations like reading, we restore time, process, and action to our account of human endeavour. (1987: 221)

This is not to dismiss textual analysis, but it is to indicate the limitations of its place in cultural studies, especially the limits of its critical reach. Engaging in textual analysis allows a researcher to establish not the 'true' meaning of a text, but the way a text, although polysemic, is nonetheless structured so as to generate a 'preferred reading'.

Consumption

The practice of cultural consumption is governed by agency. By agency I mean the capacity, within structures inherited from the past and lived in the present, to act in a purposive and reflexive manner; to act in a way that at times may modify what is inherited and that which is lived. Structures are like languages (and language is itself a structure); they both enable and constrain. That is, they enable us to be agents and they confine the limits of our agency. There is of course a sense in which the question of agency in matters of cultural consumption is not really the point. As Roger Silverstone reminds us, 'The key issue is not so much whether the audience is active but whether that activity is significant' (1994: 153). Ien Ang makes much the same point, 'audiences may be active, in myriad ways, in using and interpreting media, but it would be utterly out of perspective to cheerfully equate "active" with "powerful", in the sense of "taking control" at an enduring, structural or institutional level' (Ang 1996: 243). We need to be cautious in our claims about the 'activity' of cultural consumption. In my opinion, recognition of agency, although fundamental to the cultural-studies project, is not in itself enough. What matters, as Ang and Silverstone point out, is the nature and extent of the agency involved. This is not something we can decide in advance of actual 'ethnographic' investigation, but this does not mean that we dissolve all theoretical authority, and trust instead in the 'descriptive realism' of the ethnographic gaze. A commitment to ethnography must always be theoretically informed, structuring both our reasons for going and the nature of the questions we intend to ask when there.

I will end this section with a discussion of Daniel Miller's thesis regarding the relationship between cultural consumption and the making of culture. It provides, in my view, an excellent means to understand the 'agency' of cultural consumption, without losing sight of the question of 'structure'. Miller is concerned with what he identifies as

> the very active, fluid and diverse strategies by means of which people transform resources . . . purchased through the market . . . into expressive environments, daily routines and often cosmological ideals: that is, ideas about order, morality and family, and their relationships with the wider society. (1987: 8)

He works with a definition of culture which sees it not as a collection of objects to be judged good or bad, authentic or inauthentic, but as a process, involving a dynamic social relationship between subject and object. He claims, using Hegel's theory of objectification,[4] that the 'process of consumption is [potentially] equivalent to the Hegelian concept of sublation . . . the movement by which society reappropriates its own external form – that is, assimilates its own culture and uses it to develop itself as a social subject' (17).

According to Miller, 'For Hegel, the subject develops through a process of objectification in which the external is first created through an act of positing, then reincorporated in an act of sublation' (35). Objectification is thus a dual process of externalisation followed by internalisation. In Hegel's usage, objectification is deployed to explain an ongoing process of social development in which what we create is first seen to exist outside ourselves (externalisation: we create something outside ourselves) and is then only gradually recognised to be part of ourselves (internalisation: it becomes a part of our sense of social identity).

Miller uses Hegel's concept of objectification to develop a theory of cultural consumption. He argues that to make culture requires that societies must first produce (externalise), and then sublate (internalise) what they have produced. In other words, it is by consuming what is produced that we make culture. Moreover, culture is a dynamic process, one which requires both production and consumption, both object and subject; neither on its own can claim to *be* culture; culture is the dynamic and mutually constitutive relationship between the two. This is culture as human practice. To see this in terms of individual acts of cultural consumption is to say that we make ourselves (cultural identities and social formations) from objects which appear to be outside and independent of ourselves (cultural commodities, products of our social formation), and in this dynamic relationship we both make culture and are made by culture. Whereas for Marx[5] self-realisation is the promise of production (we create ourselves in our work), Miller sees this potential in the practices of cultural consumption. As he explains,

> In consumption, quite as fully as in production, it is possible, through use of the self-alienation which created the cultural world, to emerge through a process of reappropriation towards the full project of objectification in which the subject becomes at home with itself in its otherness. (192)

To explain this in another way, although the culture industries, for example, produce commodities which are 'alienated', particular practices of consumption have 'the potential to produce inalienable culture' (17). In this way, Miller argues that human self-creation and the making of culture (culture as human practice) are not confined to production but are also a characteristic of cultural consumption. To know my self, for example, is to learn from that which I have first externalised from my self. For example, if I write a poem it is in my consumption of the poem that I recognise my *self* as poet. It is the poem that makes me a poet. But to know this I must first consume the poem. Without this externalisation, this objectification, followed by a process of sublation, I would not know myself as poet. Similarly, to know myself as a supporter of Manchester United, I must first externalise (or at least recognise externally) Manchester United, and by consuming (internalising) what I have objectified, I become a supporter and thus enter into a social relationship (collective or antagonistic) with other supporters. In other words, unless something is objectified, given recognisable form, it cannot be internalised by the agency of a subject, and therefore it cannot become part of the process of becoming what we call culture. Marcuse identifies a similar process at work in modern practices of cultural consumption (as we saw in Chapter 2 above). The crucial difference between Miller and Marcuse is this: what Marcuse sees as a negative development, Miller sees as a process that is both necessary and unavoidable – it is the making of culture.

For Miller, then, culture is not simply a collection of objects made by people, nor is it the people who consume these objects – culture is a result of the process of cultural consumption itself. In this way, using objectification, Miller argues for a theory of culture in which 'there is no prior subject or object, but rather a process of mutual construction which always takes place in history' (32). It is in this mutually constitutive process that culture is made – from externalisation as form and sublation or internalisation of this form. By insisting on the mutually constituting relationship between object and subject, he succeeds in not reducing culture to the simple outcome of either production or cultural consumption. To make culture, he argues, both processes are necessary. His is an account of cultural consumption as the making of culture which favours neither objectivism nor subjectivism but insists on an active relationship between both structure and agency.

Miller also rejects a view of cultural consumption which reduces it to discussions of the commodity in which the only role played by consumers is to purchase. Against such arguments he locates the moment of purchase as only

> the start of a long and complex process, by which the consumer works upon the object purchased and recontextualizes it, until it is often no longer recognisable as having any relation to the world of the abstract and becomes its very negation, something which could be neither bought nor given. (190)

The 'work' of consumption is a process of translation in which the object is translated 'from an alienable to an inalienable condition; that is, from being a symbol of estrangement and price value to being an artefact invested with particular inseparable connotations' (ibid.). For example, my daughter Jenny has had since birth a rag doll called Ruby. Ruby began life as a commodity; she is the identical copy of many thousands of other rag dolls. Once a commodity, by the work of cultural consumption, Ruby has now been thoroughly recontextualised and translated. To Jenny, she is very special; for almost 10 years now she has been a constant source of comfort and companionship, especially at bedtimes. Although to love an object in this way, to invest in its very being, is a wonderful thing, it is not unique; there are many other children with dolls like Ruby. The point I am making is that these other 'Jennys' with their own recontextualised and translated 'Rubys' form a particular and significant aspect of what we might call, at least in the West, a *culture* of childhood. This is a culture made in practices of cultural consumption. The work of consumption is 'the continual struggle to appropriate goods and services made in alienating circumstances and transform them into inalienable culture' (193). Moreover, as Miller observes, 'The diversity of the products of this process of consumption is unlimited, since goods which are identical at the point of purchase or allocation may be recontextualized by different social groups in an infinite number of ways' (196).

In this way, Miller argues,

Mass goods represent culture, not because they are merely there as the environment within which we operate, but because they are an integral part of that process of objectification by which we create ourselves as an industrial society: our identities, our social affiliations, our lived everyday practices. The authenticity of artefacts as culture derives, not from their relationship to some historical style or manufacturing process – in other words, there is no truth or falsity immanent in them – but rather from their active participation in a process of social self-creation in which they are directly constitutive of our understanding of ourselves and others. The key criteria for judging the utility of contemporary objects is the degree to which they may or may not be appropriated from the forces which created them, which are mainly, of necessity, alienating. This appropriation consists of the transmutation of goods, through consumption activities, into potentially inalienable culture. (215)

For Miller, the work of consumption, its recontextualisation and translation, contains the potential to produce inalienable culture.

However, to conclude discussion of Miller's approach on a less optimistic note, he observes that, 'under present conditions, consumption only rarely amounts to the ideal model developed here, which is based on its potential as evident in certain cases, and is not a description of general practice' (213–14). Despite this qualification it is my contention that seeing cultural consumption (if only potentially) as the practice of making culture is a useful addition to cultural-studies thinking on this question.

Gramscian Cultural Studies and Cultural Consumption

In this, the final section of the book, I will draw together and make explicit what has perhaps been implicit throughout this volume, the Gramscian cultural-studies approach to questions of cultural consumption.

Gramscian cultural studies is committed to the study of cultural consumption for two reasons. The first is a theoretical reason. To know how cultural texts[6] are *made to mean* requires a consideration of cultural consumption. This will take us beyond an interest in the *meaning* of a text, to a focus on the range of meanings that a text makes possible. Cultural studies has never really been interested in the *meaning* of a cultural text; that is, meaning as something 'essential', inscribed and guaranteed. Cultural studies has always been more concerned with the *meanings* of cultural texts; that is, their 'social' meanings, how they are appropriated and used in practice: meaning as ascription, rather than inscription. This point is often missed in critiques of ethnography (or what passes for ethnography) in cultural studies. Cultural-studies ethnography is not a means to verify the 'true' meaning of a text; rather, it is a means to discover the meanings people make; the meanings which circulate and become embedded in the lived cultures of people's everyday lives. Working with hegemony theory may at times lead to a certain celebration of the lived cultures of ordinary people, but such celebrations are always made in the full knowledge that what in one context is 'resistance' can become very easily in another 'incorporation'.

Cultural studies views cultural consumption as a form of 'agency' which takes place within the confines of specific structures. Agents are mostly aware of what they are actively doing when they consume; and to understand this we need to undertake ethnographic study. But agents may well not be aware of the full significance of the structures in which they consume. Now this is not to suggest that agents are always passively positioned by the structures determining the limits of cultural consumption. But it is to suggest that in order to understand the structural conditions in which specific practices of cultural consumption may take place, we need to deploy cultural theory. As Anthony Giddens observes in a discussion of Paul Willis's *Learning to Labour*, working-class boys are aware of their location in the power structures of the school and react against this by various acts of rebellion. What they are less conscious of are the structures of power outside the school and how these might relate to the power structure of the school. Moreover, their success in resisting the power structure of the school results in them receiving an education that directs them to unskilled and unrewarding labour. In this way, as Giddens observes, their actions facilitate 'the reproduction of some general features of capitalist-industrial labour. Constraint, in other words, is shown to operate through the active involvement of the agents concerned, not as some force of which they are passive recipients' (1984: 289). The boys would soon become all too aware of how their 'resistance' to education prepared them for particular patterns of work. What Willis's cultural theory brings to the situation is an understanding of how their actions also contribute to the structural needs of industrial capitalism. As social anthropologists George Marcus and Michael Fischer observe,

> Willis is explicitly concerned both with the remarkable insights of his working-class subjects about the nature of capitalist process and with the limited self-understanding that they display concerning the ironic implications of their rebellious behaviour at school. In learning to resist the school environment, his lads establish the kinds of attitudes and practices that lock them into their class position, foreclosing the possibility of upward mobility. Resistance is thus an intimate part of the process of reproducing capitalist-class relations. The linkage of the local situation of cultural learning and resistance at the level of the school to the situation of labor in capitalist production at the level of the shop floor is thus one of unintended consequences. (1986: 82)

Angela McRobbie makes a similar point about how the 'anti-school culture' of adolescent working-class girls may operate as 'the most effective agent of control . . . pushing them into compliance with that role which a whole range of institutions in capitalist society also, but less effectively, directs them towards' (1978: 104).

For these reasons ethnographic research, if all that is intended by the term is an uncritical listening followed by a report on what has been heard, is not enough. Cultural studies informed by Gramscian hegemony theory always insists that there is a dialectic between the processes of production and the activities of cultural consumption. A consumer, situated in a specific social context, always confronts a commodity in its material existence as a result of determinate conditions of production. But in the same way, a commodity is confronted by a consumer, situated in a specific social context, who appropriates as culture and 'produces in use' the range of possible meanings the commodity can be made to bear – these cannot just be read off from the materiality of a commodity or from the means or relations of its production.

'Production in use' is obviously a shorthand term for a process that may involve desire, purchase/appropriation, use and incorporation into the lived culture of the consumer. Roger Silverstone offers a convincing elaboration of the range of possible moments which may come into play in the practice of cultural consumption. In an argument that is in some ways similar to Miller's (as outlined above), Silverstone distinguishes six moments in the practice of consumption: commodification, imagination, appropriation, objectification, incorporation and conversation (1994: 123). He acknowledges that these moments are 'neither discrete, nor necessarily as evenly present, in all acts of consumption' (123–4). He sees these moments as forming a cycle beginning and ending with commodification. Commodification is the commercial processes of production for profit of the texts we consume. This is followed by 'imagination'. At one level this refers to the work of advertising in seeking to make a commodity an object of desire. But it also involves the work of desire and imagination engaged in by consumers prior to consumption (for discussion of this process see Chapters 1 and 7 above), and of course informed but not controlled by the activities of advertisers (for failure to achieve control, see Fiske 1989a, Storey 1997).

Appropriation refers to the moment at which a commodity is taken out of the world of market exchange and into the possession of a consumer. This is the moment when the commodity is translated from something for sale in the marketplace into something which is owned by the consumer. Silverstone describes this as a transition from the 'formal' economy of production and distribution to the 'moral' economy of the consumer (1994: 126), which is marked by 'the withdrawal of objects from public to private space' (1994: 127). The attraction of 'window shopping' is undoubtedly in imagining this moment. Again this is a process which is rehearsed and promised in the discourse of advertising. How this moment is decoded – whether determined by advertising or in terms of the situated fantasies of the consumer, for example – is open to question. Objectification is articulated in usage; how an object is displayed, where it is located in the moral economy of the consumer. Incorporation refers to the ways in which over time the object finds its place in the daily routines of the consumer's moral economy. Clearly there is considerable overlap between objectification and incorporation. Silverstone marks the difference in terms of space and time: 'objectification principally identifies the spatial aspects of the moral economy, incorporation focuses . . . on its temporalities' (129). Finally, conversion draws attention to the way in which an object once appropriated, objectified and incorporated can be used to articulate public meanings. Silverstone maintains that it is by market researchers paying attention to the moments of appropriation, objectification, incorporation and conversion that these processes are fed back into the processes of production and distribution. In this way, the six moments of consumption can be seen to form a cycle.

Articulation

The dominant mode in cultural studies for understanding the 'compromise equilibrium' of the field of cultural consumption is Stuart Hall's (1982, 1996b) concept of 'articulation'. Articulation is the key concept in Gramscian cultural studies. Lawrence Grossberg even calls it 'the practice of cultural studies' (1993: 90). It is a concept which insists on context: 'cultural studies is committed to a radical contextualism, a contextualism that precludes defining culture, or the relations between culture and power, outside of the particular context into which cultural studies imagines itself to intervene' (ibid.).

Hall plays on the word's double meaning. As he explains, it

has a nice double meaning because 'articulate' means to utter, to speak forth, to be articulate. It carries that sense of language-ing, of expressing, etc. But we also speak of an 'articulated' lorry (truck): a lorry where the front (cab) and back (trailer) can, but need not necessarily, be connected to one another. (1996b: 141)

It is this play on both expression and connection that is central to the Gramscian cultural-studies use of articulation. Using articulation, the first point Hall makes is that cultural texts are not inscribed with meaning, meaning has to be 'articulated'; that is, meaning has to be *made*. This is articulation as expression. Hall's second point is that meanings are always made in the confines of a context. This is articulation as connection, the argument that when and where something is done impact on how it is done. In other words, as I have already insisted, cultural texts are not inscribed with meaning, guaranteed by authorial intention or mode of production; meaning has to be articulated; that is, actively produced in a practice of cultural consumption.

Hall's model is also informed by the work of the Russian theorist Valentin Volosinov (1973). According to Volosinov, cultural texts are always 'multi-accentual'. That is, they can always be made to speak with different 'accents'.[7] In this way, meaning is always a social production – the world has to be *made* to mean. Furthermore, because different meanings can be ascribed to the same cultural text, meaning will always be a site of struggle and negotiation. According to Hall, the cultural field is marked by this struggle to articulate, disarticulate and re-articulate cultural texts for particular ideologies and particular social interests. For example, when a black radical uses the word 'nigger' to attack institutionalised racism, it is articulated with an 'accent' very different from the 'accent' used in the Neanderthal ramblings of a neo-Nazi. This is not simply a question of linguistic struggle, a matter of semantic difference; it is the sign of political struggle about who can claim the power and authority to define social reality (i.e. *make* the world mean). On a larger scale, we might think of how 'nationalism' or 'democracy' can be articulated to serve the competing interests of different social groups. In *Mechanic Accents* Michael Denning uses Hall's mixture of Gramsci and Volosinov to critically assess the 'place and function' of dime novels 'within working-class cultures' in the United States in the nineteenth century (1987: 3). Denning recognises the novels as 'products of the culture industry', but he refuses to locate them as simply operating on one side of a binary opposition of incorporation or resistance. In a Gramscian move informed by the work of Volosinov he insists that the novels

> can be understood neither as forms of deception, manipulation, and social control nor as expressions of a genuine people's culture, opposing and resisting the dominant culture. Rather they are best seen as a contested terrain, a field of cultural conflict where signs with wide appeal and resonance take on contradictory disguises and are spoken in contrary accents. Just as the signs of a dominant culture can be articulated in the accents of the people, so the signs of the culture of the working classes can be dispossessed in varieties of ventriloquism. (ibid.)

Using the concept of 'articulation', therefore, is to insist that a cultural text is not the issuing source of meaning but a site where the articulation of meaning – variable meaning(s) – can be produced in a specific context for particular competing social interests.

The second reason Gramscian cultural studies is concerned with cultural consumption is political. Cultural studies has always rejected the 'pessimistic elitism' which haunts so much work in cultural theory and analysis (I have in mind Leavisism, the Frankfurt School, most versions of structuralism, economistic versions of Marxism, political economy) which always seem to want to suggest that 'agency' is always overwhelmed by 'structure'; that cultural consumption is a mere shadow of production; that audience negotiations are fictions, merely illusory moves in a game of economic power. Moreover, 'pessimistic elitism' is a way of thinking which seeks to pass off itself as a form of radical cultural politics. But too often this is a politics in which attacks on power end up being little more than self-serving revelations about how *other* people are always 'cultural dupes' (see Williams 1958: 289 for a similar argument with regard to the deployment of the term 'masses'). Although cultural studies recognises that the culture industries are a major site of ideological production, constructing powerful images, descriptions, definitions, frames of reference for understanding the world, Gramscian cultural studies rejects the view that those who consume these productions are 'cultural dupes', victims of 'an up-dated form of the opium of the people' (see Hall 1998).

Although we should never lose sight of the manipulative powers of capital and the authoritarian, and authoring, structures of production, we must insist on the active complexity and situated agency of cultural consumption. Culture is not something already made which we 'consume'; culture is what we *make* in the varied practices of cultural consumption. Consumption is the *making* of culture; this is why it matters. Moreover, it is a central argument of cultural studies that making culture is complex and contradictory, and cannot be explained by simple notions of determination, false consciousness (whether capitalist, imperialist or patriarchal), co-option and manipulation. Meanings are never definitive but always provisional, always dependent on context.

Gramscian cultural studies is informed by the proposition that people *make* culture from the repertoire of commodities supplied by the culture industries. Making culture – 'production in use' – can be empowering to subordinate and resistant to dominant understandings of the world. But this is not to say that cultural consumption is always empowering and resistant. To deny the passivity of cultural consumption is not to deny that sometimes cultural consumption is passive; to deny that the consumers of the commodities produced by the culture industries are not cultural dupes is not to deny that the culture industries seek to manipulate. But it is to deny that culture of everyday life is little more than a degraded landscape of commercial and ideological manipulation, imposed from above in order to make profit and secure social control. Gramscian cultural studies insists that to decide on these matters requires vigilance and attention to the details of the active relationship between production and cultural consumption. These are not matters that can be decided once and for all (outside the contingencies of history and politics) with an elitist glance and a condescending sneer. Nor can they be read off from the moment of production (locating meaning, pleasure, ideological effect, incorporation, resistance in, variously, the intention, the means of production or the production itself): these are only aspects of the contexts for cultural consumption as 'production in use'; and it is, ultimately, in 'production in use' that questions of meaning, pleasure, ideological effect, incorporation or resistance can be (contingently) decided.

The introduction of hegemony theory into cultural studies has provided the means for a way of seeing cultural consumption always in terms of an active relationship between production and consumption. However, perhaps it is now time to suggest that this is a relationship which should no longer be thought of exclusively in terms of 'incorporation' and 'resistance', but more neutrally, in a way which does not necessarily prejudge the range of possible outcomes, as an active relationship of 'structure' (production) and 'agency' (cultural consumption).[8] Certainly, there can be no doubt that there are already, as I have observed elsewhere (Storey 1996b, 1998), many different ways of thinking, different ways of using, what Hall calls 'the enormously productive metaphor of hegemony' (1992: 280). Hegemony theory in cultural studies has never quite operated as first formulated by Gramsci. The concept has been expanded and elaborated to take into account other areas and relations of negotiation and struggle. Whereas for Gramsci the concept is used to explain and explore relations of power articulated in terms of class, recent formulations in cultural studies have extended the concept to include, for example, gender, race, meaning and pleasure. What has remained constant (or relatively constant under the impact of political and theoretical change, from left-Leavisism to debates about postmodernism) is a particular guiding principle of cultural analysis. It is first found in what Michael Green quite rightly calls Richard Hoggart's 'remarkably enduring formulation' (1996: 52): 'Against this background may be seen how much the more generally diffused appeals of the mass publications connect with commonly accepted attitudes, *how they are altering those attitudes and how they are meeting resistance*' (Hoggart 1970: 19; my italics). In the 1960s it is given a culturalist accent by Hall and Whannel: 'Teenage culture is a contradictory mixture of the authentic and the manufactured: *it is an area of self-expression for the young and a lush grazing pasture for the commercial providers*'

(1998: 63; my italics). In the 1970s it is found in the more formally Gramscian tones of John Clarke *et al.*:

> Men and women are . . . *formed, and form themselves* through society, culture and history. So the existing cultural patterns form a sort of historical reservoir – a pre-constituted 'field of possibilities' – which groups take up, transform, develop. Each group *makes something of its starting conditions* – and through this 'making', through this practice, culture is reproduced and transmitted. (1976: 11; my italics)

In the 1980s we hear it in the Foucauldian analysis of Mica Nava: 'Consumerism is far more than just economic activity: it is also about dream and consolation, communication and confrontation, image and identity . . . Consumerism is a discourse through which *disciplinary power is both exercised and contested*' (1987: 209–10; my italics). In the 1990s it is there in Marie Gillespie's account of the relationship between media consumption and the cultures of migrant and diasporic communities, demonstrating how young Punjabi Londoners are '*shaped by but at the same time reshaping the images and meanings* circulated in the media' (my italics) – what she calls 're-creative consumption' (1995: 2, 3). In every decade in the history of cultural studies the point has been repeatedly made. It is the 'Gramscian insistence' (before, with and after Gramsci), learned from Marx, that we make culture and we are made by culture; there is agency and there is structure. It is not enough to celebrate agency; nor is it enough to detail the structure(s) of power. We must always keep in mind the dialectical play between agency and structure, between production and cultural consumption.

Notes

1   John B. Thompson makes the pertinent and perceptive observation that

> It is all too easily assumed that, because individuals have been treated as passive consumers of images and ideas, they have *become* passive consumers . . . This assumption . . . commits the fallacy of internalism: it unjustifiably infers, on the basis of the production and characteristics of a particular cultural product, that this product will have a given effect when it is received by individuals in the course of their everyday lives. (1990: 116)

2   Fiske's position has been the subject of much criticism in cultural studies (see Storey 1996b). In my view, the problem (if there is one) is not in the theory but in the practice; Fiske's own work tends to privilege the cultural economy.

3   This is often informed by what we might call 'textual determinism': the view that the value of something is inherent in the thing itself. This position can lead to a way of working in which certain texts and practices are prejudged

to be beneath the legitimate concerns of a critical gaze. Against such thinking, I would contend that what really matters is not the object of study, but how the object is studied.

Michel de Certeau makes an interesting observation about how the notion of a text containing a hidden meaning can help sustain a certain power relationship in matters of pedagogy:

> This fiction condemns consumers to subjection because they are always going to be guilty of infidelity or ignorance when confronted by the mute 'riches' of the treasury. . . . The fiction of the 'treasury' hidden in the work, a sort of strong-box full of meaning, is obviously not based on the productivity of the reader, but on the social institution that overdetermines his [and her] relation with the text. Reading is as it were overprinted by a relationship of forces (between teachers and pupils . . .) whose instrument it becomes. (1984: 171)

This may in turn produce a teaching practice in which 'students . . . are scornfully driven back or cleverly coaxed back to the meaning "accepted" by their teachers' (172).

4 Miller's primary source is Hegel's *Phenomenology of Spirit*, first published in 1807.

5 Marx makes a similar argument (like Miller, also drawing on Hegel) in his discussion of alienation. He argues that the nature of work under industrial capitalism (especially the division of labour) is such that workers are unable to create themselves in it, and are therefore forced to find themselves in practices of cultural consumption. As he explains,

> What then constitutes the alienation of labour? . . . the fact that labour is external to the worker, i.e. it does not belong to his essential being; that in his work, therefore, he does not affirm himself but denies himself, does not feel content but unhappy, does not develop freely his physical and mental energy but mortifies his body and ruins his mind. The worker therefore only feels himself outside his work, and in his work feels outside himself. . . . It [work] is therefore not the satisfaction of a need; it is merely a *means* to satisfy needs external to it. (1963: 177)

The difference between Marx and Miller is that Marx sees this as a loss which communism will overcome, whereas Miller sees it as inevitable and necessary for the making of culture.

6 I am using the concept of text as elaborated by John Frow and Meaghan Morris. See Chapter 6, note 3.

7 Multi-accentuality is similar to polysemy in that both point to the possibility of multiple meanings. The difference between the two concepts is that polysemy is a property of a text (different voices are discovered in the text), whereas multi-accentuality is what is done to a text (it is made to speak with different voices).

8 The concept of 'resistance' was developed in cultural studies in the 1970s as a way of understanding, and possibly more significantly, as a means to value subcultural forms of cultural consumption. I think its use now needs to be a great deal more circumspect. My preferred term is 'recontextualized' (Miller 1987). This allows discussion of resistance, without prejudging the issues at stake.

Bibliography

Abrams, M. H. 1953. *The Mirror and the Lamp: Romantic Theory and the Critical Tradition*. New York: Oxford University Press.

Adorno, T. W. 1991.*The Cultural Industry: Selected Essays on Mass Culture*, ed. with intro. J. M. Bernstein. London: Routledge.

Adorno, T. W. 1994. *The Stars Down to Earth and Other Essays on the Irrational in Culture*, ed. S. Crook. London: Routledge.

Adorno, T. W. 1998. On Popular music. In J. Storey (ed.) *Cultural Theory and Popular Culture: A Reader*, 2nd edn. Hemel Hempstead: Harvester Wheatsheaf.

Adorno, T. W. and Horkheimer, M. 1977. The Culture Industry: Enlightenment as Mass Deception. In J. Curran, M. Gurevitch and J. Woollacott (eds) *Mass Communication and Society*. London: Edward Arnold.

Adorno, T. W. and Horkheimer, M. 1979. *Dialectic of Enlightenment*. London: Verso.

Althusser, L. 1969. *For Marx*. London: Penguin.

Althusser, L. 1998. Ideology and Ideological State Apparatuses. In J. Storey (ed.) *Cultural Theory and Popular Culture: A Reader*. Hemel Hempstead: Harvester Wheatsheaf.

Anderson, B. 1983. *Imagined Communities*. London: Verso.

Ang, I. 1985. *Watching Dallas: Soap Opera and the Melodramatic Imagination*. London: Methuen.

Ang, I. 1990. *Desperately Seeking the Audience*. London: Routledge.

Ang, I. 1995. *Living Room Wars*. London: Routledge.

Ang, I. 1996. Culture and Communication: Towards an Ethnographic Critique of Media Consumption in the Transnational Media System. In J. Storey (ed.) *What is Cultural Studies? A Reader*. London: Arnold.

Ang, I. 1998. Feminist Desire and Female Pleasure. In J. Storey (ed.) *Cultural Theory and Popular Culture: A reader*. Hemel Hempstead: Harvester Wheatsheaf.

Appleby, J. 1993. A Different Kind of Independence: The Post-war Restructuring of the Historical Study of Early America. *William and Mary Quarterly* 50: 245–67.

Bakhtin, M. 1984. *Rabelais and His World*. Bloomington: Indiana University Press.

Barthes, R. 1967. *Elements of Semiology*. London: Jonathan Cape.

Barthes, R. 1973. *Mythologies*. London: Jonathan Cape.

Barthes, R. 1977. *Image-Music-Text*. London: Routledge.

Baudrillard, J. 1988. *Selected Writings*, (ed.) M. Poster. Cambridge: Polity Press.

Bausinger, H. 1984. Media, Technology and Everyday Life, *Media, Culture and Society* 6.4.

Bennett, T. 1979. *Formalism and Marxism*. London: Methuen.

Bennett, T. 1982. Popular Culture: Themes and Issues. In *Popular Culture U203*. Milton Keynes: Open University Press.

Bennett, T. 1983. Text, Readers, Reading Formations. *Literature and History* 9.2.

Bennett, T. and Woollacott, J. 1987. *Bond and Beyond: The Political Career of a Popular Hero*. London: Macmillan Education.

Bermingham, A. 1995. The Consumption of Culture: Image, Object, Text. In A. Bermingham and J. Brewer (eds) *The Consumption of Culture 1600–1800: Image, Object, Text*. London: Routledge, 1–20.

Bettelheim, B. 1991. *The Uses of Enchantment*. Harmondsworth: Penguin.

Bobo, J. 1995. *Black Women as Cultural Readers*. New York: Columbia University Press.

Bourdieu, P. 1984. *Distinction: A Social Critique of the Judgement of Taste*, trans. R. Nice. Cambridge, MA: Harvard University Press.

Bowlby, R. 1985. *Just Looking: Consumer Culture in Dreiser, Gissing and Zola*. London: Methuen.

Brecht, B. 1978. *Brecht on Theatre*. London: Methuen.

Brewer, J. and Porter, R. (eds) 1993. *Consumption and the World of Goods*. London: Routledge.

Brown, M. E. 1990. Motley Moments: Soap Opera, Carnival, Gossip and the Power of the Utterance. In M. E. Brown (ed.) *Television and Women's Culture: The Politics of the Popular*. London: Sage Publications.

Buckingham, D. 1987. *Public Secrets: EastEnders and Its Audience*. London: British Film Institute.

Campbell, C. 1983. Romanticism and the Consumer Ethic: Intimations of a Weber-style Thesis. *Sociological Analysis* 44.4: 279–95.

Campbell, C. 1987. *The Romantic Ethic and the Spirit of Modern Consumerism*. Oxford: Basil Blackwell.

Campbell, C. 1993. Understanding Traditional and Modern Patterns of Consumption in Eighteenth-century England: A Character-action Approach. In J. Brewer and R. Porter (eds) *Consumption and the World of Goods*. London: Routledge, 40–57.

Campbell, C. 1995. The Sociology of Consumption. In D. Miller (ed.) *Acknowledging Consumption: A Review of New Studies*. London: Routledge, 96–126.

Certeau, M. de 1984. *The Practice of Everyday Life*. Berkeley, CA: University of California Press.

Certeau, M. de 1998. The Practice of Everyday Life. In J. Storey (ed.) *Cultural Theory and Popular Culture: A Reader*. Hemel Hempstead: Harvester Wheatsheaf.

Chambers, I. 1986. *Popular Culture: The Metropolitan Experience*. New York: Methuen.

Chaney, D. 1995. *The Cultural Turn*. London: Routledge.

Chodorow, N. 1978. *The Reproduction of Mothering*. Berkeley: University of California Press.

Clammer, J. 1992. Aesthetics of the Self: Shopping and Social Being in Contemporary Urban Japan. In R. Shields (ed.) *Lifestyle Shopping: The Subject of Consumption*. London: Routledge, 195–215.

Clarke, G. 1990. Defending Ski-jumpers: A Critique of Theories of Youth Subculture. In S. Frith and A. Goodwin (eds) *On Record: Rock, Pop and the Written Word*. New York: Pantheon.

Clarke, J., Hall, S., Jefferson, T. and Roberts, B. 1976. Subcultures, Cultures and Class. In S. Hall and T. Jefferson (eds) *Resistance Through Rituals: Youth Subcultures in Post-war Britain*. London: Hutchinson.

Cohen, P. 1980. Subcultural Conflict and Working-Class Community. In S. Hall, D. Hobson, A. Lowe and P. Willis (eds) *Culture, Media, Language*. London: Hutchinson.

Corrigan, P. 1997. *The Sociology of Consumption*. London: Sage Publications.

Cruz, J. and Lewis, J. (eds) 1994. *Viewing, Reading, Listening: Audiences and Cultural Reception*. Boulder, Colo.: Westview Press.

Curran, J. and Gurevitch, M. (eds) 1991. *Mass Media and Society*. London: Arnold.

Curran, J., Gurevitch, M. and Woollacott, J. (eds) 1977. *Mass Communication and Society*. London: Edward Arnold.

Denning, M. 1987. *Mechanic Accents: Dime Novels and Working-Class Culture*. London: Verso.

Docker, J. 1994. *Postmodernism and Popular Culture*. Cambridge: Cambridge University Press.

Douglas, M. and Isherwood, B. 1996. *The World of Goods: Towards an Anthropology of Consumption*. London: Routledge.

Dyer, R. 1977. Victim: Hermeneutic Project. *Film Forum* 1.2.

Dyer, R. 1981. Entertainment and Utopia. In R. Altman (ed.) *Genre: The Musical: A Reader*. London: Routledge & Kegan Paul.

Eagleton, T. 1983. *Literary Theory: An Introduction*. Oxford: Blackwell.

Engels, F. 1998. Letter to Joseph Bloch. In J. Storey (ed.) *Cultural Theory and Popular Culture: A Reader*. Hemel Hempstead: Harvester Wheatsheaf.

Ewen, S. 1976. *Captains of Consciousness: Advertising and the Social Roots of the Conscious Society*. New York: McGraw-Hill.

Ewen, S. and Ewen, E. 1982. *Channels of Desire*. New York: McGraw-Hill.

Featherstone, M. 1991. *Consumer Culture and Postmodernism*. London: Sage.

Fekete, J. 1987. Introductory Notes for a Postmodern Value Agenda. In J. Fekete (ed.) *Life After Postmodernism*. New York: St Martin's Press.

Fine, B. and Leopold, E. 1990. Consumerism and the Industrial Revolution. *Social History* 15.2: 151–79.

Fish, S. 1980. *Is There a Text in This Class? The Authority of Interpretative Communities*. Cambridge, MA: Harvard University Press.

Fiske, J. 1987. *Television Culture*. New York: Routledge.

Fiske, J. 1989a. *Understanding Popular Culture*. Boston, MA: Unwin Hyman.

Fiske, J. 1989b. *Reading the Popular*. Boston, MA: Unwin Hyman.

Fiske, J. 1989c. Moments of TV: Neither the Text nor the Audience. In E. Seiter, H. Borchers, G. Kreutzner and E.-M. Warth (eds) *Remote Control: Television, Audiences and Cultural Power*. London: Routledge.

Fiske, J. 1992. The Cultural Economy of Fandom. In L. Lewis (ed.) *The Adoring Audience: Fan Culture and Popular Media*. London: Routledge.

Fornas, J. 1995. *Cultural Theory and Late Modernity*. London: Sage.

Foucault, M. 1981. *The History of Sexuality. volume one: An Introduction*, trans. R. Hurley. Harmondsworth: Penguin.

Foucault, M. 1980. *Power/Knowledge: Selected Interviews and Other Writings 1972–77*. New York: Pantheon.

Foucault, M. 1982. What is Enlightenment? In P. Rabinow (ed.) *The Foucault Reader*. Harmondsworth: Peregrine.

Franklin, S., Lury, C. and Stacey, J. (eds) 1991. *Off-Centre: Feminism and Cultural Studies*. London: HarperCollins.

Frazer, E. 1987. Teenage Girls Reading *Jackie*. *Media, Culture and Society* 9: 407–25.

Frith, S. 1996. Music and Identity. In S. Hall and P. du Gay (eds) *Questions of Cultural Identity*. London: Sage.

Frith, S. and Goodwin, A. (eds) 1990. *On Record: Rock, Pop and the Written Word*. New York: Pantheon.

Frith, S., Goodwin, A. and Grossberg, L. (eds) 1991. *Sound and Vision: The Music Television Reader*. Boston, MA: Unwin Hyman.

Frith, S. and Horne, H. 1987. *Art into Pop*. London: Methuen.

Frow, J. and Morris, M. (eds) 1994. *Australian Cultural Studies: A Reader*. St Leonards: Allen & Unwin.

Frow, J. and Morris, M. 1996. Australian Cultural Studies. In J. Storey (ed.) *What is Cultural Studies? A Reader*. London: Arnold.

Gadamer, H.-G. 1979. *Truth and Method*. London: Sheed & Ward.

Garnham, N. 1997. Political Economy and the Practice of Cultural Studies. In M. Ferguson and P. Golding (eds) *Cultural Studies in Question*. London: Sage.

Giddens, A. 1984. *The Constitution of Society*. Cambridge: Polity.

Gillespie, M. 1995. *Television, Ethnicity and Cultural Change*. London: Routledge.

Gilroy, P. 1987. *There Ain't No Black in the Union Jack*. London: Hutchinson.

Gilroy, P. 1993a. *The Black Atlantic: Modernity and Double Consciousness*. London: Verso.

Gilroy, P. 1993b. *Small Acts: Thoughts on the Politics of Black Culture*. London: Serpent's Tail.

Gilroy, P. 1996. British Cultural Studies and the Pitfalls of Identity. In H. A. Houston, M. Diawara and R. H. Lindeborg (eds) *Black British Cultural Studies: A Reader*. Chicago: University of Chicago Press.

Gilroy, P. 1997. Diaspora and the Detours of Identity. In K. Woodward (ed.) *Identity and Difference*. London: Sage.

Glennie, P. 1995. Consumption within Historical Studies. In D. Miller (ed.) *Acknowledging Consumption: A Review of New Studies*. London: Routledge, 164–203.

Golding, P. and Murdock, G. 1991. Culture, Communication and Political Economy. In J. Curran and M. Gurevitch (eds) *Mass Media and Society*. London: Arnold.

Golding, P. and Ferguson, M. (eds) 1997. *Cultural Studies in Question*. London: Sage.

Gramsci, A. 1971. *Selections from Prison Notebooks*, ed. and trans. Q. Hoare and G. Nowell-Smith. London: Lawrence & Wishart.

Gramsci, A. 1998. Hegemony, Intellectuals and the State. In J. Storey (ed.) *Cultural Theory and Popular Culture: A Reader*. Hemel Hempstead: Harvester Wheatsheaf.

Gray, A. 1992. *Video Playtime: The Gendering of a Leisure Technology*. London: Routledge.

Green, M. 1996. Centre for Contemporary Cultural Studies. In J. Storey (ed.) *What is Cultural Studies? A Reader*. London: Arnold.

Grossberg, L. 1992. *We Gotta Get Out of this Place: Popular Conservatism and Postmodern Culture*. London: Routledge.

Grossberg, L. 1993. Can Cultural Studies Find True Happiness in Communication? *Journal of Communication* 43.4: 89–97.

Grossberg, L. 1996. Identity in Cultural Studies – Is This All There Is? In S. Hall and P. du Gay (eds) *Questions of Cultural Identity*. London: Sage.

Grossberg, L. 1997. Wandering Audiences, Nomadic Critics. In L. Grossberg *Bringing It All Back Home: Essays on Cultural Studies*. Durham, NC: Duke University Press.

Grossberg, L., Nelson, C. and Treichler, P. (eds) 1992. *Cultural Studies*. London: Routledge.

Hall, S. 1978. Some Paradigms in Cultural Studies. *Annali*, 3.

Hall, S. 1980. Encoding and Decoding. In S. Hall, D. Hobson, A. Lowe and P. Willis (eds) *Culture, Media, Language*. London: Hutchinson.

Hall, S. 1982. The Rediscovery of 'Ideology': Return of the Repressed in Media Studies. In M. Gurevitch, T. Bennett, J. Curran and J. Woollacott (eds) *Culture, Society and the Media*. London: Methuen, 56–90.

Hall, S. 1986. Introduction. In D. Morley *Family Television: Cultural Power and Domestic Leisure*. London: Comedia.

Hall, S. 1990. Cultural Identity and Diaspora. In J. Rutherford (ed.) *Identity: Community, Culture, Difference*. London: Lawrence & Wishart.

Hall, S. 1992. Cultural Studies and its Theoretical Legacies. In L. Grossberg, C. Nelson and P. Treichler (eds) *Cultural Studies*. London: Routledge.

Hall, S. 1996a. Introduction: Who Needs 'Identity'? In S. Hall and P. du Gay (eds) *Questions of Cultural Identity*. London: Sage.

Hall, S. 1996b. On Postmodernism and Articulation. In D. Morley and K.-H. Chen (eds) *Stuart Hall: Critical Dialogues in Cultural Studies*. London: Routledge.

Hall, S. 1996c. The Meaning of New Times. In D. Morley and K.-H. Chen (eds) *Stuart Hall: Critical Dialogues in Cultural Studies*. London: Routledge.

Hall, S. 1996d. Minimal Selves. In H. A. Houston, M. Diawara and R. H. Lindeborg (eds) *Black British Cultural Studies: A Reader*. Chicago: University of Chicago Press.

Hall, S. 1996e. The Problem of Ideology – Marxism Without Guarantees. In D. Morley and K.-H. Chen (eds) *Stuart Hall: Critical Dialogues in Cultural Studies*. London: Routledge.

Hall, S. 1996f. When Was 'the Post-colonial'? Thinking at the Limit. In L. Chambers and L. Curti (eds) *The Post-colonial Question*. London: Routledge.

Hall, S. 1996g. Cultural Studies: Two Paradigms. In J. Storey (ed) *What is Cultural Studies? A Reader*. London: Arnold.

Hall, S. 1998. Notes on Deconstructing 'The Popular'. In J. Storey (ed.) *Cultural Theory and Popular Culture: A Reader*. Hemel Hempstead: Harvester Wheatsheaf.

Hall, S. and du Gay, P. (eds) 1996. *Questions of Cultural Identity*. London: Sage.

Hall, S. and Jefferson, T. (eds) 1976. *Resistance Through Rituals: Youth Subcultures in Post-war Britain*. London: Hutchinson.

Hall, S. and Whannel, P. 1964. *The Popular Arts*. London: Pantheon Books.

Hall, S. and Whannel, P. 1998. The Young Audience. In J. Storey (ed.) *Cultural Theory and Popular Culture: A Reader*. Hemel Hempstead: Harvester Wheatsheaf.

Hall, S., Critcher, C., Jefferson, T., Clarke, J. and Roberts, B. 1978. *Policing the Crisis: Mugging, the State and Law and Order*. London: Macmillan.

Hall, S., Hobson, D., Lowe, A. and Willis, P. 1980. *Culture, Media, Language*. London: Hutchinson.

Hebdige, D. 1979. *Subculture: The Meaning of Style*. New York: Routledge.

Hegel, G. 1977. *Phenomenology of Spirit*. Oxford: Oxford University Press.

Hermes, J. 1995. *Reading Women's Magazines*. Cambridge: Polity Press.

Hirsch, Jr., E. D. 1967. *Validity in Interpretation*. New Haven: Yale University Press.

Hobson, D. 1982. *Crossroads: The Drama of a Soap Opera*. London: Methuen.

Hobson, D. 1990. Women Audiences and the Workplace. In M. E. Brown (ed.) *Television and Women's Culture: The Politics of the Popular*. London: Sage Publications.

Hodge, B. and Tripp, D. 1986. *Children and Television: A Semiotic Approach*. Cambridge: Polity Press.

Hoggart, R. 1970. *The Uses of Literacy*. New York: Oxford University Press.

Huyssen, A. 1986. *After the Great Divide: Modernism, Mass Culture and Postmodernism*. London: Macmillan.

Iser, W. 1974. *The Implied Reader*. Baltimore: Johns Hopkins University Press.

Iser, W. 1978. *The Act of Reading: A Theory of Aesthetic Response*. London: Routledge & Kegan Paul.

Jameson, F. 1984. Postmodernism, Or the Cultural Logic of Late Capitalism. *New Left Review* 165: 53–92.

Jauss, H. R. 1982. *Toward an Aesthetic of Reception*. Brighton: Harvester.

Jenkins, H. 1992. *Textual Poachers*. London: Routledge.

Jenson, J. 1992. The Adoring Audience. In L. Lewis (ed.) *The Adoring Audience: Fan Culture and Popular Media*. London: Routledge.

Johnson, R. 1996. What is Cultural Studies Anyway? In J. Storey (ed.) *What is Cultural Studies? A Reader*. London: Arnold, 75–114.

Kaplan, C. 1986. *Sea Changes: Culture and Feminism*. London: Verso.

Lacan, J. 1977. *Ecrits: A Selection*. London: Tavistock.

Laclau, E. and Mouffe, C. 1985. *Hegemony and Socialist Strategy*. London: Verso.

Laermans, R. 1993. Learning to Consume: Early Department Stores and the Shaping of the Modern Consumer Culture (1860–1914). *Theory, Culture & Society* 10: 79–102.

Langman, L. 1992. Neon Cages: Shopping for Subjectivity. In R. Shields (ed.) *Lifestyle Shopping: The Subject of Consumption*. London: Routledge, 40–82.

Leavis, F. R. 1933. *For Continuity*. Cambridge: Minority Press.

Leavis, F. R. 1998. Mass Civilisation and Minority Culture. In J. Storey (ed.) *Cultural Theory and Popular Culture: A Reader*. Hemel Hempstead: Harvester.

Leavis, F. R. and Thompson, D. 1977. *Culture and Environment*. London: Chatto & Windus.

Leavis, Q. D. 1978. *Fiction and the Reading Public*. London: Chatto & Windus.

Lefebvre, H. 1984. *Everyday Life in the Modern World*, trans. S. Rabinovitch. New Brunswick: Transaction Books.

Lefebvre, H. 1991. *Critique of Everyday Life*, vol. 1. London: Verso.

Lewis, L. (ed.) 1992. *The Adoring Audience: Fan Culture and Popular Media*. London: Routledge.

Liebes, T. and Katz, E. 1993. *The Export of Meaning: Cross-cultural Readings of Dallas*, 2nd edn. Cambridge: Polity Press.

Light, A. 1984. 'Returning to Manderley': Romance Fiction, Female Sexuality and Class, *Feminist Review*, 16, 7–25.

Long, E. 1987. Reading Groups and the Postmodern Crisis of Cultural Authority. *Cultural Studies*, 1.3.

Lovell, T. 1998. Cultural production. In J. Storey (ed.) *Cultural Theory and Popular Culture: A Reader*. Hemel Hempstead: Harvester Wheatsheaf.

Lowenthal, L. 1961. *Literature, Popular Culture and Society*. Palo Alto: Pacific Books.

Lunt, P. and Livingstone, S. M. 1990. *Mass Consumption and Personal Identity*. Buckingham: Open University Press.

Lury, C. 1996. *Consumer Culture*. Cambridge: Polity Press.

Lyotard, J.-F. 1984. *The Postmodern Condition*. Manchester: Manchester University Press.

McCracken, G. 1990. *Culture and Consumption*. Bloomington and Indianapolis: Indiana University Press.

McGuigan, J. 1992. *Cultural Populism*. London: Routledge.

McKendrick, N. 1974. Home Demand and Economic Growth: A New View of the Role of Women and Children in the Industrial Revolution. In N. McKendrick (ed.) *Historical Perspectives: Studies in English Thought and Society in Honour of J. H. Plumb*. London: Europa Publications, 152–210.

McKendrick, N. 1982a. Introduction. In N. McKendrick, J. Brewer and J. H. Plumb (eds) *The Birth of a Consumer Society*. London: Europa Publications, 1–6.

McKendrick, N. 1982b. Commercialization and the Economy. In N. McKendrick,

J. Brewer and J. H. Plumb (eds) *The Birth of a Consumer Society*. London: Europa Publications, 9–194.

McKendrick, N., Brewer, J. and Plumb, J. H. 1982. *The Birth of a Consumer Society*. London: Europa Publications.

McRobbie, A. 1978. Working-class Girls and the Culture of Femininity. In Women's Study Group: Centre for Contemporary Cultural Studies, University of Birmingham (eds) *Women Take Issue*. London: Hutchinson.

McRobbie, A. 1991. New Times in Cultural Studies, *New Formations*, Spring: 1–17.

McRobbie, A. 1994. *Postmodernism and Popular Culture*. London: Routledge.

McRobbie, A. 1996. Looking Back at New Times and Its Critics. In D. Morley and K.-H. Chen (eds) *Stuart Hall: Critical Dialogues in Cultural Studies*. London: Routledge.

McRobbie, A. (ed.) 1997. *Back to Reality? Social Experience and Cultural Studies*. Manchester: Manchester University Press.

Maffesoli, M. 1996. *The Time of the Tribes: The Decline of Individualism in Mass Society*. London: Sage.

Malinowski, B. 1922. *Argonauts of the Western Pacific*. New York: Dutton.

Marcus, G. E. and Fischer, M. J. 1986. *Anthropology as Cultural Critique: An Experimental Moment in the Human Sciences*. Chicago: University of Chicago Press.

Marcuse, H. 1968. *One Dimensional Man*. London: Sphere.

Marx, K. 1963. *Selected Writings in Sociology and Social Philosophy*, ed. T. Bottomore. Harmondsworth: Penguin.

Marx, K. 1973. *Marx in His Own Words*, ed. E. Fischer. Harmondsworth: Penguin.

Marx, K. 1976. *Preface and Introduction to A Critique of Political Economy*. Peking: Foreign Languages Press.

Marx, K. 1977. *The Eighteenth Brumaire of Louis Bonaparte*. Moscow: Progress Publishers.

Marx, K. 1998. Base and Superstructure. In J. Storey (ed.) *Cultural Theory and Popular Culture: A Reader*. Hemel Hempstead: Harvester Wheatsheaf.

Mennell, S. 1985. *All Manners of Food: Eating and Taste in England and France from the Middle Ages to the Present*. Oxford: Basil Blackwell.

Mercer, K. 1990. Welcome to the Jungle. In J. Rutherford (ed.) *Identity: Community, Culture, Difference*. London: Lawrence & Wishart.

Miller, D. 1987. *Material Culture and Mass Consumption*. Oxford: Basil Blackwell.

Miller, D. 1995a. Consumption as the Vanguard of History. In D. Miller (ed.) *Acknowledging Consumption: A Review of New Studies*. London: Routledge.

Miller, D. 1995b. Consumption Studies as the Transformation of Anthropology. In D. Miller (ed.) *Acknowledging Consumption: A Review of New Studies*. London: Routledge.

Miller, D. (ed.) 1995c. *Acknowledging Consumption: A Review of New Studies*. London: Routledge.

Miller, M. B. 1981. *The Bon Marché: Bourgeois Culture and the Department Store, 1869–1920*. Princeton: Princeton University Press.

Moores, S. 1993. *Interpreting Audiences*. London: Sage.

Moores, S. 1996. *Satellite Television and Everyday Life: Articulating Technology*. Luton: University of Luton Press.

Morley, D. 1980. *The 'Nationwide' Audience: Structure and Decoding*. London: British Film Institute.

Morley, D. 1986. *Family Television: Cultural Power and Domestic Leisure*. London: Comedia.

Morley, D. 1992. *Television, Audience and Cultural Studies*. London: Routledge.

Morley, D. 1995. Theories of Consumption in Media Studies. In D. Miller (ed.) *Acknowledging Consumption: A Review of New Studies*. London: Routledge.

Morley, D. and Chen, K.-H. 1996. *Stuart Hall: Critical Dialogues in Cultural Studies*. London: Routledge.

Morris, M. 1988a. Things to Do with Shopping Centres. In S. Sheridan (ed.) *Grafts: Feminist Cultural Criticism*. London: Verso.

Morris, M. 1988b. At Henry Parkes Motel, *Cultural Studies* 2.1: 1–47.

Morris, M. 1988c. *The Pirate's Fiancée*. London: Verso.

Morris, M. 1996. Banality in Cultural Studies. In J. Storey (ed.) *What is Cultural Studies? A Reader*. London: Arnold, 147–67.

Mort, F. 1996. *Cultures of Consumption*. London: Routledge.

Munns, J. and Rajan, G. (eds) 1995. *A Cultural Studies Reader*. London: Longman.

Murdock, G. 1997. Base Notes: The Conditions of Cultural Practice. In P. Golding and M. Ferguson (eds) *Cultural Studies in Question*. London: Sage.

Nava, M. 1987. Consumerism and its Contradictions, *Cultural Studies* 1.2.

Nava, M. 1997. Modernity's Disavowal: Women, the City and the Department Store. In P. Falk and C. Campbell (eds) *The Shopping Experience*. London: Sage Publications, 56–91.

Nightingale, V. 1996. *Studying Audiences: The Shock of the Real*. London: Routledge.

Parkin, F. 1971. *Class Inequality and Political Order*. New York: McGibbon and Kee.

Perkin, H. 1968. *The Origins of Modern English Society*. London: Routledge & Kegan Paul.

Plumb, J. H. 1982. Commercialization and Society. In N. McKendrick, J, Brewer and J. H. Plumb (eds) *The Birth of a Consumer Society*. London: Europa Publications, 265–334.

Polan, D. 1988. Complexity and Contradiction in Mass Culture Analysis, *Camera Obscura*, 16: 160.

Pressdee, M. 1986. *Agony or Ecstasy: Broken Transitions and the New Social State of Working-class Youth in Australia*. Occasional Paper, South Australia Centre for Youth Studies, South Australia College of Adult Education, Magill, South Australia.

Radway, J. 1986. Reading is Not Eating: Mass Culture, Analytical Method, and Political Practice, *Communication* 9.1: 93–123.

Radway, J. 1987. *Reading the Romance: Women, Patriarchy, and Popular Literature*. London: Verso.

Radway, J. 1988. Reception Study: Ethnography and the Problems of Dispersed Audiences and Nomadic Subjects, *Cultural Studies*, 2.3: 359–67.

Radway, J. 1990. The Scandal of the Middlebrow: the Book-of-the-Month Club, Class Fracture, and Cultural Authority, *South Atlantic Quarterly*, Fall: 703–7.

Radway, J. 1994. Romance and the Work of Fantasy. In J. Cruz and J. Lewis (eds) *Viewing, Reading, Listening: Audiences and Cultural Reception*. Boulder, Colo.: Westview Press.

Ricoeur, P. 1981. *Hermeneutics and the Human Sciences*. New York: Cambridge University Press.

Riesman, D. 1990. Listening to Popular Music. In S. Frith and A. Goodwin (eds) *On Record: Rock, Pop and the Written Word*. New York: Pantheon.

Rutherford, J. (ed.) 1990. *Identity, Community, Culture, Difference*. London: Lawrence & Wishart

Sahlins, M. 1976. *Culture and Practical Reason*. Chicago: University of Chicago Press.

Sarup, M. 1996. *Identity, Culture and the Postmodern World.* Edinburgh: Edinburgh University Press.

Saussure, F. de 1974. *Course in General Linguistics.* London: Fontana.

Seiter, E., Borchers, H., Kreutzner, G. and Warth, E.-M. (eds) 1989. *Remote Control: Television, Audiences, and Cultural Power.* London: Routledge.

Shelley, P. B. 1973. A Defence of Poetry. In H. Bloom and L. Trilling (eds) *Romantic Poetry and Prose.* New York: Oxford University Press.

Sheridan, S. (ed.) 1988. *Grafts: Feminist Cultural Criticism.* London: Verso.

Shields, R. 1992. The Individual, Consumption Cultures and the Fate of Community. In R. Shields (ed.) *Lifestyle Shopping: The Subject of Consumption.* London: Routledge, 99–113.

Silverstone, R. 1994. *Television and Everyday Life.* London: Routledge.

Silverstone, R. and Hirsch, E. 1992. *Consuming Technologies.* London: Routledge.

Simmel, G. 1957. Fashion, *American Journal of Sociology,* 62.6: 541–58.

Simmel, G. 1964. The Metropolis and Mental Life. In K. H. Wolff (ed.) *The Sociology of Georg Simmel.* New York: The Free Press, 409–24.

Sontag, S. 1966. *Against Interpretation.* New York: Stein and Day.

Stacey, J. 1994. *Star Gazing: Hollywood and Female Spectatorship.* London: Routledge.

Storey, J. 1985. Matthew Arnold: The Politics of an Organic Intellectual, *Literature and History* 11.2: 212–28.

Storey, J. 1992. Texts, Readers, Reading Formations: 'My Poll and My Partner Joe' in Manchester in 1841, *Literature and History* 1.2: 1–18.

Storey, J. 1996a. *Cultural Studies and the Study of Popular Culture: Theories and Methods.* Edinburgh: Edinburgh University Press.

Storey, J. (ed.) 1996b. *What is Cultural Studies? A Reader.* London: Arnold.

Storey, J. 1997. *An Introduction to Cultural Theory and Popular Culture,* 2nd edn. Hemel Hempstead: Prentice Hall/Harvester Wheatsheaf.

Storey, J. (ed.) 1998. *Cultural Theory and Popular Culture: A Reader.* Hemel Hempstead: Harvester Wheatsheaf.

Suleiman, S. 1980. Introduction. In S. Suleiman (ed.) *The Reader in the Text.* Princeton: Princeton University Press.

Taylor, J. T. 1943. *Early Opposition to the English Novel: The Popular Reaction from 1760–1830.* New York: King's Crown Press.

Thompson, E. P. 1961. Review of *The Long Revolution. New Left Review,* 9: 24–33.

Thompson, J. B. 1990. *Ideology and Modern Culture.* Cambridge: Polity Press.

Thompson, J. B. 1995. *The Media and Modernity: A Social Theory of the Media.* Cambridge: Polity.

Thornham, S. 1997. *Passionate Detachments: An Introduction to Feminism and Film Theory.* London: Arnold.

Tulloch, J. 1990. *Television Drama: Agency, Audience and Myth.* London: Routledge.

Tulloch, J. 1995. 'But He's a Time Lord! He's a Time Lord!' Reading Formations, Followers and Fans. In J. Tulloch and H. Jenkins (eds) *Science Fiction Audience: Watching Doctor Who and Star Trek.* London: Routledge.

Tulloch, J. and Moran, A. 1986. *A Country Practice: 'Quality Soap'.* Sydney: Currency Press.

Turner, G. 1996. *British Cultural Studies: An Introduction,* 2nd edn. London: Routledge.

Veblen, T. 1994. *The Theory of the Leisure Class.* Harmondsworth: Penguin.

Vickery, A. 1993. Women and the World of Goods: A Lancashire Consumer and her Possessions, 1751–81. In J. Brewer and R. Porter (eds) *Consumption and the World of Goods.* London: Routledge, 274–301.

Volosinov, V. N. 1973. *Marxism and the Philosophy of Language*. London: Seminar Press.

Weber, M. 1930. *The Protestant Ethic and the Spirit of Capitalism*. London: Unwin University Books.

Weber, M. 1965. *The Sociology of Religion*. London: Methuen.

Williams, R. 1958. *Culture and Society 1780–1950*. London: Chatto & Windus; (1963) Harmondsworth: Penguin.

Williams, R. 1961. *The Long Revolution*. London: Penguin.

Williams, R. 1980. *Problems in Materialism and Culture*. London: Verso.

Williams, R. H. 1982. *Dream Worlds: Mass Consumption in Late Nineteenth Century France*. Berkeley: University of California Press.

Williamson, J. 1978. *Decoding Advertisements: Ideology and Meaning in Advertising*. London: Marion Boyars.

Williamson, J. 1986. *Consuming Passions: The Dynamics of Popular Culture*. London and New York: Marion Boyars.

Willis, P. 1977. *Learning to Labour: How Working Class Kids Get Working Class Jobs*. Farnborough: Saxon House.

Willis, P. 1978. *Profane Cultures*. London: Routledge & Kegan Paul.

Willis, P. 1990. *Common Culture*. Milton Keynes: Open University Press.

Wilson, T. 1993. *Watching Television: Hermeneutics, Reception and Popular Culture*. Cambridge: Polity Press.

Woodward, K. (ed.) 1997. *Identity and Difference*. London: Sage.

Wolff, J. 1985. The Invisible Flaneuse: Women in the Literature of Modernity. *Theory, Culture & Society* 2:3, 37–46.

Wolff, J. 1990. *Feminine Sentences: Essays on Women and Culture*. Cambridge: Polity Press.

Wolff, J. 1993. *The Social Production of Art*, 2nd edn. Basingstoke: Macmillan.

Women's Studies Group, Centre for Contemporary Cultural Studies 1978. *Women Take Issue: Aspects of Women's Subordination*. London: Hutchinson.

Index